A Century of Gamecocks

MEMORABLE BASEBALL MOMENTS

A portion of the author's royalties are being donated
to the University of South Carolina
Department of Athletics

Also by Tom Price
The '84 Gamecocks: Fire Ants and Black Magic (1985)
A Century of Gamecocks: Memorable Football Moments (1995)
A Century of Gamecocks: Memorable Basketball Moments (1995)

A
Century
of
Gamecocks

Memorable Baseball Moments

by Tom Price

Summerhouse Press
Columbia, South Carolina

Dedication

**This book is dedicated to all the coaches and their players,
whose performances on the field created the thrills
that made these memorable moments possible,
and to the great Gamecock fans who
made them worthwhile.**

FIRST EDITION

ISBN # 1-887714-02-2 (Paperback)

Manufactured in the United States of America
by Wentworth Printing Company, Inc.
Columbia, South Carolina

Contents

Contents

Foreword

A century contains a lot of memories, and there have been many memorable moments in the more than 100 year history of athletics at the University of South Carolina.

Baseball was a pioneer in the development of competitive sports at Carolina with evidence that the sport was played on campus as early as 1875. The first organized teams appeared in the early 1890s and the first documented intercollegiate competition dates back to 1895.

In *A Century of Gamecocks: Memorable Baseball Moments*, and in prior volumes covering football and basketball, I have tried to recapture some of those memories.

Long time followers of South Carolina teams may relive past thrills and experiences, or perhaps learn for the first time of a few thrilling events that occurred long ago. For newcomers to the Gamecock scene, accounts of memorable triumphs can be a history lesson.

It is hoped that *A Century of Gamecocks: Memorable Baseball Moments*, and its companion books, *Memorable Football Moments* and *Memorable Basketball Moments* will bring reading pleasure to fans of all ages.

There have been many more memorable games than those cited and readers may have other favorites and may disagree with some of the selections. However, those chronicled on these pages are some of my favorites, either through personal experience or from reading accounts in newspapers and from other sources.

Some memorable moments occurred before I came on the Carolina scene. The short life and career of James McCutchen James (Doc McJames) near the turn of the century fascinated me and I am indebted to several persons who contributed to the research into his intriguing life.

Lindsay Smith of Irmo, an ardent baseball historian, contributed much to this research as did two members of the James family, Mac James—the ballplayer's grand nephew—and Watson Chamblin, both of Columbia.

John Hammond Moore, a researcher and author, set me on the trail of early baseball competition on the Carolina campus, and two members of the Caroliniana Library staff—Daniel Boice and Thelma

Hayes—were always patient and helpful during long periods of microfilm study.

The newspaper clippings of recent seasons compiled by Fred Brinkman were of great value.

From Doc McJames in the 1890s, to the first no-hit game pitched by Milton "Babe" Adams in 1914; from the 1930s genius of Billy Laval who was a winner whether he coached baseball, football or basketball; to the All-America performances of Earl Bass, Hank Small, Randy Martz, Mookie Wilson and many others; to the highly successful programs developed by Bobby Richardson and June Raines; it has been a century to remember.

Thanks to the many journalists whose accounts of happenings on the fields were used as source material and to the Caroliniana Library and the Richland County Library for making available their microfilm and other archived material.

Thanks, also, to the University of South Carolina Sports Information Office for access to score books, scrap books, box scores, photographs and other material, and to all others who made available scrap books, photographs and other information. Special thanks to Jim Covington for his photo copy work.

Thanks to Summerhouse Press for publishing *A Century of Gamecocks*, my trilogy history of football, basketball and baseball at the University of South Carolina.

TP...

The Beginning

Football and to a lesser extent basketball command more attention from Gamecock fans and the media in the late 20th century, but more than 100 years ago, baseball was the first game played against outside competition by students at the University of South Carolina, possibly as early as 1875, and around the turn of the century was the predominant sport.

University archives contain a faded photograph marked "Baseball 1890," with notation that team members were named Legare, McGowan, Sam Evans, Laney, Walker, B. Rhett, Griffin, Hamer, A. Rhett, James and Shand.

The archives also have a photograph from the 50th anniversary edition of *The State* newspaper in 1941 which pictures a baseball team from 1891. M. L. Hanahan, who sent the photo to the newspaper, said he didn't remember the names of all in the photograph, but he did identify Jimmy Jones, first base; Otis Withers, pitcher-third base; Bob Shand, catcher; Akin Rhett, Marion Hanahan (apparently the writer of the letter); Bunny Rhett, Al Walker, Singleton Green, George Legare, Sam McGowan, manager of athletics; Sam Evans, manager; and Al Laney.

Hanahan stated the team played Wofford but he didn't mention a score or any other games played against intercollegiate competition. The oldest intercollegiate score documented was a 7-4 loss to Wofford May 2, 1895. However, several earlier games against non-collegiate teams from the Columbia area in 1892 and 1893 have been documented and there is evidence that an organized baseball team did exist on the Carolina campus as early as 1890.

That would be two years prior to the first known football game —a Christmas Eve 1892 meeting between a pickup team of Carolina students and Furman's organized team that claimed a 44-0 victory. That game was played at Charleston and the South Carolina College—now the University of South Carolina—fielded its first organized football team in 1894.

There is evidence that "class football or rugby" was played by college and high school students in Columbia as early as 1883 and baseball was played on the University of South Carolina campus in 1875, some fifteen years or more before a documented college team was organized.

The decade following the War Between the States was a period of reconstruction and among the results was racial integration of state government, the student body at the University of South Carolina, and the establishment in 1872 of the Agricultural and Mechanical Institute at Orangeburg in connection with Claflin University, an institution for Negroes that had been established by the Methodist Episcopal Church in 1869.

The Charleston *News & Courier* carried a story about an Aug. 24, 1875 baseball game between a team from Orangeburg—believed to be made up of Claflin students—and a team of University of South Carolina students. The game was played on the garrison grounds in Columbia with the South Carolina team winning 41-10.

The Orangeburg *News & Times* of Aug. 28, 1875, alluded to that game with this brief item:

"Some of our baseballists (colored) went over to Columbia on Tuesday to try the skill of one of the clubs there. We have not heard from them what the result of the battle was, but the *Union-Herald* says they got badly beaten. The whole truth of the matter is, and we presume to give the advice to all of our clubs, you want to practice, practice, practice."

The following brief item appeared in the June 16, 1876 issue of the *Columbia Register:* "Base Ball. The nameless base ball club of Winnsboro, will arrive here this afternoon on the half past 3 o'clock train. The game will commence at half past 4 o'clock precisely, and is expected to be intensely exciting, as both are crack clubs. There

This 1890 photograph is the oldest known University of South Carolina team photo in any sport. —*USC Archives*

will be seats provided for the ladies, and the clubs hope to see them out in full force. The game will be played on the garrison grounds."

The garrison grounds were the area now occupied by the Russell House and the Cooper Library on the Carolina campus, so called because federal troops were garrisoned there when Gen. William T. Sherman occupied Columbia in 1865. The same area was later the site of Melton Field, a football facility, and Davis Field, which held a baseball diamond and running track until the 1950s.

Controversy

The athletics program at the University of South Carolina has been no stranger to controversy throughout its existence and it took just three days after *The State* newspaper came into existence for an athletic controversy to appear in print.

The State published its first issue on Wednesday, Feb. 18, 1891 with N.G. Gonzales as editor and manager, and Ambrose E. Gonzales listed on the masthead as "general agent."

The edition of Friday, Feb. 20 carried a story under a headline that stated: "Trouble At The University," with a sub-head that added: The Students Can't Play Ball—Several Expulsions."

The text of the story read: "The series of base ball games arranged for centennial week between the Charleston and University teams cannot now be played—at least, the students will have to be counted out.

"The University council is now enforcing all rules and regulations to the letter, and have ordered the students to cease playing base ball in any shape. This, of course, kills the University Club and will prevent it from crossing bats with the Charleston team as was expected. The club plans to ask manager Rideout of the 'Mechanics' to take up the cudgels and play the centennial week series.

"The enforcement of the regulations at the University resulted this week in the expulsion of eight students for violating different rules. It is understood that the council is also pushing its crusade against the students taking part in certain classes of public entertainment."

The following day, in its Saturday edition, *The State* clarified its earlier story, saying in effect, the council hadn't banned the students from organizing a baseball team but had ruled that all members of the team had to be legitimate students and proper procedures had to be followed.

The top headline on the story stated: "A University Ball Team Only," and the lengthy sub-head added, "The Council Edict Not So Stringent. The University Statement—No Mixed Base Ball Teams— No Students 'Expelled.' They Were Sent Home."

The story explained the controversy: "In *The State* of yesterday a brief statement was made of trouble at the State University, about the students playing base ball and other matters. In view of the fact that only one (side) was given, *The State's* special University Correspondent made a full investigation of the facts yesterday, and the following account from him shows the main facts to be as reported, only they are not near so broad in their application.

THE UNIVERSITY

When the students read that the University Council had issued an edict that there could be no baseball played by them this year— Freshman and Senior alike—were just indignant at the apparent tyrannical use of authority; and all day long the common topic of conversation was how could they express their indignation.

But later in the day it was discovered that no such action as was supposed had been taken by the University authorities. The professors composing the council are among the most popular in college, and the students were no little gratified to find they had not overstepped the bounds of reason and justice. So far from forbidding baseball and other innocent amusements, the members of the council are desirous of encouraging all such amusements when carried on in the proper manner.

There is a by-law of the University that requires in all such matters that the students must make formal petition to the council for permission before they proceed. The council is perfectly willing for the students to organize a baseball team, or as many as they desire, but they do object most seriously, and in this most of the students agree with them, to having the team composed in the large measure of residents of the city having no connection with the University, and yet calling it the 'University Baseball Team.'

But this is not the main cause of the recent trouble. In the words of one in a position to know, the real trouble was that the council objected to any student proent (sic) proceeding, without authority (of) either the council or to perfect arrangements for a series of games by a University team, composed partly of non-university men, when no team had been organized at the University, without complying with the by-law that required permission to be first obtained from the council. This is the whole trouble and the students and the public generally are assured that the council has no desire in any manner to lessen the rightful enjoyment of the students. Further, *The State* is authorized to say that if the students desire to form an intercollegiate baseball association, or to play any respectable non-professional team during the centennial, they have only to petition the council to that effect, and the request will be considered just as any other.

In regard to the statement that several students had been expelled, the truth is that this session as is the case every year, several students were sent home on account of the unsatisfactory result of their recent examinations. The council has no power to expel. That is vested in the trustees.

All the above comes from the University, and shows the trouble in another and far more satisfactory light, yet the main facts are the same."

In its first story and the sub-head and first paragraph of the second, the newspaper spelled baseball as two words, but in the body of the second story shortened it to one word as it is spelled today.

Columbia was chartered as the site of a new state capital for South Carolina in 1786 and permanently populated in 1791 and the city fathers planned a gala centennial celebration in the spring of 1891.

The State, in tracing the history of the centennial, noted that on March 22, 1786, an act was passed for removing the seat of South Carolina's government from Charleston to a town to be built on the Congaree River to be called Columbia. A convention called to establish a new constitution met in the newly laid out capital in 1790.

The State of Tuesday, May 12, 1891 printed the schedule of events for the centennial the following day. The program was to begin at 6 a. m., with the firing of twenty one aerial bombs. General Wade Hampton was the "orator of the day."

It was requested that citizens ring all bells in the city for half an hour and other events included fireworks, trade displays, the Peoples' Ball, etc.

A baseball series between the University team and a team from Charleston was on the original centennial schedule but, perhaps due to the aforementioned controversy, the university team withdrew and the Mechanics, a local team, were substituted.

The centennial program for May 13, 1891 listed "A base ball game at the ball park on Elmwood Ave., between the Mechanics and Charleston."

However, the Charleston team balked over financial and game time arrangements and the series was at first canceled, then rescheduled.

The games as well as the horse racing which was to have featured the centennial never occurred as rainy weather washed out much of the centennial celebration.

The State declared the centennial, "A week of unalloyed pleasure—except for the rain," adding, "The centennial weather disappeared, the sun burst forth in all its glory and main street dried off in a few hours, until not a sign of mud was visible."

City officials reported more than 4,000 rode the street cars during the centennial and hotels were jammed, but the rain "made the horse races a complete failure in every respect." No mention was made of the rained out centennial baseball series.

Columbia fielded a professional team in the South Atlantic League in the early 1890s, and *The State* carried accounts of an exhibition game between the South Carolina College team and the professionals, April 25, 1892 and an April 28, 1892 game against an amateur team that included some of the college players as well as a 14-8 college win over the Mechanics on April 8, 1892.

The professionals won by scores of 9-2 and 31-5.

The State's report on the April 8, 1892 game read:

> The first game of baseball of the season was played at the ball park at the fair grounds, yesterday afternoon. Although none expected to see a finely fought amateur game, when 'play ball' was called the grand stand was filled, many of the spectators being ladies, thus attesting the great amount of enthusiasm which has been aroused by the league prospects.
>
> The game was umpired by the retired pitcher, Mr. Jack Fetner, and it was a beautiful battle. For the first two innings the college boys played badly. Then they got on to Waites, and bunching their hits, assisted by loose playing on the part of the Mechanics, in two innings they broke down the Mechanics' lead of six and ended the fourth with a lead of one. This lead they swelled and won the game, goose egging their larger competitors until the seventh, when the game was called. The feature of the game was James pitching, he standing aside (striking out) 15 men in seven innings, yielding only five hits, and giving only two bases on balls.
>
> The official score tells the story of the game. The entire score is not given as it is not deemed necessary.

Doc McJames

The South Carolina pitcher in the April 8, 1892 win over the Mechanics, as well as in the exhibitions against the professional team and in four documented games played in 1893 was James McCutchen James, who between 1895 and 1901, would pitch in the National League under the name "Doc" McJames as probably South Carolina's first alumnus to play major league baseball.

James, or McJames as he was known in professional baseball, won 27 games for the Baltimore Orioles in 1898 and compiled a lifetime 79-80 record in six seasons with Washington, Baltimore and Brooklyn. His career and his untimely death from complications following injuries suffered in a runaway horse accident in September 1901 make up one of the most fascinating stories in South Carolina athletics history.

Three baseball encyclopedias list James' date and place of birth as Aug. 27, 1873 in Williamsburg County. *The Ballplayers*, a collection of brief biographies on 600 major leaguers, also lists James' year of birth as 1873. However, his gravestone in St. David's Episcopal church yard at Cheraw lists his birth date as one day short of a year later, Aug. 26, 1874.

James was the right guard on the pickup team that played South Carolina's first football game on Christmas Eve 1892. It was in baseball, however, that he excelled. A story in the *Columbia Sunday Record*, Nov. 8, 1925, commemorating the 1892 football game with Furman mentions James and his subsequent baseball career and states he was "believed to have been the discoverer of the first curve ball."

Baseball lore, however, credits Arthur "Candy" Cummings, a 5-9, 120 pound righthander who played more than twenty years before James with inventing the curve ball. Cummings' reputation as the inventor of the curve resulted in his election to the Baseball Hall of Fame in 1939, although his two year National League record (1876-77) showed only 21 wins and 22 losses. Counting play in the old National Association (1872-75) his lifetime record was 124-72.

Although he lost a 9-2 decision to the Columbia professional team in 1892, James struck out 13 and in the 31-5 rout by the professionals he struck out six before being relieved after four innings and switching to second base. He was reached for seven first inning runs but allowed only two more in his four innings before being relieved by Jim Campbell who gave up fifteen runs in the fifth inning and seven more in the sixth.

James was the pitcher in all four documented South Carolina College games in 1893. The college defeated the Mechanics 5-2 and 10-3, Orangeburg 12-4, and Frost Mill 22-6.

The box score of the first Mechanics game doesn't indicate strikeouts, but James fanned 15 Orangeburg batters and struck out 14 Mechanics in the second game. *The State* did not print a box score of the Frost Mill game but the story indicated that James pitched a no hitter despite Frost Mill scoring 6 runs.

"Yesterday afternoon perhaps the last game of the season was played on the South Carolina College grounds, and the college boys closed the season without being beaten a single time," the newspaper reported.

"The record of the game is interesting. By innings the score was: "Frost Mill 103 101 00—6; "College 713 125 3X—22

"James, the college pitcher, did not yield a single base hit, while the college made twenty base hits off Tarrar and Frost."

Two years after leaving South Carolina College, James arrived on the major league scene, appearing in two 1895 games with Washington and compiling a 1-1 record with a 1.59 earned run average in 17 innings.

James was pitching at Petersburg, Va., at the time he was promoted to Washington, and used his correct name in the two 1895 games that he pitched for Washington.

In his first start, James lost a 6-5 decision to New York Sept. 24, 1895 and the *New York Times* the following day reported, "James James, a new pitcher from the Virginia League, pitched for Washington to-day, and while extremely wild was hit safely only five times."

Four days later, Sept. 28, James defeated Boston 8-5 for his first major league victory.

After the 1895 season, his name was listed as McJames. His grand nephew, Mac James of

James McCutchen James
(Doc McJames)
—James Family Album

Columbia, theorized that perhaps James slightly altered his surname so his mother wouldn't know he was playing baseball as professional ballplayers were not held in very high social esteem during the times.

A story that appeared April 24, 1927 in *The Columbia Record* credited Mendel L. Smith with signing James to his first professional contract. Smith, who later served as speaker of the South Carolina House of Representatives and as a circuit judge, had a barnstorming team known as the "Midgets" in the early 1890s.

"Another interesting story told about this barnstorming tour was the launching of Mack James into the baseball world," *The Record* story related.

"Later James became a great pitcher in the big league and in professional baseball. Mack James was a pitcher at the University of South Carolina. During one of his summer vacations he was signed by Manager Mendel L. Smith and it is said that it was at Florence or some other town hereabouts that James received his first dollar for pitching, he having been paid that sum which was 'good money' in those days for playing a game. This together with James' career at Carolina marked the stepping stone to his big league advent."

He had a 12-20 record with Washington in 1896 and was 15-23 in 1897 but led the National League in strikeouts with 156 in 324 innings.

James apparently worked himself into shape and at the same time instructed the South Carolina baseball team before reporting to Washington for the 1896 season. *The State* of March 18, 1897, published the following:

"Mr. J. Mack James, South Carolina's star National League pitcher, who has attended the Charleston Medical College during the past season, will leave in a few days for Washington, says *The Charleston Post*. James was a student at the South Carolina College here when he first began to pitch, and has hundreds of admirers in the city. Last year he did his training here acting at the same time as trainer for the South Carolina College baseball team."

James (or McJames) was sold to the Baltimore Orioles in 1898 and blossomed into stardom with a 27-15 record. He pitched 40 complete games in 42 starts and 45 appearances and had an earned run average of 2.36 while working 374 innings. His 178 strikeouts ranked second in the league and he was fourth in earned run average and complete games.

After the 1898 season, the owners of the Baltimore Orioles—Harry Von der Horst and Ned Hanlon—saw an opportunity to move into the more lucrative Brooklyn market. According to the encyclopedia *Total Baseball*, they purchased a half interest in the Brooklyn

Bridegrooms. The news media dubbed the team the Superbas after Hanlon's Superbas, a popular vaudeville act.

Hanlon maintained his presidency of the Baltimore club but took over as manager at Brooklyn, taking along with him the best players from the Baltimore team. *Total Baseball* identified them as "shortstop Hughie Jennings and outfielders Joe Kelley and Willie Keeler —plus its two best pitchers, Jim Hughes and Doc McJames."

Present day rules wouldn't tolerate such activity but McJames and the others mentioned shifted to Brooklyn where Doc compiled a 19-15 record despite, according to his biography in The Ballplayers, a month long attack of malaria "which curtailed his 1899 season."

He was the opening day pitcher April 15, 1899 and on Sept. 9— in the final game of the season—he came within out of pitching a no-hit game, defeating Boston 4-0. Future Hall of Famer Hugh Duffy of the Beaneaters (forerunner of the Braves) spoiled the no-hit bid with a two out ninth inning single.

T*he New York Times* edition of Sept. 10, 1899 carried this account that that game:

"More than 12,000 persons were at Washington Park, Brooklyn yesterday to see the final game of the season between the Brooklyns and the Bostons. As in Friday's game, the Bostons were beaten without making a run. It was one of the best exhibitions of pitching on the part of McJames, the home pitcher, that was ever seen on a local ball field. He had the Bostons guessing throughout, not allowing a base hit until two were out in the ninth inning, when Duffy managed to make the Bostons' solitary base hit."

The Superbas won the National League pennant and James, who had attended the Medical College of South Carolina at Charleston during the off-season, quit baseball to join his father and brother in practice at Cheraw in 1900. His brother, Dr. Thomas H. James, died the following March, however, of meningitis.

A year away from the game he loved was apparently all the young doctor could stand and on April 7, 1901 the *Charleston Sunday News* carried the following headline:

"BETTER THAN MEDICINE. Dr. James, the Famous Pitcher, Signs For a Season of Five Months With the Brooklyn Team."

A brief story with a Cheraw dateline read:

"Dr. McD (sic) James, the famous base ball pitcher, who left the field some months back to settle in Cheraw to practice medicine, and who had succeeded in building up a lucrative practice, has seen no peace since, being constantly importuned to toss again. Dr. James finally yielded to-day and signed with Brooklyn for the season of five months, and will leave on Wednesday to begin his work. It is reliably reported that Dr. James gets $5,000 for a few months work."

He appeared in 13 games for Brooklyn in 1901, starting 12, and pitched 6 complete games. His record was 5-6, when he suffered heat exhaustion while pitching on a hot day in St. Louis and soon returned to his Cheraw home to recuperate.

The St. Louis episode occurred July 9, when McJames lost to the Cardinals, 5-3. He had one more start, July 13, but was rocked for four first inning runs by Cincinnati. The next day, "The Brooklyn club to-day gave pitcher McJames his ten day notice of release."

That epitaph to a short, but outstanding, major league career was the last sentence of the New York Times story reporting a 7-0 loss to Cincinnati by the Brooklyn team.

James' obituary in the Charleston News and Courier had this to say about the illness that sent him home:

"At the St. Louis game in early July, during the insufferable torrid heat that swept over that part of the country, Dr. James succumbed to the heat at the end of the third inning. (The box score in the New York Times shows he pitched a complete game in a 5-3 loss.) He never fully recovered from the shock his system sustained at that time. He was advised to lay off for a few weeks and he complied with the admonition tendered by his friends. He returned to his home and resumed the practice of medicine with his father."

Back in Cheraw, James joined the local team about a month after leaving the big leagues and pitched in several games that summer. A report of a 4-3 Cheraw win over Anderson, printed in the Charleston *News and Courier* Aug., 21, 1901, stated "Dr. McJames was in fine form today, and pitched with his old-time force and vigor."

In late August of 1901, while driving a spirited horse in Cheraw, James was thrown from a buggy when the horse ran away and suffered a broken left arm and collar bone and other injuries. He was transported by train to Charleston for treatment by doctors he knew from medical school.

The News and Courier printed this account on Sept. 2, 1901:

"Dr. James Mack James, the well known physician and base ball player, is lying at the Charleston Hotel, suffering from serious injuries sustained last Saturday in a runaway accident at Cheraw, S. C. Dr. James arrived in the city late Saturday night and went at once to the hotel, where he was attended by several doctors. His left arm is broken in two places and a shattered collar bone adds much to his suffering. While the doctor's injuries are serious and very painful, they are by no means dangerous, and unless some unlooked for complications arise it is expected that Dr. James will be able to be out in a few days."

However, James contracted pneumonia and was hospitalized

at St. Francis Xavier Infirmary where he died Sept. 23, 1901, some 4 weeks after the accident and 27 or 28 days after his birthday. He was either 27 or 28 years old.

James apparently never married. He is buried at Old St. David's, an historic Episcopal church in Cheraw that dates back to 1768 and was the last parish established in colonial South Carolina.

The James family album, donated to the University of South Carolina's Caroliniana Library some years ago, contains letters from two of James' Brooklyn teammates solicited by the Cheraw Chronicle to commemorate the 20th anniversary of his death.

Former pitcher Wild Bill Donovan wrote in 1921:

"Your letter in reference to Jimmy McJames, or Doc as I always knew him, recalled to my mind a man who in my opinion was one of the greatest pitchers that ever wore a base ball uniform, and I think I can say without fear of contradiction that if Doc were alive and in the game at the present time he would take rank with the great pitchers of today. He was gifted with tremendous speed and had the best and fastest breaking curve ball that I have ever seen. I remember him as a big, good natured lovable character and I am sure that the city of Cheraw and the Old National game sustained a big loss when the Great Umpire of the Universe called the last out on our dear old friend and pal, Doctor Jimmy McJames."

Shortstop Hugh Jennings wrote:

"Jimmie (Doc) McJames was a fine character. The type of man who made friends rapidly and kept them. He was one of the star pitchers of his day and would compare favorably with any of the leading pitchers of today. Base ball cannot well afford to lose many men of Jimmie McJames caliber."

The family album at the Caroliniana Library contains a 1926 story from an unidentified newspaper which quotes memories of James by W. C. Cothran, a teammate at South Carolina College.

"Judge Cothran, who was playing second base for the team, said no college catcher could 'hold' the big, robust right-hander who had a wicked fast ball and a bewildering old-fashioned 'drop' curve," the story said.

Some years later, the Cheraw Chronicle printed the following feature story about James and his baseball career:

"James McCutchen James was born in 1874 in Williamsburg County and came here in 1884 when his father, Dr. J. A. James, moved his family to Cheraw. Mack, as he was called, pitched on the local baseball team. He was then signed by Petersburg of the Virginia League, and from there he went to Washington. He was bought from Washington by Baltimore, at that time in the National League.

"The Baltimore team, known as the Orioles, some contend was

the best baseball club of all time. James was its ace pitcher. The club at that time had such players as John McGraw, afterwards manager of the Giants, Hughie Jennings, later to manage the Cleveland club, Wild Bill Donovan, later to manage the Phillies, Willie Keeler and other stars of the base ball world. Baltimore was so much better than the other clubs that fans quit attending the games, both at home or on the road, so the franchise was transferred to Brooklyn, and they won the pennant for the Dodgers. (Actually they were known as the Superbas then).

"At the time James was playing he was attending medical school in the winter, and graduated at the Medical College of South Carolina in 1900 and quit base ball and practiced his profession here, but in September 1901 he died of pneumonia.

"To show the difference in the way professional base ball was regarded forty years ago and today, he played under the name 'Jimmie McJames,' as the profession was not regarded highly. The pay then was small; it is said he was paid $2,500 a year and was regarded as the best pitcher of his day, and his was about the top salary paid in the National League.

"One provision that his mother insisted that he make in his contract was that he would never play on Sunday. He was a great ball player and inspired the interest in the game in this section which is still felt. He is buried in the James family plot in St. David's cemetery."

Family records and his mother's tombstone indicate she died in 1899, two years before he signed a contract to return to the big leagues.

Records at the Medical University of South Carolina in Charleston indicate that James attended the University of South Carolina (then South Carolina College) for three years and the medical school for three years, graduating in 1899.

While James McCutchen James was the first University of South Carolina alumnus to play major league baseball, at least eight other Gamecocks reached the big leagues during the half century between the beginning of the game at Carolina and World War II.

Sydney Smith, who played on South Carolina teams of 1902-03, appeared in 146 major league games as a catcher-infielder between 1908 and 1915 with the Philadelphia Athletics, St. Louis Browns, Cleveland Indians and Pittsburgh Pirates. He coached the Carolina team briefly in 1915 before leaving to rejoin the Pirates where he ended his major league career by appearing as a pinch hitter in one game. Smith also played football at Carolina.

Alfred H. "Fritz" Von Kolnitz, another football player, played two seasons of college baseball, 1912-13, and appeared in 115 major league games as a catcher-third baseman-first baseman-outfielder, with the Cincinnati Reds and Chicago White Sox, 1914-16. Von Kolnitz was inducted into the University of South Carolina Athletic Hall of Fame in 1967.

Bert Edgar Chapman, who played professional baseball under the name Bert Edgar (Chappy, Ed) Chaplin, attended Carolina 1912-14, and played 35 major league games, 1920-22, as a catcher with the Boston Red Sox.

Sumpter Ellis Clarke, who starred in both football and baseball for the Gamecocks, 1915-18, was a third baseman-outfielder in 47 major league games, 1920-24, with the Chicago Cubs and Cleveland Indians.

Wade Eure "Roxy" Snipes, who attended Carolina 1921-24 and received a law degree, had one pinch hitting appearance with the White Sox in 1923.

Elzie Clise Dudley, who attended Carolina 1923-24, pitched in 100 major league games between 1929 and 1933 with three National League clubs, Brooklyn, Philadelphia and Pittsburgh. His lifetime record was 17-33.

David Lamar Coble, a Carolina student, 1933-34, caught 15 major league games in 1939 with the Phillies, and batted .280.

George Edward Jeffcoat, who quit baseball to become a Baptist preacher, attended Carolina in 1933. He pitched in 70 major league games with the Dodgers and Boston Braves between 1936 and 1943. Primarily a relief pitcher, Jeffcoat's lifetime major league record was 7-11.

In the middle 1950s, while working for United Press, I interviewed the Rev. George Jeffcoat at his West Columbia home for a feature story about his leaving the pitcher's mound for the pulpit. He told me he had once been a hell raiser who ran with catcher Frenchy Bordagaray, legendary party boy with the Dodgers and other major league teams, but had been converted and "swapped fast balls for faith."

After Jeffcoat there wouldn't be an alumnus of the University of South Carolina in a major league box score until Gary Lance, a shortstop with the Gamecocks, 1969-70, pitched two innings for the Kansas City Royals in 1977.

Over the next eighteen years, the University of South Carolina would send at least sixteen more alumni to the major leagues.

First baseman Hank Small, an All America choice at South Carolina in 1974 and 1975, played one game for the National League Atlanta Braves in 1978. Jeff Twitty had a 2-1 record as a lefthanded relief pitcher for the American League champion Kansas City Royals in 1980 and was on the World Series roster but didn't appear in a game. Catcher Greg Keatley played in two games for the 1981 Royals.

Outfielder Garry Hancock played in 272 American League games between 1978 and 1984 with the Boston Red Sox and Oakland Athletics.

Righthanded pitcher Jim Lewis had brief stints in the American League between 1979 and 1985, appearing in eleven games with Seattle, New York and Minnesota.

Righthander Randy Martz, All America at Carolina and winner of the Lefty Gomez Plate as the nation's best amateur player in 1977, pitched three seasons for the National League Chicago Cubs and one game for the American League Chicago White Sox between 1980 and 1983.

Righthanded pitcher Ed Lynch pitched in 248 National League games with the New York Mets and Chicago Cubs between 1980 and 1987, and became general manager of the Cubs in 1995.

Righthanded pitcher Don Gordon appeared in 78 American League games between 1986 and 1988 with the Toronto Blue Jays and the Cleveland Indians.

Infielder Jim Pankovits played in 316 National League games with the Houston Astros between 1984 and 1988, and appeared in two American League games with the Boston Red Sox in 1990. A third baseman in college, Pankovits played primarily at second base in the major leagues.

Kent Anderson played two seasons, 1989-90, in the American League with the California Angels, appearing in 135 games. He played both shortstop and second base in the majors.

Outfielder Mookie Wilson had a twelve year major league career, appearing in 1,403 games, 1,116 in the National League with the New York Mets and in 287 American League games with the Toronto Blue Jays. Wilson played in four league championship series and the 1986 World Series when the Mets won the world championship.

Righthanded relief pitcher Bill Landrum had an eight year National League career, 1986-93, appearing in 268 games with Cincinnati, Chicago, Pittsburgh and Montreal.

Righthanded pitcher Mike Cook pitched in 41 American League games between 1986 and 1993 with California, Minnesota and Baltimore.

Three former Gamecocks were active on major league rosters in 1995. Shortstop Tripp Cromer was in the National League with the St. Louis Cardinals. Righthanded pitcher Brian Williams, with Houston, 1991-94, was traded to the San Diego Padres before the 1995 season.

Dave Hollins, a third baseman in college, has played third, first and the outfield in the major leagues. He played for the Philadelphia Phillies, 1990-95, making the National League all-star team and appearing in the World Series in 1993. Hollins was traded to the American League Boston Red Sox in mid-season 1995.

Former Gamecocks Ed Lynch and Mookie Wilson were teammates with the New York Mets.—*NY Mets*

The Agrarian Revolution

The Agrarian Revolution, spearheaded by Edgefield County farmer and later Governor Benjamin R. "Pitchfork Ben" Tillman contributed indirectly to the development of athletics at South Carolina College. The movement resulted in the creation of Clemson College and the downgrading of the University of South Carolina to South Carolina College.

The act of 1890 restricted South Carolina and The Citadel to the teaching of "law, literature, classics and theoretical science," according to the two volume history of the University of South Carolina's first 150 years written by Dr. Daniel Walker Hollis.

Clemson was to be devoted to training in agriculture, engineering and the industrial arts, while Winthrop was to educate young women to be teachers and instruct them in practical matters.

"Intramural games won the sanction of the faculty in 1890 when the students obtained permission to convert half of the eight acre tract bounded by Sumter, Devine, Bull and Green streets—heretofore planted in cotton as part of the University's farm—into a playing field," Hollis wrote.

With the teaching of agriculture about to be transferred to Clemson, Carolina's cotton field—site of the present Russell House and Thomas Cooper Library—was no longer needed and the student body obtained its first playing field. James McCutchen James and other early baseball players, as well as Carolina's first football teams, honed their skills there.

The Columbia Record, in an Oct. 4, 1934 special edition commemorating the first game in what is now Williams-Brice Stadium, shed additional light on the University of South Carolina's first on campus athletic field and how it was financed and built. The newspaper printed the following:

"The first football gridiron in Columbia was located where University field now stands and was first used in 1890.

"Class football or rugby, as it was known then, was played here as early as 1883, contests being engaged in by high school boys and some students at the South Carolina College.

"Prof. Harry Davis of the university faculty recalls playing rough and tumble football during those days at the old Taylor school ground. The ball was not carried but was kicked exclusively. Three of the outstanding players in those days were Lee Hagood, James S. Verner and Julius Taylor.

"The ball then was round, apparently in the shape of a basketball and had to be inflated by lung power. There were no pumps or valves.

"In 1889, a meeting with G.S. Legare presiding, (was) held at which plans were discussed for a football and baseball field.

"The faculty of S.C. College decided at this meeting that the students would be given the right to use the field south of the wall, which is the present University field.

"The students organized into a company with a capital stock of 200 shares at $2 a share. Up to December 8, 1889, approximately 100 shares had been sold, records at the university library show.

"In 1890 the students of the college organized class rugby games and according to an account in the college weekly the game grew steadily in interest and enthusiasm among the spectators and players."

The information that the ball was round and "was not carried but kicked exclusively" indicates the game was perhaps more akin to today's soccer than to rugby.

The departure of ace pitcher Mack James to professional baseball, the sharp decline in enrollment due to the reduction of the University to South Carolina College, and a faculty ban on playing games away from Columbia apparently resulted in baseball being limited to an intramural basis in 1894. No record of games against outside teams has been found but *The State* of March 22, 1894 carried this brief story:

"Yesterday afternoon the fifth baseball game of the season was played on the college grounds. The freshman team met a team composed of men representing the sophomores, juniors and lawyers and after a hard fought battle succeeded in downing the combination by a score of 8 to 7."

The faculty relaxed its ban on travel by suggesting in late 1895 that athletic teams be permitted to "visit occasionally other institutions to play Match games," and the trustees agreed.

The first documented road trip was the March 28, 1896 trip to Spartanburg to return Wofford's 1895 visit to Columbia. However, the controversy over the eligibility of Wofford's pitcher resulted in Carolina playing against a team designated as "Spartanburg" but including the Wofford players minus the challenged player.

South Carolina made a second road trip in 1896, traveling to Greenville where South Carolina defeated Furman 10-7 on April 1. That apparently was the school's first ever baseball road victory.

The South Carolina College baseball team also received its first official uniforms for the 1896 season. A story in *The State* of March 24, 1896 reported:

"The suits for the S.C. College baseball team arrived yesterday. The material is of grayish color with garnet belt and stockings and cap. On the breast is printed in letters of garnet, 'South Carolina,' an idea that is being adopted by all ball teams this season."

The first documented game against an intercollegiate opponent, a 7-4 loss to Wofford, had occurred the previous year, May 2, 1895 in Columbia. South Carolina was scheduled to travel to Spartanburg to open the 1896 season at Wofford but a controversy over the eligibility of Wofford's pitcher arose.

Carolina manager E. R. Wilson wrote Wofford refusing to play if pitcher Chrietzenburg participated. Wilson alleged that Chrietzenburg was a professional who had been paid to play. When the South Carolina team arrived in Spartanburg for the March 28 game Wofford refused to play under the Wofford College name if Chrietzenburg was barred.

As a compromise the team competed under the name "Spartanburg" and, without Chrietzenburg, won the game 18-6.

Other schools in the area also became involved in eligibility disputes. A story in *The State* filed from Clemson said Clemson refused to play Furman because Furman was not a member of the Southern Intercollegiate Athletic Association. Adjacent was a story filed from Furman stating that Clemson had forfeited the game by failing to show up.

The 1896 South Carolina College baseball team—*USC Archives*

In a May 8, 1902 account, the Augusta, Ga, YMCA accused the University of North Carolina of using two players—first baseman Holt and shortstop Carr—who had played the previous year for the Augusta Y "for salary."

The Augusta YMCA also threatened to expose "The Tech" (Georgia Tech) and the University of Georgia for similar offenses.

There were also some non-athletic scandals involving colleges in the area. A front page story in *The State* April 30, 1902, reported 69 of 74 members of Clemson's sophomore class had quit in protest over the suspension of Cadet Thornwell of Fort Mill for taking four glass test tubes from a chemistry laboratory without permission.

The 1896 season also apparently produced South Carolina's first attempt at marketing and promotion to boost attendance. The State's advance story before the May 2 game against Georgia reported, "A brass band will be furnished and free ice water will be dispensed."

The story also noted that ladies were usually admitted free but, "due to heavy guarantee," would be charged to see the Georgia game. Admission was 25 cents.

Admission remained at 25 cents until 1913 when, for big games, a graduated admission of 25 to 50 cents was charged. Ladies continued to be admitted free to some games and were charged 15 cents to see the major contests.

Virtually all team travel was by train and in the late 1890s and for a number of years after the turn of the century there were plenty of rail lines to choose from.

The State reported that in 1894 there were 182,710 miles of steel rail in the United States and an additional 38,917 miles of iron rail. A trip from Columbia to Washington on the Seaboard Airline Railway required sixteen hours via Raleigh, Petersburg and Richmond.

The year 1894 also apparently spawned the first sporting goods store in Columbia. A June 10, 1894 advertisement in *The State* said:

"Just Received at Indian Girl Cigar Store, a fresh line of baseball goods! Bats, Balls, Belts, Caps, Mitts, Masks."

Brooklyn Superbas

A year after Mack James' final season, his old team—the Brooklyn Superbas—chose Columbia and the University of South Carolina campus as its spring training site.

The State of Feb. 27, 1902 reported:

"Yesterday, Mr. Edward Hanlon, manager of the Brooklyn National League baseball team,, was in the city and practically completed all arrangements for bringing his team to Columbia for spring practice. Mr. Hanlon has been offered good inducements in other southern cities, but has selected this city because of the climate and the accommodations.

"The party, numbering about 20 in all, will arrive on April 1st and remain here until April 15th, the league season opening a few days afterwards."

The story reported that eight members of Brooklyn's 1901 pennant winning team would be back and Hanlon would have "seven or eight youngsters who under the eye of the older and more experienced men will develop into regular National Leaguers."

The Brooklyn team was housed in the Columbia Hotel and *The State* reported the entire cost of two weeks of spring training, including "railroad fare, hotel bills, etc.," would "be about $1,500." The story added that "Mr. A. Yager," a sportswriter for The Brooklyn Eagle, accompanied the team to Columbia.

A follow up story in *The State* the next day reported "The South Carolina College Athletic Association has invited the Brooklyn National League baseball team to use their grounds, gymnasium, etc., during their regular two weeks of practice previous to the opening of the baseball season."

The National League team was to "have the use of the college park, gymnasium, baths, etc. The management of the college team will prepare the park, such as scraping the infield, clearing the outfield and making repairs in general and the Brooklyn management will keep them in order."

The Brooklyn team had the grounds for practice from 9:30 a.m., until 4:30 p.m., and agreed to furnish coaches for the college team and to arrange "at least three match games" with the collegians, "so that lovers of baseball in this city may have the opportunity to see the champions play."

Hanlon was not present when the Superbas opened spring training in Columbia. He was in New York attending a meeting scheduled to set the 1902 National League schedule and plot strategy to counter the raids the fledgling American League had been making on National League talent.

"Manager Hanlon is in New York city attending a meeting of the managers of the National League," *The State* reported.

The meeting is mainly for the arrangement of the schedule but other matters may be introduced and manager Hanlon himself in view of the recent troubles intends to try and institute a decided movement against the American League, which has stolen away so many of the National League's crack-a-jacks. Mr. Hanlon believes that the American is nothing more than a big bubble which must burst in time, but he intends to pop it by getting back the players which the National needs. Even a baseball player can be induced to consider a monetary consideration larger than the one he gets at the time of the offer."

The 1902 South Carolina team played three exhibition games against the National League champions, losing 5-2, 12-6, and 6-4. Against collegiate competition, Carolina had a 6-4 record managed by George Bell Timmerman who years later would become a prominent lawyer and judge. He was the father of George Bell Timmerman, Jr., who served as South Carolina's governor in the middle 1950s.

During the time the Brooklyn National League team held spring training in Columbia, the team nickname was Superbas. Brooklyn was known by a number of nicknames, including Dodgers, before permanently settling on Dodgers in 1932.

A locker display in the Baseball Hall of Fame in Cooperstown, N. Y., lists the following nicknames for the Brooklyn franchise: Bridegrooms/Trolley Dodgers, 1890-98; Superbas, 1899-1910; Dodgers, 1911-13; Robins, 1914-31; Dodgers, 1932-57.

The franchise was moved to the West Coast in 1958 and became the Los Angeles Dodgers. Newspapers dubbed the team the Robins during the tenure of manager Wilbert Robertson, 1914-31. The term Trolley Dodgers was used to describe fans who "dodged" the trolley cars installed on Brooklyn's streets in 1893.

The practice sessions of the Superbas were attended by many Columbians, young and old, who appeared in awe of the major leaguers. *The State* of April 3, 1902, reported:

"Yesterday the Brooklyn team was again at the college park indulging in light batting practice. The small boys crowded the field gazing with open mouthed admiration at the erstwhile champions and a number of older heads were out to watch the Leaguers at their practice."

While having a major league baseball team in spring training occupied the attention of Carolina students and Columbians alike, there were other big 1902 doings in South Carolina. The Charleston Exposition, the port city's world fair, was in full swing and March 15, 1902 was "Columbia Day," with round trip rail fare from Columbia to Charleston priced as $2.75.

On April 8, 1902, three weeks after Columbia Day, President Theodore Roosevelt visited the Charleston Exposition.

Two days after the president's visit to Charleston, Wade Hampton—South Carolina's civil war hero and former governor—died. *The State* devoted its entire front page and most of page two to his obituary.

The state appropriations bill of 1902 provided a salary of $3,000 per year for the governor, $1,350 for his private secretary and $400 for a stenographer. The state treasurer and attorney general salaries were listed at $1,900. The state railroad commissioner's job was apparently considered much more important. He made $5,000.

The budget bill also cut Winthrop College's annual appropriation by $10,000, hinting at retaliation for suffragette activities at the state college for women.

South Carolina College opened the 20th century with four consecutive winning seasons, 7-4 in 1900, 6-3 in 1901, 6-4 in 1902, and 8-3-1 in 1903, the first year that the team had a head coach. W. Augustus Lee coached the 1903 and 1904 Gamecocks, posting a break-even, 3-3, record his second year.

Despite the winning records the baseball played by the University of South Carolina and its opponents in the early 1900s was not a finesse game. The Gamecocks committed 16 errors April 4, 1903 but still managed to defeat Newberry College 10-9. Newberry committed 24 errors March 30, 1900 in a 23-0 loss to South Carolina, which stole 10 bases in the game.

The Brooklyn team returned to Columbia for spring training in 1903 and 1904. *The State* quoted Manager Ned Hanlon as saying Columbia was selected because of its climate.

"In the estimation of Mr. Hanlon the climate of Columbia is exactly right for his purposes," the newspaper reported.

"It is not enervating as in the cities further south, nor is it cold and penetrating as in the towns farther north. On the contrary, the climate is balmy and invigorating, while the warm sun makes it possible for the men to perspire freely, an important adjunct to the regular course pursued by athletes getting down to perfect form."

The 1903 South Carolina team played two exhibition games against the Superbas, losing 8-2 and 12-5, but there is no documented record of the Gamecocks playing the Brooklyn National League team in 1904.

However, the collegians did benefit from instruction furnished by the major leaguers. *The State* reported that "each afternoon when they leave the field one of the men will be left behind to assist Mr. H.N. Edmunds and Prof. H.L. Spahr in getting the Carolinians into shape."

While the Superbas didn't return to Columbia after 1904, the South Carolina campus did serve one more season as the spring training site for a team from Brooklyn. The Brooklyn team of the short-lived Federal League trained in Columbia in 1914 and played one exhibition game against the Gamecocks, defeating the collegians 14-1.

Other major league teams trained in nearby cities such as Augusta during the early 1900s.

The Boston Braves played the University of South Carolina an exhibition game March 28, 1912, winning 13-2.

That game was played the day before Cy Young, beginning his 23rd major league season, celebrated his 46th birthday. Young, who won 511 major league games and for whom the Cy Young Award is named, did not pitch against the University or against the Columbia Sally League team the following day although *The State* newspaper, perhaps in an attempt by club management to boost attendance, listed him as the probable starting pitcher before both games.

Ty Cobb visited the University of South Carolina baseball diamond April 13, 1913 while holding out in a salary dispute with the Detroit Tigers. During his holdout Cobb organized a barnstorming team that played against a number of teams in Georgia and South Carolina.

The Gamecocks defeated Cobb's stars, 3-0, with the celebrated Georgia Peach collecting one single in three official at bats. One of the greatest outfielders of all time, Cobb played first base against the Gamecocks. He ended his holdout twelve days later, signing with the Tigers April 25, 1913.

Babe Ruth played a game on the University of South Carolina baseball field April 5, 1920 when the New York Yankees lost an exhibition game to the Brooklyn Robins (Dodgers), 9-3. The Bambino went hitless in two official at bats as Jeff Pfeffer, Rube Marquard and George Mohart combined to limit the Yankees to eight hits, including a home run by first baseman Wally Pipp. Centerfielder Hi Myers homered for the Dodgers. Ruth went on to hit 54 home runs that season.

Nickname

For a short time the University of South Carolina shared its Gamecock nickname with professional baseball.

Columbia fielded a professional team for several seasons in the 1890s and returned to the Sally League in 1905 using the nickname Gamecocks. *The State* referred to the college team as "Little Gamecocks." The college teams had been referred to by a number of nicknames in the early years, including "Jaguars" and simply "The College Boys."

The nickname "Gamecocks" when first applied to the University of South Carolina appeared about 1903 when a newspaper account of a football game said the Carolina team "fought like game cocks." *The State* newspaper shortened the nickname to one word and for nearly a century University of South Carolina teams have been known as Gamecocks.

Unlike today when teams and franchises adopt nicknames and mascots for marketing visibility, early team nicknames were coined by enterprising journalists and headline writers. Newspapers called Brooklyn fans "Trolley Dodgers" after trolley cars were introduced in the borough in 1893. The team became the Superbas when managed by Ned Hanlon because there was a famed vaudeville act called Hanlon's Superbas, and newspaper headlines called the Brooklyn team "Robins" when it was managed by Wilbert Robertson.

The same was true of teams at the University of South Carolina when a newspaper account said "they fought like game cocks."

A gamecock, of course, is a fighting rooster known for its spirit and courage. A cock fight, which was a popular sport throughout the United States in the 19th century, would last until the death of one of the combatants. Cock fighting has been outlawed in most states for humanitarian reasons, but it is still conducted surreptitiously in some areas.

The University of South Carolina is one of only two universities in the United States with a gamecock as its mascot. The other is Jacksonville State, an NCAA Division II school in Alabama.

The state of South Carolina has long been associated with the breeding and training of fighting gamecocks. General Thomas Sumter, one of two guerrilla commanders from South Carolina in the American Revolution, was known as "The Fighting Gamecock,"

33

and Sumter High School teams also are known as the gamecocks.

The baseball "Little Gamecocks" played three exhibition games against the pros in 1905, losing the first two 6-1 and 4-0, but winning the third, 6-4, on April 14.

By 1909, the professional team had shed the Gamecock label and was called the Palmettos, or Pals. That franchise was shifted to Charleston where it operated for a number of years as the Pals and a new professional team was organized in Columbia. The Columbia morning newspaper referred to the 1910 professional team as the Blues.

A fan contest to select a better nickname for the professional team was held in 1911 with the winning entry being the Commissioners because Columbia was the only city east of the Mississippi river with a commissioner form of government.

Within a few weeks the newspaper shortened the nickname to "Comers," and that name was used for a number of years and confusion with the University of South Carolina Gamecocks was permanently eliminated.

Subsequent professional teams in Columbia have used the nicknames Sandlappers, Senators, Reds, Gems, Mets and Bombers.

The Twentieth Century

With the departure of the Superbas after 1904 spring training, the Gamecocks didn't play exhibitions against any major leaguers until 1912 when Carolina lost a 13-2 decision to the Boston Braves. The 1914 game with the Brooklyn Federal League team was South Carolina's last game condition competition against major leaguers, but the Gamecocks often played exhibitions against minor leaguers, most against the Columbia Sally League team but others against other teams training in the area.

Against collegiate and other amateur opponents, the schedule during the 1890s varied from a single game against Wofford in 1895 to a nine game slate in 1899 when South Carolina closed the 19th century by stumbling to a 1-8 record.

The first northern team to come south for spring training and compete against South Carolina was Lafayette College of Easton, Pa., which played two games each in Columbia in 1898 and 1899. The Pennsylvanians swept the series both years, winning 11-10 and 21-5 in 1898 and 15-14 and 33-2 in 1899. The 33 runs scored by Lafayette April 1, 1899 remain the most ever allowed by a South Carolina baseball team.

Hobart College of Geneva, N. Y., split a pair of games at South Carolina in 1902. Hobart won on March 27, 7-5, with South Carolina prevailing the next day, 9-5.

It would be ten years before another northern team visited Columbia. Lafayette returned in 1912 and split a pair with the Gamecocks. South Carolina won 11-6 on March 25 and Lafayette won, 5-3, March 26. Lafayette returned in 1913, '14, and '15, playing the Gamecocks three times each year. South Carolina won only one of those nine games, a 9-7 decision in 1914.

South Carolina swept a two game series from West Virginia Wesleyan in 1914, 3-0 and 3-2, and also in 1915, 6-4 and 6-5.

Most of the early collegiate competition in the first quarter century, however, was against colleges in the Carolinas, Georgia, Virginia and Tennessee.

The oldest rivalries include Wofford, 1895; Furman and Georgia, 1896; Wake Forest and Erskine, 1897; Sewanee, Clemson and College of Charleston, 1899; and The Citadel and Davidson, 1900.

During the 1890s, South Carolina compiled a 14-20 record against colleges and other amateur teams. The first decade of the 20th century was much kinder, the Gamecocks recording eight winning seasons, one losing year, and a break-even season from 1900 through 1909, the composite record for the decade being 68-46-3.

The number of games played fluctuated from 6 in 1904, when the record was 3-3, to 17 in 1907 and 1909, each seasons producing an 11-6 record. The only losing season during the decade was 1906, when the record was 1-7.

The second decade produced four winning seasons and a break-even record the first five years, but five consecutive losing seasons followed and the composite record for the 1910-19 decade was dead even at 95-95-4. The most games in a season during the period were 24 in 1918, when the record was 11-13.

World War I had some affect on the number of games scheduled and travel was curtailed. In the spring of 1917, as the nation geared up for war, University officials announced that the remainder of the baseball schedule would be canceled "to provide more time for military training."

There were eight games remaining on the schedule when the announcement appeared in *The State* April 17, 1917. However, the Gamecocks played four games before terminating competition for the year.

The Gamecocks made no out of state trips in 1917, when a 13 game schedule resulted in a 4-7-2 record. The 1918 schedule showed 24 games played, the most ever, with a record of 11-13. The only out of state games were a five day trip to North Carolina, April 23-27, when the Gamecocks played Trinity (later Duke) twice and North Carolina and Davidson once each, losing all four games.

The 1918 schedule included two military teams, the Officers' Training School and the 81st Division from Fort Jackson, resulting in a win and a loss. This was in sharp contrast to the World War II years when the schedule was heavily curtailed by travel restrictions and many of the games were against Military teams.

Many athletes and coaches left Carolina during World War II for military service and by the spring of 1943 the entire athletics program was in doubt. When director of athletics and football coach Rex Enright was called to active duty by the Navy, a committee of the board of trustees, chaired by Sol Blatt of Barnwell, met to determine the future of intercollegiate athletics at the University of South Carolina.

A headline in the March 17, 1943 issue of *The State* gave the answer: "Carolina to Carry on in Athletics," albeit on a curtailed basis.

The story beneath the headline read, "The University of South

Carolina's major athletic program, including intercollegiate football, baseball and track (basketball was not mentioned) was apparently pulled from the fire yesterday afternoon when a special committee of the board of trustees voted for the continuance of intercollegiate athletics and inserted a paragraph in the formal statement that the committee at a later meeting will select a football coach and fix a schedule of games for the coming season."

Six of eleven baseball games played to a 5-6 record in 1943 were against military teams. Three others were against Columbia Mills and another against the Columbia Police Department. The only collegiate opponent that year was Newberry and the team was directed by student player-coach Kay Kirven.

The 1944 team was made up entirely of Navy trainees coached by Ensign H. W. Klocker and five of eight games played for a 4-4 record were against military teams. The Gamecocks met Newberry College twice and Presbyterian once and the only road trip was to Newberry, only forty miles from Columbia.

By 1945, as the war neared its end, the baseball schedule was up to a dozen games and an 8-4 record under coach Johnnie McMillan.

The schedule returned to normal with 23 games in 1946, only three against military teams, and Michigan State of the Big Ten conference visited Columbia for a two game series.

Through 1902, teams were administered by a manager who handled business affairs such as scheduling and travel arrangements while the captain took care of on the field functions such as starting lineups, substitutions and game strategy.

Many of the early coaches were professional players who instructed the collegians until time to report to their pro teams and then turned the team over to the captain. Among these were Dicky James (1907), Bill Breitenstein (1910), Syd Smith (1915), Bill Clark (1916 and 1921-24), and perhaps there were others.

Faculty members and others also apparently contributed to the coaching and administration at times as evidenced by the reference to Professor H.L. Spahr and Mr. H.N. Edmunds being assisted by Brooklyn Superba players "in getting the Carolinians into shape" in 1902.

The first full-time university employee to coach baseball apparently was James G. Driver who compiled records of 11-11 in 1912 and 11-8-1 in 1913. A Virginian, Driver served the University in a number of capacities, including business manager and head basketball coach, 1911-12, when his record was 3-4, and 1912-13 when the Gamecocks had a 2-3 record in a five game basketball schedule.

Eventually, the coaching of baseball was assigned to a member of the football staff, sometimes the head football coach and sometimes an assistant. The first of four head football coaches to also coach baseball was Dixon Foster, who was less than successful in three seasons, posting 11-13, 9-13, and 3-18 records, 1918-20. Foster coached football two seasons with equally undistinguished results, 3-5 in 1917 when his captain was future major league baseball player Sumpter Clarke, and 1-7-1 in 1919. Clarke also captained the 1918 baseball team with Foster as head coach.

Branch Bocock, head football coach, 1925-26, coached the Gamecock baseball squad three seasons, 1925-27, with records of 4-9, 6-4 and 7-8.

By far the most successful combination football-baseball coach at Carolina was Billy Laval. His football teams had seven consecutive winning seasons, 1928-34, and his only losing baseball season was his first, 7-8-1 in 1928. From 1929 through 1934, Laval's baseball teams recorded seasons of 8-4, 14-5, 15-3, 16-7, 17-3 and 12-3. His career winning percentage of .728 (89-33-1) is the best among South Carolina's 27 head coaches through 1995, excluding Frank Lohr who won 75 per cent of his games (10-3-1) in only one season, 1908.

Laval also coached basketball one season, leading the Gamecocks to a 17-2 record and the Southern Conference championship in 1933. Before coming to the University of South Carolina Laval coached with much success at Furman and, after leaving Carolina, he was at Emory and Henry before finishing his career at Newberry College.

The decade of the 1920s was a dismal period in South Carolina's baseball history, producing a 63-86-3 composite record. The program began to come out of its slump the final two years of the decade, the first two of Billy Laval's seven year tenure as head coach.

Laval won nearly 78 per cent of his games during the first five seasons of the 1930s decade, and although the Gamecocks had four losing seasons the final five years, 1935-39, under Dutch Stamman and Catfish Smith, the entire decade showed a 114-64-1 record representing success 64 per cent of the time.

Johnnie McMillan coached the war time 1945 baseball team to an 8-4 record before he became head football coach for one year, taking the Gamecocks to the inaugural Gator Bowl game on New Year's day 1946 despite a below .500 record of 2-4-3. McMillan was also the head basketball coach one season, 1944-45, and led the Gamecocks to one of their best ever records, 19-3.

Vernon "Catfish" Smith and Ted Petoskey were two assistant football coaches who put in two separate tenures each as head baseball

Coach Ted Petoskey—*Garnet & Black*

coach. Smith coached baseball, 1938-39 and 1946-47 and Petoskey was head baseball coach, 1940-42, and 1948-56. His 12 season record was 113-118-1. Smith, in four seasons, compiled a mark of 40-48.

Petoskey was also head basketball coach, 1935-40.

The 1940s, which included the World War II years, were a losing period with the Gamecocks compiling an 80-90 decade, which was salvaged somewhat by a 15-6 record under Coach Ted Petoskey in 1949. That represented the most win in a season since Billy Laval compiled a 17-3 record in 1933.

Joe Grugan, a former Gamecock pitcher, 1939-41, was a physical education professor who coached baseball on a part-time basis for seven seasons, 1957-63 with limited success, compiling a 51-93 career record.

The 1950s, seven seasons under Petoskey and three under Joe Grugan, were also a losing decade. Petoskey's 16-9-1 record in 1950, and 9-8 in 1952 were the only winning seasons, although Petoskey broke even in 1954, 1955 and 1956, and Grugan had break-even seasons in 1957 and 1959. The record for the decade showed 96 wins, 117 losses and 1 tie.

Bob Reising split his time between teaching English and coaching baseball for two seasons and produced Carolina's first winning seasons in 12 years, 15-12 in 1964 and 16-12 in 1965. Grugan's teams had been 4-18 in 1960, 3-15 in '61, 9-11 in '62, and 7-14 in 1963.

Football assistant Dick Weldon took over the baseball program for the 1966 season and had a 15-8 record. Another football assistant, Jack Powers, followed for three years, 1967-69, with records of 21-8, 14-11 and 12-21-1.

The total record for the decade of the 1960s was 116-130-1 but over the final six seasons the record was 93-72-1 despite a 12-21-1 record in 1969.

Athletics Director Paul Dietzel in 1970 brought in South Carolina's first full-time head baseball coach, former New York Yankee all-star second baseman and South Carolina folk hero Bobby Richardson from Sumter. The budget for baseball was beefed up considerably and the schedule gradually expanded with the Gamecock baseball program rapidly rising to national prominence.

Richardson had his only losing record his first year, 14-20 in 1970. The highlight of that season was the appearance of South Carolina's first black scholarship baseball player, Ansel Eugene "Jackie" Brown of Jonesville, N.C.

Brown was on the baseball squad only one season. He played in 22 games, managing only 1 hit in 22 at bats, but he was used often as a courtesy runner when speedup rules were in force and he scored 13 runs. He also played briefly as an infielder and outfielder.

Brown walked on the football squad after the 1970 baseball season, and became a three year starter, 1971-73, at wide receiver for Coach Paul Dietzel. His scholarship was switched to football.

While Jackie Brown's baseball career at South Carolina was short, he opened the door for a succession of African American Gamecock stars, including future major leaguers Mookie Wilson and Brian Williams. After graduation, Brown became a Baptist minister in his native North Carolina and died of cancer at an early age.

Richardson improved to 18-12 in 1971, 25-16 in 1972, 26-15 in 1973, 48-8 in 1974 when South Carolina made its first appearance in the NCAA playoffs, a school record 51-6-1 in 1975 with an NCAA regional championship and a second place finish in the College World Series, and 38-14 in 1976 with a third consecutive NCAA playoff appearance.

After seven seasons Richardson resigned to run unsuccessfully for the U.S. House of Representatives and June Raines replaced him as South Carolina's second full-time head baseball coach. Richardson won more than 70 per cent of his games, compiling a 220-91-2 record in seven seasons.

Raines, through 1995, had won 738 games, lost 352 and tied 2 in 19 seasons, and had taken the Gamecocks to the NCAA playoffs 11 times with 4 trips to the College World Series, including a second place finish in his first season, 1977. He and Richardson had combined for 25 consecutive winning seasons, 998 victories, and more than 62 per cent of the 1,600 plus games that South Carolina had won since 1892.

Raines was a former minor league catcher who quit professional baseball at the age of 30 after a 10 year career to return to college. He earned bachelors and masters degrees at South Carolina while serving as a student assistant coach, first under Jack Powers and then under Bobby Richardson.

Raines returned to professional baseball for four years as an instructor in the Philadelphia Phillies organization before coming back to the University of South Carolina as head coach in 1977.

Raines attended Furman University as a freshman but then signed with the Cleveland Indians organization. He played as a catcher from the Class D to the AAA levels in the Cleveland and Washington Senators systems. Called up to the majors once as bench insurance when a Cleveland catcher was injured, Raines spent five days warming up big league pitchers but never got into a major league game.

Among his many professional baseball thrills was catching two future major league star pitchers, "Sudden Sam" McDowell and Luis Tiant at Burlington, N.C., in the Carolina League. Raines was the catcher in a Carolina League no-hit game pitched by "El Tiante."

South Carolina

vs

Guilford

April 3, 1914—South Carolina 1, Guilford 0
At Columbia (No Hit Game)

The headline in *The State* newspaper on the morning of April 4, 1914 declared: "Not a Single Hit Did Adams Allow."

Milton "Babe" Adams, a big righthander, had pitched the University of South Carolina's first no hit, no run game against a collegiate opponent.

Since Adams' feat, a 1-0 victory over Guilford College April 3, 1914, five other no-hitters had been accomplished by Gamecock pitchers through the 1995 season, the final two being back-to-back no-hitters, March 25-26, 1975 by lefthander Tim Lewis, 10-0 versus Old Dominion, and righthander Ray Lavigne, 8-0, against George Mason.

"University Pitcher Twirled Great Game against Guilford, Winning 1-0," a sub-head over *The State's* story reported, with additional sub-heads adding, "Dozen Players Fan, Three Reach First. The Only Score of the Contest was made in the First Inning. Only Twenty Nine Men Face the Boy Wonder."

As the winds of war gathered in Europe, baseball was the topic of conversation in South Carolina in early 1914. For the first time in ten years a major league baseball team chose the University of South Carolina campus and Columbia as its spring training site. The National League Brooklyn Superbas, who gradually evolved into the Dodgers, had trained in South Carolina's capital city for three seasons, 1902-04.

Another Brooklyn team, a member of the new Federal League, decided to set up shop on University Field. *The State* of Feb. 27, 1914, reported the following:

"Pending the action of the athletic board of the University of South Carolina, John M. Ward, business manager of the Brooklyn Federal League team, returned yesterday to Richmond and will go from there to Chicago. Mr. Ward stated unequivocally that should the University authorities permit the Brooklyn club to use the grounds the players would train in Columbia.

"He was pleased with Columbia and more especially with the advantages that the campus, field and nearby gymnasium had to offer as a training camp. Mr. Ward also went to the fairgrounds and though struck by its level surface, yet from a baseball standpoint he saw disadvantages in having to go so far for practice."

The hastily put together Brooklyn franchise had no official nickname but was sometimes referred to as "Tiptop," since the club was financed by the bakers of Tiptop bread.

The Federal League had signed 210 players to league contracts, raiding the rosters of the established National and American leagues and league officials met in Chicago to divide the players.

The Brooklyn team announced intentions to try and sign New York Giants ace pitcher Christy Mathewson as player-manager. Hal Chase of the Chicago White Sox was also being sought as a Federal League manager and Federal officials had designs on seven members of the Giants and White Sox who were on a world wide tour.

They planned to meet the ocean liner carrying the barnstorming teams when it docked in New York. All of this was to be accomplished by the time spring training began between March 8-12.

Mathewson put the Federal Leaguers off by saying he would give Giants manager John McGraw a chance to counter the Federal offer, reported to be $65,000 for three years. Mathewson decided to remain with the Giants without revealing terms of his contract and Brooklyn settled on Bill Bradley as the manager of its new team.

Bradley was a veteran third baseman who played 1,461 major league games but appeared in only 6 games as a player with the Brooklyn Federals. Other big league names in Columbia for spring training included Jim Delehanty, one of five Delehanty brothers in the major leagues, pitcher Thomas Seaton who had led the National League with 27 wins for the Phillies in 1913, outfielder Arthur "Solly" Hofman, and first baseman Hap Myers.

Delehanty reportedly objected to being listed by team management simply as "Delehanty" on the hotel register, saying, "that won't do," as he wrote "Mr. James Delehanty" on the register.

The Brooklyn team played one exhibition game against the University of South Carolina, defeating the collegians 14-1.

Other sports news in early 1914 included a story March 3 that "Alfred Holmes Von Kolnitz, star baseball and football star at the University of South Carolina, has retired from college and leaves at 7 o'clock this morning to train with Cincinnati."

Fritz Von Kolnitz had graduated the previous year with a law degree and had played minor league baseball with Morristown of the Appalachian League, batting .412 with a fielding average of .989 as a catcher.

"He set the circuit afire afield and at bat," *The State* reported and Cincinnati manager Buck Herzog sought his services but "From the beginning the young catcher was a holdout—because his father wanted him to practice law rather than play baseball.

"But his father agreed to his trying for the Cincinnati team after urgent appeals from manager Herzog."

Von Kolnitz appeared in 115 major league games over three seasons, 1914-16, with Cincinnati and the Chicago White Sox as an infielder, outfielder and catcher.

The 1914 South Carolina team was coached by G.I. Guerrant who doubled as secretary of the Columbia YMCA.

The pitching ace of the 1914 team was John Mills with Adams the number two starter. Other regulars included catcher Burnet Stoney, first baseman and captain Welser Edens, second baseman Fred Rudisill, third baseman John Shuler, shortstop Bill Rudisill, left fielder Bruce Barksdale, center fielder Arthur Plaxico, and right fielder William Graydon.

South Carolina defeated Lafayette 9-7 in the season opener but lost the next two games of the series to the visitors from Easton, Pa.

The Gamecocks won a two game series from West Virginia Wesleyan to take a 3-2 record into a two game home series with Guilford College which *The State* described as "one of the oldest and most famous institutions of the old north state.

Guilford won the first game of the series, 6-4, with a five run seventh inning "by taking full advantage of two passes, two boots and two hits."

"Breaking down the doors of the hall of fame, Milton Adams walked boldly in after the game yesterday afternoon between the University of South Carolina and Guilford College," *The State* reported.

"For nine exciting innings the Columbia boy held the North Carolinians without a hit or a run and at the conclusion the 'home nine' was returned the winner 1 to 0. Adams pitched superb ball throughout, only three men reaching first, two by passes and one when an outfielder (left fielder Bruce Barksdale) dropped a fly ball."

Arthur Plaxico led off the South Carolina first inning with an infield single and moved to third base on a sacrifice. The newspaper story doesn't explain how he advanced two bases on a bunt. Welser Edens struck out but Bill Rudisill singled to left field to drive in the game's only run.

South Carolina

vs

Clemson

April 28, 1930—South Carolina 18, Clemson 2

At Columbia

Billy Laval was a busy man in March of 1930.

Alabama defeated Duke 31-24 to win the Southern Conference basketball championship at the tournament in Atlanta and Laval, as South Carolina's director of athletics, was there attending a meeting that announced the creation of "a basketball league within the Southern Conference."

The defection by 13 members to form the Southeastern Conference was still nearly 3 years away and, for scheduling purposes, 10 members of the far flung Southern Conference announced the league within a league. Members were South Carolina, Clemson, Auburn, Alabama, Florida, Georgia Tech, Georgia, Kentucky, Tennessee and Vanderbilt. It didn't last long as the Southeastern Conference was created in December 1932 with all but South Carolina and Clemson going to the SEC.

As head football coach, Laval was in the midst of seven weeks of spring practice.

Addressing a gathering of upstate alumni in Spartanburg on March 18, Laval "painted a brilliant picture" of the University of South Carolina's athletic future.

An early baseball game against Columbia Mills was rained out and the Gamecocks were scheduled to begin play March 28 with a two game series against Erskine.

Laval called the 1930 South Carolina squad, "the best baseball team I ever coached."

One of the team's top stars was third baseman Buddy Laval, the coach's son, who *The State* called "a chip off the old block when it comes to a love for baseball and there are few college players who look as much at home on the diamond."

The team's three man pitching staff included lefthander Hugh Stoddard, Bill Brighman and Lucius B. "Bo" Keels. The catchers were N. B. "Swetto" Hicks and Barney Smith, the team captain.

Besides Laval at third, the infield included Eddie Sikes at first base, Archie Vaughn at second and Hap Edens at shortstop. Bill Harley was in left field and Stoddard played center field when not pitching. Hubert Nolan opened the season in right field but was replaced late in the season by Jim Porter. Bru Boineau also saw outfield duty as did several others.

South Carolina won the season opener, 5-3, over Erskine with the two hit no walk pitching of Stoddard dominating despite eight errors committed by the defense. *The State* said Stoddard "pitched a jam up game for Carolina despite a slippery ball caused by the drizzling rain." Hap Edens hit the season's first home run.

Brigham pitched a three hitter the next day as South Carolina won 14-1. The Gamecocks shut out Presbyterian 9-0 on Stoddard's five hitter, and split a two game series with Georgia Tech, losing 2-1 despite Stoddard's four hitter, and winning 5-4 behind Bigham.

An 11-0 loss at Furman left the Gamecocks with a 5-2 record going into a two game series at Clemson. Rain washed out the first day and a doubleheader was scheduled the next day.

Brigham lost the first game 4-1 but Stoddard won the second 9-2, with two more games against the Tigers coming up in Columbia April 28-29.

The seventh inning of the first game of that series produced one of the largest offensive explosions in Gamecock baseball history.

Clemson took a 1-0 lead in the top of the second inning but Bru Boineau's triple started a three run South Carolina third and the Gamecocks added two runs in the sixth to take a 5-2 lead.

"The big seventh was the stanza that put the game on ice for Carolina," *The State* reported. "Laval singled and was out at second on a fielder's choice (by Bill Harley). Hicks popped out to (Batson) Hewitt (second base). Then the lid busted off the Carolina pyrotechnics and the scorer clicked off 13 more runs before Vaughn's grounder to J. D. Gibson (Clemson shortstop) brought the spree to a halt."

Some sixty years later, Jim Porter—the Carolina right fielder—recalled that with two out and Bill Harley on first base Laval flashed the steal sign but then changed it to a hit and run.

"With me hitting left handed, Coach Laval put on the steal but as the pitcher threw he said there he goes, hit with him. As the shortstop covered second I hit through where he left and the fun began. Boineau scored the 13th run of the inning and would you believe Laval made the third out with the bases full."

The newspaper account published April 29, 1930 differed slightly from Porter's memory, saying Vaughn's grounder made the final out. The number of batters in the inning tended to support Porter's memory over the newspaper account. If South Carolina scored 13 runs after 2 were out and left the bases loaded, 19 Gamecocks would have batted in the inning. If Laval led off the inning with a single, he would have been up for the third time as the 19th batter.

The nine South Carolina starters played the entire game and Clemson, except for using two relief pitchers, also did not substitute. Stoddard allowed only four hits and was the only South Carolina batter without at least one hit.

Clemson starting pitcher G.C. Hoffman allowed 13 of South Carolina's 18 hits in 6 2/3 innings. Despite the 19 batter, 13 run, inning, the game was played in the fast time of 2 hours and 15 minutes.

Harley led the South Carolina attack with 4 hits, his only failure being his fielder's choice for the first out of the big seventh. Hap Edens had 3 hits, including a double, and Boineau also had 3 hits, including a triple. Laval, Porter and second baseman Archie Vaughn had 2 hits each, with catcher N.B. "Swetto" Hicks and first baseman Eddie Sikes each gettting 1 hit.

The State went several paragraphs into its game story before discussing the thirteen run inning, beginning: "Amid all the characteristic enthusiastic applause of a typical Carolina-Clemson contest, the Gamecocks piled up their hits and tightened up their defense to defeat the Tigers in the first of a two game series on Melton Field yesterday afternoon 18-2.

"The hitting of the Birds deserves plenty of praise, but first mention should go to Carolina's ever calm lefthander, Hugh Stoddard, who held the visiting team to four scattered safeties and fanned seven batters."

Each of the 9 Gamecocks scored with Boineau scoring 4 runs, Porter 3, Edens, Stoddard, Harley and Sikes 2 each, with Vaughn, Laval and Hicks each scoring once.

The fourth and final game against Clemson the next day went into extra innings before Harley's line drive to the center field fence in the bottom of the tenth drove in Laval to give the Gamecocks a 4-3 win and 3 victories in the 4 game series for the season.

Coach Billy Laval—*Garnet & Black*

The State's description of the winning hit said, "Harley's hit was a terrific drive and would have been good for the complete circuit had the game not officially ended when Laval touched home plate." Gamecock pitcher Bill Brigham allowed 8 hits, struck out 13 and walked none, but constantly pitched with Clemson runners on base as the Gamecocks committed 6 errors.

South Carolina lost close games on a road trip to North Carolina, 3-1 at Chapel Hill and 5-4 at Davidson and Games with North Carolina and Duke were rained out before defeating Furman 7-4 in Columbia and sweeping two games from The Citadel on neutral fields, 11-6 at Orangeburg and 14-4 at Florence to finish the 1930 season with a 14-5 record.

A headline in *The State* of May 14, 1930 declared: "Carolina Wins State Intercollegiate Baseball Title."

The Gamecocks were 11-2 against in-state teams, Newberry was 7-5, Erskine 7-6, and Clemson was fourth with an 8-7 record.

Buddy Laval led the team in batting with a .415 average on 34 hits in 82 at bats. Jim Porter batted .409 but had only 22 at bats. Archie Vaughn hit .395, captain Barney Smith .333 in only 27 at bats. Shortstop Hap Edens hit .286, sophomore outfielder Bill Harley .281, first baseman Eddie Sikes .200, catcher Swetto Hicks .181, outfielder Hubert Nolan .178, and outfielder Bru Boineau .174 with 3 of his 10 hits coming in the 18-2 win over Clemson.

Stoddard had a 7-2 pitching record in addition to batting .288 and was elected to captain the 1931 team with Bo Keels, who had a 2-0 record as the third pitcher in 1930, named alternate captain. Bill Brigham's pitching record was 5-3.

The team Billy Laval had called in pre-season "the best baseball team I have ever coached" was invited to play at the U. S. Naval Academy on May 28, 1930 for a guarantee of $400 but turned the invitation down because the date fell in the midst of final examinations.

Bill Harley—*Garnet & Black*

South Carolina

vs

Georgia Tech

April 3, 1931—South Carolina 4, Georgia Tech 3
At Atlanta, Ga.

Most long time followers of the University of South Carolina athletics program remember Bill Ouzts as the voice of the Carolina (later Williams-Brice) Stadium public address system on football Saturdays.

For 44 years his golden tones identified the ball carriers and tacklers. Ouzts was also a prominent attorney, city councilman for 34 years and Columbia's mayor pro-tempore.

For those whose memory goes back to the early 1930s, Bill Ouzts is also remembered as one of the finest righthanded pitchers to play baseball for the Garnet and Black. He played under coach Billy Laval, 1931-33, when the Gamecocks compiled some of their finest baseball records. During Ouzts' varsity career, team records were 15-3 in 1931, 16-7 in 1932, and 17-3 in 1934, at that time a record for most wins in a season. The three year record added up to 48-13.

Ouzts shared star billing on the pitching staff with Bill Brigham in 1931 and with Grayson Wolf in 1932-33. Ouzts compiled a 5-1 record as a sophomore, 4-3 as a junior, and 7-3 as a senior for a career record of 16-7. He should best be described as a finesse pitcher with control rather than a power pitcher.

"I had a good curve ball and control but didn't have the high, hard one," is the way Ouzts described his pitching tools.

"I do remember beating Georgia Tech in Atlanta, 4-3. I pitched real well that day," he recollected. Microfilm of *The State* newspaper account of an April 3, 1931 game confirmed Ouzts' recollection. The result was probably forever etched in Bill Ouzts' memory because it was the very first start and first victory of his collegiate career. South Carolina opened the season and a two game series in Atlanta with an 11-1 victory over Georgia Tech behind the three hit pitching of Bill Brigham.

The next day it was Bill Ouzts turn and the AP account of his first collegiate game reported:

"Effective hurling by Ouzts, who allowed the opposing batters eight hits but kept them well scattered, aided by the early stickwork of his teammates, won the game for South Carolina against Georgia Tech. Carolina nicked Baker for six hits and did its scoring in the first five innings. Tech staged a ninth inning rally but failed to knot the count."

The brief wire story in *The State* was accompanied by a box score which indicated that two of the three runs allowed by Ouzts

Bill Ouzts—*Garnet & Black*

came on home runs by Baker, the Georgia Tech pitcher, and Harper. No first names were listed. South Carolina's only extra base hit was a double by third baseman Buddy Laval, the only Gamecock with two hits. Laval, shortstop Hap Edens, first baseman Eddie Sikes,and left fielder Porter Richards scored the South Carolina runs.

While the 4-3 win over Georgia Tech was memorable in that it was Bill Ouzts first collegiate victory, many wins and outstanding pitching performances were to follow.

In his second start, South Carolina scored fourteen runs in the first inning and Ouzts coasted to an 18-6 victory over Erskine. Junior outfielder Bill Harley had six hits in six at bats in that game— five singles and a double—to establish a school record that was still on the books in 1995.

Harley would finish the 1931 season with 33 hits in 75 at bats, a .440 average that in 1995 remained the highest season batting average for any University of South Carolina player. His twelve career triples, although tied, 1991-94 by Mac White, are a school record.

Ouzts defeated Presbyterian 10-2 in his third start to improve his record to 3-0, and a weekend series with Clemson was canceled due to a quarantine of the Clemson campus following an outbreak of meningitis. Ouzts pitched a four hitter to beat The Citadel 17-1, beat Davidson 13-3, lost an 8-7 decision to The Citadel, and finished his sophomore season with a 5-1 record by beating Clemson 5-1, as the meningitis quarantine had been lifted.

His junior record was 4-3 including a non-collegiate 4-0 shutout of the Veterans Hospital team in which his pitching opponent was his brother, Kenneth. Kenneth, who was known by his initials, "K.K.," would play one season as a first baseman for South Carolina, 1934, before leaving for professional baseball and in later years would umpire college games.

The three other wins by Bill Ouzts in 1932 were over Erskine, Clemson and Newberry. He lost to Newberry and twice to Clemson.

Grayson Wolf, the other half of coach Billy Laval's two man starting rotation, pitched a no-hit game in 1932, defeating Presbyterian 22-1. Newspaper accounts reveal that the no-hitter was preserved by a Presbyterian base running error and thus was slightly tainted.

The account in *The State* read:

"Hurling masterful baseball and striking out at least one batter every inning, Grayson Wolf pitched a no-hit game for Carolina yesterday to beat Presbyterian College on University field 22 to 1.

"The complete shutout was almost averted by a long drive by Copeland, the Blue Hose twirler, that brought Barrett home in the fifth inning. The ball went down the third base line and would have been good for two bases but Copeland failed to touch first base and was declared out."

South Carolina banged out nineteen hits in the 22-1 rout with left fielder Ernest Correll collecting two home runs and a triple. Right fielder Bill Harley homered and doubled, and center fielder Roy Blair had a pair of triples. Outfielder Porter Richards also tripled.

The day after he pitched the no-hitter, Wolf relieved Ouzts and got the win when Carolina edged Presbyterian 9-8 in 14 innings.

Bill Ouzts compiled a 7-3 record as a senior, 6-2 against college teams. Against non-collegiate opponents he defeated the Graniteville mill team 4-1 in the season opener but was the losing pitcher in a 19-4 rout by Barnwell in a game that dedicated a new baseball park for the town of Barnwell.

He beat Furman and Newberry twice and claimed single wins over Clemson and Erskine. His collegiate losses were to Furman in relief as the Gamecocks dropped a 6-5 decision in 11 innings, and another 6-5 decision to Newberry. Ouzts also saved a game for basketball All-America Freddie Tompkins, who claimed a 9-8 win over Erskine for his only pitching victory in 1933.

Ouzts was actually the losing pitcher in all three losses of South Carolina's 17-3 season. Wolf had an 8-0 record and Ouzts was 7-3. Tompkins and another basketball star, Dana Henderson, had 1-0 records to account for the other two wins.

Wolf and Ouzts also contributed substantially to the Gamecock offense when they were on the mound. In 1933 Wolf had 12 hits in 28 at bats for a .429 batting average while Ouzts collected 7 hits in 24 at bats for a .292 average.

Among the everyday position players, third baseman Bob Robbins had 27 hits in 70 at bats for a .386 average. Second baseman Harry Hamilton was 24-66, .364; Fred Hambright 24-67, .358; Roy Blair 26-79, .329; Bill Jenkins 20-61, .327; Ernest Correll 20-74, .270; John Munn 18-67, .269; and Walker Yonce 19-76, .250. Correll hit 3 of the team's 10 home runs.

South Carolina went into its final scheduled two game series against Presbyterian with three of its regulars ineligible. Catcher Bill Jenkins, outfielder Ernest Correll and first baseman Roy Blair had played for a semi-pro team from Lockhart the previous weekend and were declared ineligible under a Southern Conference rule against outside competition.

Despite the loss of three starters, the Gamecocks defeated Presbyterian 8-3 behind Grayson Wolf and the second game of the series, and final game of the season, was rained out. The 17-3 record in 1933 represented the most wins ever for a University of South Carolina baseball team at that time.

That would remain a school record for 34 years until the 1967 Gamecocks, coached by Jack Powers, would win 21 games.

In 1929, while a senior at Columbia High School, Ouzts worked for 35 cents an hour as a carpenter's helper on the crew building the Lake Murray dam and pitched for the Broad River Power Co., team in the city league.

In 1934 he was in law school and had completed his collegiate eligibility. Billy Laval managed the Columbia South Atlantic League team that summer and signed Ouzts but his professional baseball career was short. The franchise was shifted to Asheville, N. C., in mid-summer and after several weeks Ouzts returned to Columbia to resume his law studies.

"The Greenwood semi-pro team in the Mid-Carolina League offered me $25 to pitch on weekend for them and the St. Matthews team gave me $15 to pitch Wednesday games," Ouzts recalled. "It was during the depression and I was getting rich making $40 a week to play baseball."

He later pitched for semi-pro teams in Graniteville, S. C., Forest City, N. C., and the Tapp's Department Store team in Columbia.

Ouzts served as public address announcer at Capital City Park when the local Sally League team was a Columbia Reds farm, and as secretary of the Columbia Gems when the franchise was affiliated with Kansas City.

As a member of city council he was instrumental in bringing professional baseball back to Columbia and when the ball park was enlarged and upgraded as Capital City Stadium in 1991, the playing surface was named "Bill Ouzts Field."

South Carolina

vs

Clemson

May 6, 1950—South Carolina 10, Clemson 2
At Columbia

Grady Faircloth was a junior when he enrolled at the University of South Carolina in the fall of 1949, having spent two years in junior college, but he was only nineteen years old and it took him most of an undefeated season in the spring of 1950 to convince coach Ted Petoskey that he was the ace of South Carolina's pitching staff.

Most of the members of the baseball roster were World War II G.I. Bill of Rights students and were older than Faircloth.

The Gamecocks were coming off a 15-6 season in 1949, by far the best record in Petoskey's tenure as coach, and he had proven veteran pitchers in righthanders Bill "Country" Camp, football quarterback Harold "Bo" Hagan and Frank Sherer, who had pitched a no-hit, no-run game two seasons earlier against Presbyterian.

A 1950 pre-season prospectus published in *The State* said "the pitching staff should be one of the strongest in the (Southern) conference," with Camp, Hagan and Sherer. "Add to that list Grady Faircloth and (lefthander) Walker Anderson and you have a sound staff."

However, the prospectus lamented that shortstop John Sykes, center fielder Roger "Red" Wilson and catcher Gus Allen were the only experienced position players back from the strong team of 1949.

Petoskey chose to go with his veteran pitchers in early games and South Carolina split two games with Michigan State, lost one to Duke and tied the Blue Devils 5-5 in an extra inning game called by darkness, and dropped an 8-3 decision at Georgia in the first game of a five game trip during the Easter holidays.

Faircloth, in the sixth game of the season, got his first start in the second game of that trip, at Macon against Mercer University. He beat the Bears 12-6, pitching seven strong innings before being relieved by Frank Sherer.

Military teams still dotted the schedules of many colleges, a leftover from the days of World War II, and the Gamecocks moved from Macon to Jacksonville, Fla., for three games against the Naval Air Station team there. South Carolina won all three, 5-4, 7-1, and 8-2, scoring six times in the 10th inning. Faircloth didn't start any of those games, but did work three innings in relief.

His first opportunity against a contending team in the Southern Conference was against Duke at Durham, N.C., April 14, 1950, and he pitched a complete game in a come-from-behind 8-6 victory.

The Associated Press account of that game under a Durham dateline stated, "South Carolina's Gamecocks took advantage of some loose fielding on the part of the Duke infield in the eighth

Grady Faircloth—*Garnet & Black*

inning...to score five runs and defeat the Blue Devils 8 to 6 in a Southern Conference Southern Division contest."

The story noted the Gamecocks trailed by three runs going into the eighth before putting together two hits, two walks and four Duke errors "to pull the victory out of the fire."

All nine of South Carolina's hits were singles, two each by first baseman Cy Szakacsi, shortstop John Sykes and left fielder Ashley Phillips.

Faircloth's next start came in the first game of a doubleheader against The Citadel and he allowed five hits in a 3-1 win, Carolina scoring single runs in the second, fourth and fifth innings. Frank Sherer won the second game 10-3 to give the Gamecocks an 8-4-1 record at the midway point in the season. Faircloth had three of the wins.

In the first game of a two game series at Furman, South Carolina blew a six run ninth inning lead as Furman scored seven times to pull out a 12-11 decision. Faircloth was the starting pitcher the next day in the second game of the series.

He pitched a six hitter, South Carolina winning 15-0 to record the Gamecocks' only shutout of the 1950 season. The Associated Press account of the game mentioned the final score only in the line score by innings. The AP's story printed in *The State* said:

"The University of South Carolina trampled Furman University this afternoon in the final game of their two game Southern Conference series. Faircloth hurled neat, six hit ball for the victors."

The line score indicated South Carolina scored 2 runs in the first inning, 5 in the second, and 3 in the third to take a 10-0 lead after three innings. The Gamecocks added 1 run in the fifth and 2 each in the seventh and ninth.

In the spring of 1950, I was a junior in the school of journalism and wrote a column entitled, "The Price of Things" in *The Gamecock*, covered home baseball games as a stringer for *The State*, and traveled with the baseball team as its official statistician.

A scrap book yielded this column from the student newspaper after Faircloth had shut out Furman to improve his record to 4-0:

"Probably one of the best things that ever happened to baseball coach Ted Petoskey was when a young pitcher named Grady Thomas Faircloth transferred to Carolina from South Georgia Junior College last September.

"Last Saturday in Greenville, Grady shut out the Furman University Purple Hurricane 15-0 to notch his fourth win of the young season against no defeats. He had previously claimed victories over Mercer University, Duke University and The Citadel.

"Grady, a junior majoring in physical education, is only 19 years old. His home town high school in Donaldsonville, Ga., didn't have a baseball team so he joined a semipro outfit made up of men much older than himself. He was an infielder then and did all right in fast company despite his 15 years.

"In 1947 an American Legion junior team was formed in Donaldsonville and Grady reported for the first day's practice. Pitchers were scarce, so the coach stuck Grady on the mound. He had a brilliant season and enrolled at South Georgia Junior College that fall. He compiled a record of six wins and three losses in junior college baseball in 1948 and last year hung up a perfect 4-0 record."

The column went on to say the first few weeks of Faircloth's first season at South Carolina were discouraging as Coach Petoskey went with his veteran pitchers and Faircloth's only activity was in the bull pen.

"He became discouraged and even talked of quitting," the column continued, but his chance to start for the Gamecocks arrived in the game at Mercer.

"Although the weather was frigid, with the thermometer hovering around 35 degrees, and a stiff wind blew the cold right through him, Grady Faircloth set the Bears down with four hits over the first seven innings. He was rather wild, walking eight, and four Gamecock errors kept him in trouble throughout but each time, he pitched out of danger and stifled the Mercer bats."

The column noted that Faircloth had been approached by a professional scout but, on the advice of his father, rejected the overtures to finish his college education.

"If Grady Faircloth continues his current winning ways," I wrote in *The Gamecock*, Ted Petoskey will be eternally grateful that the kid from South Georgia decided to finish his schooling."

While Grady Faircloth was on his way to an undefeated season at South Carolina, former Gamecock coach Billy Laval was just as feisty in the twilight of his career as he had been when, some 18 to 30 years earlier, he had led Furman and South Carolina to many winning seasons. He was making noise at little Newberry College.

Laval took issue with newspaper accounts extolling the strengths of the South Carolina and Clemson baseball programs and, through a column by sports editor Jake Penland of *The State*, he let the world know his team would welcome the opportunity to whip either the Gamecocks or the Tigers.

"Newberry's Billy Laval wasn't talking, he was growling, 'Where do you get that stuff about Carolina and Clemson playing for the state championship'?" Penland's column began.

"'Why, we've won seven straight against opponents in the state. We beat Furman twice, Wofford twice, P.C. (Presbyterian) twice and

Erskine once. In all our games we've won 11 and lost 3. We beat Davidson of the Southern Conference twice and I'm pretty sure we're going to beat The Citadel. We can't get a game with Carolina and Clemson. They won't play us. But as far as we're concerned, they've got to play us before they start claiming the state championship'."

Laval went on to say Newberry, "can't compete against Carolina and Clemson in football and we can't in basketball either. Baseball is different, though. It gives the little fellow a break. So, we get the runaround. We tried to schedule games with Carolina and Clemson. They said they couldn't get us on their schedules, and yet, even though we've won all seven games we've played in the state, every time I pick up a paper I read about Carolina and Clemson fighting it out for the state championship.

"Ever hear about a coach who had too many players? Well, I've got too many. I've got four good lefthanded pitchers, four righthanders, three catchers, two first basemen, two second basemen, two shortstops, two third basemen and eight outfielders."

Despite all that talent—or perhaps because of all that talent—Billy Laval wasn't able to get Newberry on the schedule of either South Carolina or Clemson and the Gamecocks were off to Charleston to meet The Citadel in a two game series.

Bill Camp pitched the first day, holding the Bulldogs to three hits, and the Gamecocks won, 9-3.

Faircloth was the second game starting pitcher and he was far more successful on the pitching mound than on the base paths.

The Citadel played baseball at Stoney Field, hard by the Ashley river and within sight of the draw bridge that spanned the river. Faircloth was a runner at third base when the bridge opened to allow a boat to pass through. They didn't have any draw bridges in Donaldsonville, Ga., and Grady—with about a six foot lead—stood entranced as he watched the two sides of the bridge part and open.

The Citadel pitcher picked him off third base.

On the mound, he scattered 4 hits while South Carolina pounded out 17 and used a number of walks and Citadel errors to win 21-1.

Faircloth's record was 5-0 with a 1.03 earned run average and the team mark was 11-5-1. Except for the road win at Duke, however, he still hadn't been rewarded with a start against a conference contender.

His undefeated record was in jeopardy when he was hit hard by Davidson, but South Carolina rallied for an 8-5 victory behind relief pitcher Bill Camp.

Clemson came to Columbia for a two game series and Coach Petoskey indicated Grady Faircloth would be his starting pitcher the second day. He surprised everyone by starting Grady in the first game but, just as surprisingly, lifted him for a pinch runner in the second inning when the score was tied, 2-2.

Fred Knoebel hit for the cycle—with a single, double, triple and a home run—to lead Clemson to a 14-5 win. The only bright spot for Carolina was the pre-game crowing of Mary Ann Phillips of Abbeville as South Carolina's "Miss Baseball 1950." Catcher Gus Allen, her fiancé and soon to be husband, did the crowning.

As stringer for *The State*, the second day's game story appeared under my byline May 7, 1950.

"Grady Faircloth scattered ten Clemson singles while his University of South Carolina mates clubbed three Tiger pitchers for thirteen safeties and a 10-2 victory yesterday afternoon on University Field to take revenge for the Tigers' 14-5 Friday win," I wrote.

"The Gamecocks scored all their runs in two big innings. They drove Clemson starter Nig Griffith to the showers in the second with a five hit barrage that, coupled with two bases on balls, netted six runs.

"Blackie Kincaid opened the inning by drawing a free pass. Lloyd Chinnes also walked but Mitchell Scott and Faircloth fanned. Kincaid and Chinnes worked a double steal and Bobby Rogers beat out a roller to short to drive in Kincaid. Chinnes scored when Ken Culbertson, in an attempt to get Rogers, threw wildly past first. Rogers went to second on the error.

"Tommy Clark doubled over Fred Knoebel's head in left field to drive Rogers home and John Sykes followed with a triple to deep right center to score Clark. Cy Szakacsi singled to center to score Sykes and Ashley Phillips dropped a Texas Leaguer in center that bounced past Ray Mathews and went for a double to score Szakacsi. That was all for Griffith and Ken Kea came in and struck out Kincaid to retire the side.

"Faircloth would have had a shutout but for single unearned runs by the Tigers in the third and fifth. In the third, Clark made two bad throws to first base on grounders by Knoebel and Culbertson. Knoebel scored on the second error. In the fifth, Knoebel beat out an infield roller, stole second, went to third on a wild pitch, and scored when no Gamecock covered second base on Doug Angley's steal attempt. Angley had drawn a base on balls.

"The Gamecocks batted around again in the seventh to add their final four runs and sew up the ball game. Chinnes led off with a walk. Scott also walked and Faircloth laid down a sacrifice bunt. Kea tried to get Chinnes at third on the play but umpire Ken Ouzts ruled the Gamecock second sacker safe.

"Rogers bounced to Gene Aughtry at second and he tried to get Chinnes at the plate but threw high for an error. The bases were still loaded with no outs. Johnny Stokes drove a single to left to score Scott and Faircloth. Sykes blooped a single to center to load the bases again. Szakacsi hit a lazy liner over first and Luke Deanhardt made a nice stab for the first out. Phillips singled to center to score Rogers but Kincaid lined out to second and Chinnes flied to left to end the inning. Carolina got four runs on three hits in the frame.

"The win was Faircloth's sixth without a loss and the Gamecock righthander struck out seven while walking only two."

The Gamecocks were faced with having to win their five remaining conference games to qualify for a Southern Conference playoff tournament. They won the first three, defeating Davidson 8-1 behind Bill Camp, Furman 3-2 with Faircloth pitching a complete game for this seventh win, and Furman again, 11-5, behind seldom used pitcher Dempsey Jones.

Things got tougher with the final two game series at Clemson and South Carolina was eliminated from contention with an 11 inning, 8-7 loss. Bill Camp was the losing pitcher. Grady Faircloth wasn't involved in the series and the Gamecocks were routed in the final game, 18-9.

Final statistics showed the team with a 16-9-1 record. Faircloth's 7-0 record accounted for nearly half the wins. Dempsey Jones was also undefeated with a 2-0 mark, Bill Camp was 5-5 and Frank Sherer 2-3. Bo Hagan had an 0-1 record and two other pitchers, Bill Lattimore and Walker Anderson, did not have a decision. Faircloth's earned run average was 1.98 and he recorded 43 strikeouts and 22 bases on balls in 66 innings.

He also collected 10 hits in 27 at bats for a .370 batting average. Shortstop John Sykes led the regulars in hitting with a .353 average and hit half of the team's eight home runs. Center fielder Bobby Rogers batted .351 and first baseman Cy Szakacsi .343. Szakacsi led the team in runs batted in with 30.

Outfielder Red Wilson hit .343 but played in only eight games. Outfielder Ashley Phillips batted .337, second baseman Lloyd Chinnes .309 and third baseman Tom Clark .306.

Entering his senior season at South Carolina, Grady Faircloth hadn't lost since his freshman year in junior college. He had 11 consecutive wins, including a 4-0 junior college sophomore season and a 7-0 season with the Gamecocks.

He shut Furman out 2-0 in the 1951 season opener for his 12th consecutive win, eighth as a Gamecock. The team struggled to a 6-15 record, however, and Faircloth—although leading the team in wins—had a 3-5 senior season to finish his Gamecock career with a 10-5 record.

South Carolina

vs

Maryland

April 20, 1965—South Carolina 1, Maryland 0
At College Park, Md. (13 Innings)

University of South Carolina and Minnesota Viking football fans remember Bobby Bryant more for his exploits on the gridiron than on the diamond, but the skinny lefthander from Macon, Ga., who bore the nickname "Bones" was just as much a super star on the baseball field as in a football stadium.

When the Gamecock baseball program and other spring sports operated on very small budgets and scholarship aid as a result was quite limited, coaches in the spring sports turned to the football roster for help and many of the stars in baseball as well as track and field were on football scholarships.

Bobby Bryant was one of these and his exploits on the pitching mound as well as his sensational play as a defensive back and kick returner in football resulted in his being named the 1967 recipient of the Anthony J. McKelvin Award as the top athlete in the Atlantic Coast Conference.

In the seasons when he wasn't returning a punt a school record 98 yards against North Carolina State, making tackles or intercepting passes against other opponents, Bryant was fashioning a 16-7 career record, pitching 14 complete games, including 5 shutouts, and striking out 226 batters in 221 2/3 innings.

Long before South Carolina began playing an expanded baseball schedule of fifty or more games, Bobby Bryant became the first Gamecock pitcher to strike out 100 batters in a season. He did that his senior season, 1967, in 87 innings while fashioning a 6-2 record and leading coach Jack Powers' team to a 21-8 record.

His record as a junior was also 6-2, and as a sophomore he compiled a 4-3 mark. Bryant pitched in 36 games over his 3 year varsity career and started 28 games. His 16 career wins were over 15 different opponents.

Bobby Bryant—*USC Sports Information*

While most of Bryant's wins were as a starting pitcher, the victory over Maryland during his sophomore season was in relief and ranks as a milestone in Gamecock baseball history. He pitched the final 2 1/3 innings of that classic extra inning victory.

Almost the victim of a no-hit game by Maryland sophomore lefthanded pitcher Jerry Bark, the Gamecocks pulled out a 1-0 victory on a 13th inning home run by usually light hitting Donnie Myers, a journeyman infielder who normally performed at shortstop or third base but happened to be playing first base on April 20, 1965 at College Park, Md.

Eddie Chester, a 25-year-old sophomore six year Navy veteran was coach Bob Reising's starting pitcher against Maryland's Bark in the first game of a scheduled Atlantic Coast Conference double-header. The scheduled April 19 game at Maryland was rained out, resulting in two seven inning games being slated for the next day.

The first game of that doubleheader lasted almost twice the allotted innings. Bark held the Gamecocks hitless through nine innings until South Carolina second baseman Joe Tonelli led off the 10th with a single to left field and continued to second base when the baseball eluded Terrapin left fielder Bob McCarthy for an error.

Bark pitched out of that jam by striking out Dick Moseley, intentionally walking Dan Scarpa and then striking out Myers and Dave Corley. South Carolina's only base runners over the first nine innings were Scarpa, who walked in the second inning and was erased when Myers hit into a double play, Moseley who reached on an error in the fifth, and Scarpa who walked again in the eighth.

Chester, meanwhile, was matching Bark in pitching scoreless innings and didn't walk a batter. He gave up a two out first inning single to Lamar Davis, a single to Tom Bichy and a hit batter in the fourth, a two out double to Steve Sauve in the sixth, and a leadoff single to Bark in the eighth. Pinch hitter Gus Sclafani singled with one out in the 10th, but Bark made a double play to blunt that threat.

Bobby Northcutt pinch hit for Chester in the top of the 11th without success and Maryland mounted a serious threat in the bottom of the inning against relief pitcher Rich Grich. Paul Breslow led off with a base hit but was out attempting to steal, catcher Dan Scarpa to second baseman Joe Tonelli. Bob Isaacson was hit by a pitch and Lamar Davis singled.

Steve Ravan replaced Grich for one batter with Steve Sauve's ground ball to third baseman Dave Corley forcing Davis at second with Isaacson moving to third with the potential winning run.

Enter Bobby Bryant. He replaced Ravan on the mound for South Carolina and coaxed Mike Long to fly to center fielder Howard Brotherton to end the inning.

In the 12th, Bob McCarthy reached on an error and Bark walked with two out to mount another Maryland threat, but Breslow flied to right fielder Al Barnett for the final out.

After Scarpa popped up to second base to begin the top of the 13th inning, Myers—who batted only .207 for the season—hit a line drive over the left field fence for his only home run of the season and only the second hit off Bark, who then fanned Corley for his 15th strikeout of the game. Shortstop Dave Murrell reached on an error but Bryant made the final out of the inning by flying to left field.

Maryland got the potential tying and winning runs on base in the bottom of the 13th. Bryant retired Bob Isaacson on a ground ball to Myers at first and struck out Lamar Davis. Then, he walked Sauve and Mike Long singled to keep Maryland's hopes alive.

Tom Bichy lifted a fly ball to Barnett in right field and Bobby Bryant and the South Carolina Gamecocks had claimed a 1-0 victory despite the near perfect pitching of Maryland Jerry Bark.

The second game of the doubleheader started a little late but seven innings were completed before dark and Maryland shut out the Gamecocks 4-0 to gain a split that left South Carolina with a 13-5 overall record, 4-2 in the conference, and a break-even road trip.

Back in Columbia, *The State* newspaper's story on the events at College Park said, "Maryland ace Jerry Bark had a ho-hitter until Joe Tonelli slapped a single for USC in the 10th inning. Then, in the 13th, Myers smashed a Bark pitch over the 325 foot sign in left field. It was USC's second and last hit of the game.

"Bobby Bryant, who bailed out the Gamecocks in the 11th when the Terps reached reliever Rich Grich for two hits, stopped Maryland in the 13th to gain the victory, his second in three decisions.

"The defeat was a heartbreaker for Bark, who watched his team mates strand 12 runners while striking out 15 Carolina batters.

"Gamecock starter Eddie Chester matched Bark through ten innings, doling out six hits without a base on balls. He was lifted for a pinch hitter in the 11th."

There was no designated hitter during the years that Bobby Bryant played collegiate baseball and his superb athletic ability was demonstrated his senior season when Bryant wore a short cast on his right wrist following surgery to repair a football injury. Since he was left handed, the cast didn't hamper his pitching but Bryant couldn't grip a bat with his right hand.

Swinging with only his left hand on the bat, Bryant collected 10 hits in 37 at bats—mostly on drag bunts or opposite field line drives slapped over the third baseman's head—to hit .270 his senior season. His career batting average was .250, compiled on 23 hits in 92 at bats.

Bryant's career pitching statistics showed a 2.40 earned run average to go with his 16-7 record and 226 strikeouts.

Bryant was twice selected in the professional baseball free agent draft—once by the Boston Red Sox and once by the New York Yankees—but cast his lot with the National Football League when he was drafted by the Minnesota Vikings.

Despite his skinny physique—6 feet 2 inches tall and 170 pounds—Bryant lasted fourteen years in the NFL and played on four Viking teams that advanced to the Super Bowl. When he retired his 50 interceptions were a Viking career record.

South Carolina

vs

Georgia

March 27, 1967—South Carolina 5, Georgia 0
At Athens, Ga.(No Hit Game)

Billy Reitmeier was the starting pitcher in three of the most memorable games in South Carolina baseball history—all won by the Gamecocks—but he was credited with only one of the victories.

However, it was a big one. The chubby (5-11,185 pounds) righthander who attended high school in Atlanta but listed Honolulu, Hawaii as his home town as that's where his military father was stationed during Billy's college years, pitched a no hit, no run game against the University of Georgia Mar. 27, 1967 at Athens, Ga.

Reitmeier pitched a school record 15 1/3 innings 11 days later, April 8, 1967 when the Gamecocks set a team record by playing 17 innings before defeating North Carolina 6-5 at Columbia.

A year and 22 days later he was the starting pitcher April 30, 1968 in Columbia when South Carolina equaled its longest game in history by downing Georgia 3-2. However, Reitmeier lasted three innings, leaving for a pinch hitter with Georgia leading 2-1.

In 1967, I was in my sixth season as South Carolina sports information director and, operating as a one man staff, traveled with football and basketball, but only occasionally with baseball and track. I had planned to ride the team bus to Athens that day in late March but something came up that kept me in Columbia, and I missed a no-hitter.

Georgia used four pinch hitters in the game and the only one that hit the baseball was Jeff Corban whose ground ball to shortstop Toy McCord ended the game.

South Carolina took a 1-0 first inning lead when Wallie Jones walked, stole second and continued to third on Bulldog catcher Randy Kohn's throwing error. Jones scored on Mike Fair's two out single.

The lead grew to 3-0 in the sixth. Fair walked, moved to second on a single by Billy Cash, and third as Larry Womack's fielder's choice forced Cash at second. Fair scored on a wild pitch and Womack

64

came home when Georgia shortstop Roy Saine booted Bob Mauro's two out ground ball.

McCord's single, an infield out and Fair's RBI single made it 4-0 in the seventh and the final Gamecock run scored in the ninth inning. Jones singled, took second on an error, third on McCord's infield out, and scored on a sacrifice fly by Frank Partyka.

The State, Columbia's morning newspaper, headlined its story: "Reitmeier Fashions No Hitter as Gamecocks Rip Georgia 5-0."

The newspaper's story, datelined Athens, Ga., began, "Big Bill Reitmeier, in the second start of his collegiate career, fired a brilliant no-hitter to propel South Carolina to a 5-0 triumph over Georgia here Monday afternoon.

"Reitmeier, a sophomore righthander, completely stifled the Bulldogs and had only one close call in spinning the gem."

The close call was the near hit in the eighth inning.

"Larry McDaniel dribbled a grounder past the mound that second baseman Wallie Jones fielded and flipped to first baseman Billy Cash," the newspaper story read.

"Cash came off the base to take the throw. It was first called a hit, but changed to an error when the base umpire ruled the throw beat the runner." Cash was charged with the error for taking his foot off the base too soon.

Reitmeier's no-hitter was the fourth against a college team by a South Carolina pitcher. The first was by Milton "Babe" Adams, 1-0, over Guilford in 1914. Grayson Wolf no-hit Presbyterian in 1932, winning 22-1, and Frank Sherer pitched a 6-0 no-hitter, also against Presbyterian in 1948. The only no-hitters since Reitmeier's game, through 1995, came on consecutive days, 10-0 by Tim Lewis over Old Dominion, and 8-0 by Ray Lavigne over George Mason, March 25-26, 1975.

South Carolina has been on the losing end of four no-hitters, two of them at the hands of Clemson. Ernest "Lefty" Smith no-hit the Gamecocks 6-0 in 1924 and another lefthander, Billy Odell, did the same thing, 2-0, thirty years later in 1954. A third lefthander, Herb Busch of Virginia, pitched a 5-0 no-hit game against the Gamecocks in 1957.

Billy Reitmeier—*USC Sports Information*

The only righthander to hold South Carolina hitless was Brad Myers of Northwestern who beat the Gamecocks 4-0 in 1990.

Less than two weeks after pitching the no-hit game, Reitmeier started against North Carolina in Columbia and pitched until there was one out in the 16th inning. Through 1995 that remained the longest stint ever by a South Carolina pitcher. Eddie Chester, a 27-year-old left handed senior six year Navy veteran, pitched the final 1 2/3 innings to get the win.

Bob Spear covered that game for *The State* and the headline on his story said: Gamecocks Nip UNC in 17. Bases Loaded Walk Ends Marathon."

Spear's lead began: "South Carolina, which had clawed for survival all afternoon, bled across a 17th inning run to break up a fierce struggle and deal North Carolina a 6-5 setback here Saturday.

"The Gamecocks, who never led until the end of the Atlantic Coast Conference battle, blended a single, an intentional walk, an error with a bases-loaded two out pass to Toy McCord to scratch in the run that ran their victory string to nine, their overall record to 12-2 and their ACC mark to 2-0.

"The league's sophomore pitching sensation—USC's Billy Reitmeier and the Tar Heels' Gary Hill—staged a sharp duel for five innings, but things got sticky and the innings without threats became few and far between.

"In the 4 hour and 53 minutes between Reitmeier's first pitch on the Sunday afternoon and Chip Stone's last with darkness fast approaching, just about everything possible happened—sparkling defensive plays, clutch hits and brilliant pitching.

"The Tar Heels jumped to a 2-0 lead with single runs in the first and sixth. South Carolina pulled even with two in the sixth and then pushed across another in the seventh to deadlock things again.

"North Carolina jumped in front again in the 14th but the Gamecocks came back to knot it. The clubs did the same thing in the 16th to set the stage for South Carolina's winning run.

"Larry Womack lined a single to open the USC 17th. He moved to second on Herb Ward's bunt and the Tar Heels elected to give Bob Mauro an intentional pass. Stone replaced John Richards on the mound and promptly fanned reliever Eddie Chester, but Rod Thompson kicked Wallie Jones' grounder to third and McCord coaxed a walk to decide it."

An outstanding play by centerfielder Mike Fair, shortstop McCord and catcher Mauro prevented North Carolina from taking a two run lead in the top of the 16th and saved the game for the Gamecocks.

Reitmeier walked Danny Talbott who moved up on a sacrifice. Hull singled to score Talbott. Chester replaced Reitmeier on the mound for South Carolina. Rod Thompson forced Hull for the second out. Bruce Bolick doubled to the left centerfield gap and Thompson was cut down at the plate Fair to McCord to Mauro.

Slightly more than a year after South Carolina's first record breaking 17 inning contest, April 30, 1968, the Gamecocks were again involved in a marathon and again Billy Reitmeier was the starting pitcher.

Bill Mitchell covered that game for *The State*, and the headline on his account read: "Gamecocks nip Georgia in 17. Fair's Hit Breaks Up Marathon."

"Mike Fair's line drive single to center scored Billy Cash from second in the bottom of the 17th inning to give South Carolina a 3-2 victory over Georgia's stubborn Bulldogs at Capital City Park Tuesday afternoon," Mitchell began.

The game was played in Columbia's professional ball park due to construction at South Carolina's campus baseball stadium.

"The 17 inning contest tied an Atlantic Coast Conference record set last year by the Gamecocks and North Carolina in Columbia," Mitchell continued.

"Cash opened the 17th with a sharp single to center off hard luck loser Mike Lodgson. Lodgson then fanned Frank Partyka and got Buddy Caldwell on a fly to center. Don Stanley walked to set up Fair's decisive blow.

"Georgia scored single runs in the first and third to chase Gamecock starter Billy Reitmeier. Ronnie Evans started the fourth and pitched brilliantly through the 16th before giving way to Jimbo Smith at the start of the 17th."

Between his no-hitter and going 15 1/3 innings against North Carolina, Reitmeier pitched a one-hit, 3-0, victory over Belmont Abbey April 4, 1967. He missed pitching back-to-back no-hitters by giving up a leadoff seventh inning single to Belmont Abbey first baseman John Lawing. Reitmeier finished his sophomore season with a 5-2 record and a 2.37 earned run average to lead South Carolina to a 21-8 record.

However, he experienced difficulty his junior and senior seasons, posting an 0-4 record in 1968 and 1-2 in 1969, to graduate with a career record of six wins and eight losses.

Mar. 4, 1972—South Carolina 3, N. C. State 0
At Columbia

Apr. 25, 1972—South Carolina 6, The Citadel 0
At Charleston, S. C.

Three days before Bobby Richardson began the third season of a three year contract as head baseball coach at the University of South Carolina, Director of Athletics Paul Dietzel tore up the pact and replaced it with a new five year deal.

Terms of the new contract were not announced and the media, not being as inquisitive in 1972 as in later years, apparently didn't ask how much the former New York Yankee second baseman would be paid under the new agreement.

Things were indeed looking up for the baseball Gamecocks. After a 14-20 rookie season in 1970, Richardson had produced an 18-12 record in 1971, and with seven freshmen including such future super stars as fist baseman-outfielder Hank Small, shortstop Eddie Ford, and pitchers Earl Bass and Greg Ward, on the 1972 roster, South Carolina's diamond prospects were never brighter.

However, it would be two veteran lefthanders—juniors George Beam and Alan Hilliard—who would etch their names in the Gamecock record book in 1972.

In a pre-season story, sportswriter Bob Spear said Richardson was "really encouraged" over prospects for the season and quoted the former major league star infielder as saying, "Our practices have been good and the pitching is ready."

However, there was one cloud on the horizon. Hank Small, the big slugger from Atlanta counted on to provide long ball power to the offense, had separated his right shoulder in a physical education wrestling class and would miss a few games of the season.

Bob Kleinknecht, a sensational fielding junior from Silver Spring, Md., who had previously been used primarily as a late inning defensive replacement and had batted only seven times as a sophomore, would fill in at first base until Small's injury healed.

Richardson said senior righthander Larry Erbaugh of Staunton, Va., coming off a 6-3 season with a 2.49 earned run average, would be the opening day pitcher. Other starters were projected as junior lefthander George Beam of Charlotte, N.C., 2-3, 3.86 in 1971, junior lefthander Alan Hilliard of Greenville, S.C., 2-3, 2.31, and freshman righthander Earl Bass of Cayce, S.C.

Among the position players, switch-hitting shortstop Eddie Ford of Great Neck, N. Y., would be the only freshman starter. He was the son of former New York Yankee lefthanded pitcher, future hall of famer and Richardson's Yankee teammate, Whitey Ford.

Junior Tommy Moody of Columbia, recovered from a broken leg suffered in 1971, would be at second base with junior Bruce Pudlock of Parma, Ohio, who batted only .222 in 1971 but was outstanding defensively, would be at third base.

Seniors Pete Carpenter of Virginia Beach, Va., and Billy Petoskey of Columbia, and sophomore John Gambrell of Manning, S.C., were the projected outfield starters.

Sophomore Drew Choate of Sparta, N.C., was the starting catcher. A second round draft pick out of high school by the Philadelphia Phillies, Choate was a superb defensive player but had batted only .165 his freshman year. He would play the entire 1972 season, catching 37 of 41 games and handling 304 chances, without committing an error while batting only .212.

Bobby Richardson welcomes prize recruit Hank Small to the Gamecock Roost.—*Tom Price Files*

69

"I think we have a well balanced staff and the pitchers will get plenty of work," Richardson said.. "We have a good schedule. We don't have many days off after we get started."

The Gamecocks had scheduled 45 games including a trans-continental trip to the prestigious Riverside tournament in California.

"We're playing in perhaps the finest college baseball tournament in the country this season and we're going to get lights for our field next year," Richardson added.

On March 3, North Carolina State spoiled the Gamecock season opener when Wolfpack catcher Bill Glad broke a 4-4 tie with a solo home run in the top of the ninth inning to pin a 5-4 defeat on Erbaugh, who pitched a complete game for South Carolina.

A day later, the tables were turned in record breaking fashion. The headline in March 5 editions of *The State* told the story: "USC Blanks State; Beam Fans Record 17 Batters."

The story under Bill Mitchell's byline began, "Lefthander George Beam established a school record of 17 strikeouts and spun a neat three hitter as South Carolina managed a weekend split with N. C. State by handing the Wolfpack a 3-0 whitewashing at the Rex Enright Athletic Center Saturday afternoon."

Mitchell's story continued, "Beam, who walked four and hit a couple of batters, fanned seven straight batters in the middle of the game, including striking out the side in the fifth and sixth frames. The junior from Charlotte struck out two in the first, second, fourth and eighth innings before fanning shortstop Buddy Green for the 17th strikeout in the ninth.

North Carolina State loaded the bases in the third and eighth innings but each time Beam pitched out of trouble to preserve the shutout.

In the third, with the bases loaded and one out, Beam got center fielder Wayne Currin to bounce back to the mound for a force at the plate. Rightfielder Mike Baxter grounded into a fielder's choice to end the inning.

A hit batter, a walk and an infield single by N.C. State first baseman Rich Richardson filled the bases with two out in the eighth. Left fielder Pat Kornsrick hit a ground ball to end that threat.

South Carolina took the lead against loser Tommy Land, the first of four Wolfpack pitchers, in the second inning. John Gambrell's bloop single scored Bob Kleinknect who had singled and moved to second on an infield out.

Catcher Drew Choate provided Beam with a pair of insurance runs in the third inning with a line drive home run down the left field line after right fielder Pete Carpenter had collected a two out single.

South Carolina missed two other scoring opportunities when

runners were thrown out at the plate in the fifth and sixth innings.

Choate's home run was the game's only extra base hit and the usually light hitting Kleinknecht was the only player with two hits as South Carolina collected nine hits off four N.C. State pitchers.

Two days after Beam's strikeout record, Hank Small made his collegiate debut as a ninth inning pinch hitter against Louisville. He singled and scored on a pinch single by Bo Robinson—the sixth pinch hitter used by Richardson in the game—to give the Gamecocks a 3-2 victory.

After thirteen games, South Carolina's record was 8-5 as the Gamecocks flew to the west coast to participate in the Riverside tournament. The Gamecocks won only two of seven games against the star-studded field, but two of the losses went into extra innings and Richardson's team learned it could compete against the best.

Freshman Greg Ward earned his first collegiate win with a four hit complete game to defeat host Cal-Riverside 5-1 in the first game. Losses followed to Arizona State, 5-1; Stanford, 8-2; Cornell, 3-1 in 10 innings; UCLA, 10-4; and Santa Clara, 5-4 in 11 innings, before the Gamecocks defeated Tennessee 4-3 in their final tournament game.

There was no designated hitter rule in 1972. Bobby Richardson wanted Hank Small's bat in the lineup nonetheless and played him in right field even though Small's shoulder injury hampered his throwing. There was no impediment to his bat however as the big freshman hit safely in every game at Riverside, including a 4 for 4 day against UCLA. He batted .481 in the tournament with 13 hits in 27 at bats and was a unanimous choice for the all-tournament team.

Small would finish his freshman season with a .379 batting average, appearing in 39 of 41 games despite the painful shoulder injury. His home run total would jump from 4 as a freshman to 8 as a sophomore, 17 as a junior, and 19 as a senior and he used an aluminum bat only in his senior year.

South Carolina returned home from California with a 10-

George Beam (L) established a school record by striking out 17 batters in 1972 and Alan Hilliard tied the record in the same season.
—USC Sports Information

10 record and would win 15 of 21 games the remainder of the 1972 season to finish with a 25-16 record.

On April 25, Richardson took his team to Charleston to meet The Citadel. South Carolina had defeated the Bulldogs 11-0 at Columbia in their first game back from California. Junior lefthander Alan Hilliard was the starting pitcher at College Park in Charleston.

"Hilliard Fans 17; USC Rips Citadel," the headline in *The State* read the next morning.

"Junior lefthander Alan Hilliard tied a school record with 17 strikeouts and scattered six hits Tuesday night in pitching South Carolina to a 6-0 baseball win over The Citadel," the story's first paragraph said.

"Hilliard struck out the side in the first, second, third and sixth innings and had 16 strikeouts with one out in the seventh. However, he didn't get the 17th until the second out in the ninth when Bulldog first baseman Ron Sanders took a called third strike."

Hilliard's effort to surpass the record failed on the final out of the game when Citadel catcher Paul Plunkett grounded to second baseman Tommy Moody. Hilliard walked only 1 Bulldog batter while allowing 6 singles and striking out 17. Sophomore lefthander Rusty Booth, 5-2, took the loss for The Citadel.

South Carolina scored 2 runs each in the first and second innings and 1 each in the sixth and seventh. The Gamecocks collected 10 hits, 3 of them by Eddie Ford who drove in 2 runs. John Gambrell had 2 hits and scored 3 times.

Alan Hilliard
–USC Sports Information

Nearly a quarter of a century later, the 17 strikeouts—accomplished twice in the same season—remained a South Carolina school record for an individual pitcher. However, it was surpassed as a team record when righthanders Matt Threehouse and Rob Mosser combined to strike out eighteen batters March 16, 1993 in a 7-0 win over The Citadel at Charleston.

Threehouse had sixteen strikeouts through eight innings but gave up back to back singles with one out in the ninth. He was relieved by Mosser who struck out the final two batters.

South Carolina

vs

Georgia Tech

May 12, 1973—South Carolina 11-2, Georgia Tech 3-0
At Columbia

Greg Ward never thought of himself as an iron man, but when he told coach Bobby Richardson he felt like going a few more innings after retiring the final 19 Georgia Tech batters in the first game of a May 12, 1973 doubleheader, Richardson told him "go ahead."

Richardson didn't plan on his sophomore righthander pitching two complete games on the same day and neither did Ward. Both thought he would work a couple of innings and then give way to the bullpen. The bullpen never came into play.

When it was all over, Ward had pitched two seven inning complete games and had shut the powerful Yellowjackets out over the last 13 1/3 innings to finish his sophomore season with a 7-3 record as South Carolina finished the year with a then school record 26 victories.

Georgia Tech came to Columbia for a scheduled two day series, May 11-12, that would end the South Carolina season. Coach Jim Luck's Yellowjackets had met defeat only twice in twenty two games and were in the running for an NCAA district playoff bid. The Georgia Tech record was 19-2-1.

"Rain, hail, lightning and finally a power failure halted play after five innings Friday night with South Carolina and Georgia Tech tied at 2-2 at the Rex Enright Athletic Center baseball diamond," *The State* newspaper reported in its editions of May 12, 1973.

"The contest officially goes into the books as a tie and coaches Bobby Richardson of the Gamecocks and Jim Luck of Georgia Tech agreed to play two seven inning games Saturday beginning at 1:30 p.m., rather than the single nine inning game scheduled. Georgia Tech, now 19-2-2, is a leading contender for a district NCAA playoff berth. South Carolina, which winds up its season today, is 24-15-1."

Other news attracted far more media attention than the South

Carolina-Georgia Tech baseball series that weekend. While the abbreviated five inning tie and the resulting doubleheader appeared on the fourth page of the sports section, a story about football recruiting was the lead story on the first page of the sports section.

Also on the section's first page was an announcement that South Carolina native, Larry Doby, had been voted into the South Carolina Athletic Hall of Fame. Doby, who was born in Camden and grew up in Paterson, N.J., was the first black to play in the American League, with the Cleveland Indians, and the second in major league baseball after Jackie Robinson of the Dodgers.

Displayed prominently in the local section was a story that May 12 was graduation day at the University of South Carolina with about 2,000 degrees to be awarded.

The football recruiting story by sportswriter Ernie Trubiano said "some independent schools are seeking to beef up their football programs before next year when new scholarship limitations (105 total and 30 in one year) will be imposed by the NCAA."

Trubiano said schools that were "stockpiling" recruits included South Carolina, Florida State and Virginia Tech. He quoted football coach Paul Dietzel as saying South Carolina planned to bring in about 60 prospects but *The State* said it had learned the Gamecocks had signed 75.

Meanwhile, on the fourth page of the sports section, *The State* carried a one column photo of Greg Ward over a caption that read, "Iron Man Job."Alongside was a brief story that said:

"Sophomore righthander Greg Ward worked the iron man feat Saturday, pitching both ends of a doubleheader, as Carolina swept powerful Georgia Tech 11-3 and 2-0 to end the Gamecock season with a record 26 wins.

"Ward struck out 12 and walked none in the first game, retiring the final 19 Yellowjackets in order, and scattered five singles in the nightcap in pitching his fourth shutout of the season. The Greensboro, N.C., native struck out six and walked one in the second game. He walked only nine batters in 74 innings in compiling a 7-3 sophomore record.

"The Gamecocks completed their season with a 26-15-1

Greg Ward—*USC Sports Information*

record, surpassing by one the school record of 25 victories attained last year. Georgia Tech, which came to Columbia with a 19-2-1 record, saw its string of 13 straight games without a loss broken in convincing fashion."

After striking out the first two batters in the first inning of the opener, Ward yielded consecutive singles to Cam Bonifay and Kevin McNamara and a long home run to Randy Brown to stake Georgia Tech to a 3-0 lead.

The Gamecocks scored five times in the bottom of the first to take control of the game.

South Carolina put the game out of reach with a six run third inning, chasing Baldwin with consecutive singles by Larry Wojcicki, Ward and John Gambrell. Reliever Larry Livingston yielded three more hits and hit one batter before retiring the side.

Cam Bonifay, the Georgia Tech third baseman who twenty years later would be the general manager of the Pittsburgh Pirates, had a single in each game against Ward. The only other Georgia Tech player with more than one hit was shortstop Frank Turner, who had two of the five Tech singles in the second game.

The combined playing time of the fourteen inning doubleheader was three minutes under three hours. Ward pitched the first game in 1:32 and shaved seven minutes off that with a 1:25 time for the nightcap. He had 18 strikeouts, 1 walk, and allowed 8 hits.

The double loss knocked Georgia Tech out of contention for an NCAA playoff berth.

South Carolina—led by Ward and two time All-America righthander Earl Bass—would eclipse the school record 26 victories with 48 wins in 1974, with the Gamecocks earning their first NCAA playoff bid, and follow with 51 wins, a regional championship and a second place finish in the 1975 College World Series.

Greg Ward won 34 games, lost 13 and saved 2 during his four year collegiate career.

Ward, whose nickname was "Chico," grew up and attended high school in Greensboro, N.C., but his family lived in El Paso, Tex., during the years Ward attended South Carolina. His collegiate record showed 340 1/3 innings pitched, 7 shutouts and 25 complete games. He compiled 323 strikeouts, walked only 69.

His career earned run average was 1.74.

As a senior, when his record was 14-3 in a 51-6-1 Gamecock season, Ward defeated Eastern Michigan University freshman Bob Welch, a future major league star, 5-1, in the College World Series.

Ward signed with the Baltimore Orioles after graduation and reached class AA in professional baseball before an arm ailment ended his playing career.

South Carolina

vs

South Alabama

March 22, 1974—South Carolina 9, South Alabama 2
At Mobile, Ala.

Although they were thirty six years apart in age, University of South Carolina pitcher Earl Bass and University of South Alabama head coach Eddie Stanky had one thing in common when they squared off against each other March 22, 1974 in Mobile, Ala.

Both were competitors and winning was the most important thing.

During a colorful professional baseball career that included eleven major league seasons as an infielder and eight years as manager of three different teams, the 57-year-old Stanky had earned the nickname, "The Brat."

While playing second base he would do side straddle hops behind the bag to distract opposing hitters until the league ruled the practice illegal. As manager of the Cubs he refused to give his starting lineup to the media before game time until a rule was passed requiring release of batting orders half an hour before.

At the college level, as highly successful coach at South Alabama, Stanky wasn't above resorting to any tactic that he thought might intimidate a college age opponent. He never cut a candidate for his team and more than fifty players were in Jaguar uniforms for the series against South Carolina.

South Carolina coach Bobby Richardson and Stanky were both second basemen and both played eleven seasons in the big leagues, but there the similarity ended. Richardson was deeply religious and genteel. Stanky was as rough as a corn cob. They never played against each other as Stanky was in the National League with the Cubs, Dodgers, Giants and Cardinals and retired as a player after the 1953 season, two years before Richardson came on the American League scene with the New York Yankees.

Earl Bass, in the middle of a career that would see him win 34 collegiate games, lose only 3 and twice earn first team All-America

Gamecock Coach Bobby Richardson (L) and South Alabama Coach Eddie Stanky, both former major league second basemen.—*Tom Price Files*

honors, was just as cocky and confident at age 21 as Eddie Stanky had been throughout his baseball career. As a fashion statement, Bass liked to wear a white batter's glove—actually it was a golf glove because batter's gloves hadn't yet come into vogue—on his left hand inside his fielder's glove.

Stanky saw an opportunity to get to the 6-1, 175 pound South Carolina righthander, who batted cleanup and played first base on days he wasn't pitching, when Bass went to the mound in the bottom of the first inning of the second game of a three game series.

He protested to the umpires that Bass' glove within a glove was an illegal distraction to his hitters, and who would know more about illegal distractions than Eddie Stanky, the master of the illegal distraction. There was a meeting on the mound.

"Coach, if you don't like my glove," Bass said in a voice loud enough for all in the stands and press box to hear, "I'll take it off, but I'm still going to whip your butt."

He dramatically peeled off the glove, slowly, one finger at a time, stuffed it in his hip pocket and proceeded to pitch South Carolina to a 9-2 win.

As Bass walked off the mound after retiring Jim Hively on a pop up to shortstop to leave two base runners stranded in the bottom of the ninth inning, he was met at the foul line by Stanky who threw his arms around him and declared, "Son, you're my kind of ball player."

South Carolina, which had set a school record by winning 26 games in 1973, had begun the 1974 season with a 12 game winning streak before losing the second game of a two game series with Central Michigan, 7-6, at Columbia. The Gamecocks then reeled off a four game win streak to take a 16-1 record on a demanding five game spring break trip that included three games at South Alabama and two at Florida State.

The Gamecocks lost the first game at South Alabama, 11-7, making Bass' appearance in the middle game of the series even more important. *The State*, Columbia's morning newspaper, reported the outcome in these words:

"Righthander Earl Bass scattered nine hits and Hank Small and freshman Jim Pankovits supplied home run power Friday as South Carolina clubbed South Alabama, 9-2, to even the college baseball series at one game apiece."

The newspaper went on to say, "Bass struck out nine and walked two in going the route for his fourth win against no losses as the Gamecocks ran their season record to 17-2. Coach Eddie Stanky's Jaguars sank to 11-4. South Alabama is ranked 13th and South Carolina 16th in the latest national baseball rankings.

"South Carolina scored its first run in the third inning when Drew Choate walked, took second on an infield out, and scored on Jeff Grantz's long double. Small hit his sixth home run of the season, a 360 foot blast over the left field fence, to lead off the sixth.

In addition to pitching the victory, Bass had one hit and drove in two runs in the game.

Back home in Columbia, spring football practice attracted more attention than Earl Bass and the Gamecock baseball team. Coach Paul Dietzel welcomed 83 candidates to spring practice but his star of stars was missing. All-America quarterback candidate Jeff Grantz was in Mobile playing second base.

"I can't say I'm pleased that Jeff is not with us this spring but we knew when he came here that he would play baseball and football," Dietzel told news media covering the first practice. "I'm not complaining and really it will be a big plus to have Ron Bass as our number one quarterback during the drills."

Alex Pastore hit two home runs for South Alabama in the third game of the series and South Carolina lost, 9-2, and headed for Tallahassee with a 17-3 record. A late March cold wave hit the Florida capital and the first game of the series was postponed due to the freezing weather. A doubleheader was scheduled for the next day, March 26.

The State reported the results with this headline: Gamecocks Win Pair From FSU.

"The pitching of Greg Ward and Earl Bass fired South Carolina's Gamecocks to a doubleheader sweep over Florida State, 4-1 and 1-0, in college baseball action involving two of the top Southeastern independents," the newspaper's story began.

"The victories placed South Carolina's record at 19-3 and concluded a five game road trip to Florida and Alabama. The Gamecocks have a meeting scheduled with arch-rival Clemson Thursday on the Tigers' home field.

"Bass scattered five hits to place his record at 5-0 on the season in winning the nightcap, 1-0. The junior righthander had to pitch himself out of jams in the second and fourth innings.

"In the second frame, Florida State loaded the bases on two singles and an error, and the Seminoles got two men on in the fourth. Each time, Bass bore down and retired the side with no damage done.

"Shortstop Eddie Ford came up with the only two hits South Carolina could muster in the second game. He scored the game's only run in the sixth after lining a single to centerfield. He stole second and continued to third on a wild pitch. Bass' ground ball was bobbled by Seminole shortstop Marty Maier and Ford came in to score on the miscue."

In the first game, Greg Ward struck out six and walked one in winning his fifth decision against one loss. Five of the seven South Carolina hits off FSU pitcher Larry Rothchild were infield singles.

Second baseman Jeff Grantz and designated hitter Ray Lavigne beat out slow rollers in the first inning and Grantz scored on an error. Center fielder John Gambrell singled in the fourth, stole second, moved to third on an infield out, and scored on a wild pitch.

South Carolina added two runs in the sixth inning on bunt singles by Bass, who was playing first base, and Gambrell, plus a base on balls and catcher Drew Choate's single off the glove of FSU third baseman Guillermo Bonilla, who later played for the San Diego Padres under his first name, Juan Bonilla.

Florida State's only run in the doubleheader was unearned and came in the fifth inning of the first game. Designated hitter Jim Foxwell moved to second on another Gamecock boot, and scored on a two out single by left fielder Steve Tebbetts.

With a 3-2 record during the spring break trip and 19-3 overall, the Gamecocks headed home to Columbia for a one day break before heading upstate for a sixth consecutive road game, a confrontation with arch-rival Clemson.

South Carolina

vs

Clemson

March 28, 1974—South Carolina 3, Clemson 0
At Clemson, S.C.

The South Carolina-Clemson baseball rivalry, while not the oldest on the Gamecock schedule, has been the most prolific with the series dating back to 1899. Through 1995, the Gamecocks and Tigers had squared off against each other more than than 230 times.

Except for a one year break in 1984, one has to go back to the World War II years of 1943 and '44 to find seasons in which Carolina and Clemson didn't play, and in every other season since—with the exception of 1974 and '75—the rivals have played each other at least twice a year, sometimes as many as six times.

They met only once in 1974 and once again in 1975, and therein lies a story. Coach Frank McGuire had dropped Clemson from the South Carolina basketball schedule after the 1971-72 season citing as a reason Carolina's desire to pursue a national independent schedule after withdrawing from the Atlantic Coast Conference.

Clemson baseball coach Bill Wilhelm sought to use the same reasoning to drop the Gamecocks from his schedule. After much negotiation by the athletics directors, a compromise was reached with the teams to play a single game each season, the first game to be at Clemson. And, Wilhelm stipulated that South Carolina had to furnish the plate umpire.

As sports information director at South Carolina, I was driving to Clemson, March 28, 1974, to cover the single baseball meeting between the Gamecocks and Tigers when I spotted Bill Cummings, an umpire from Columbia, alongside his disabled automobile on Interstate Highway 26.

I stopped to lend a hand and Cummings, after explaining his predicament, hitched a ride to Clemson to umpire the ball game.

South Carolina was having its best season up to that time with a 19-3 record while Clemson was struggling with a 7-9 mark.

An advance story datelined Clemson in *The State* by Teddy Heffner set the scene:

"South Carolina seeks its 20th victory of the campaign and Clemson would like nothing better than to turn around a disappointing start with a win over the Gamecocks as the two cross-state rivals collide here this afternoon at 3 o'clock.

"Coach Bobby Richardson's Gamecocks bring a 19-3 record into the game after an out-of-state road trip which resulted in two losses in three games against South Alabama and a doubleheader sweep over Florida State.

"The Tigers of Bill Wilhelm, who has never had a losing season at Clemson, are 7-9 on the season after a 5-0 blanking of East Tennessee State Tuesday.

"Wilhelm's greatest woes this spring have been the performances of his pitching staff. The Tigers produce at the plate but have been unable to check the opposing offenses.

"South Carolina, on the other hand, has put together speed, power and pitching to enjoy the best start since Richardson took over the baseball program in 1970 and probably the best start in the Gamecocks' history.

"Earl Bass and Greg Ward lead Richardson's mound corps while Hank Small and Drew Choate have been the power hitters.

"Bass is unbeaten in five starts this season and Ward has lost but once in six times on the mound. Small has hammered six home runs this season while Choate has clouted five.

"Steve Cline's 4-1 record tops Clemson's pitching while top hitters include Smiley Sanders, Charlie Ing and Billy Wingo."

Drawing bigger play than Heffner's baseball advance in *The State* was a story announcing that Utah head basketball coach Bill Foster had been named head coach at Duke. Six years later, in 1980, Bill Foster would leave Duke to succeed Frank McGuire as head coach at South Carolina.

The second game of Clemson's series with East Tennessee State was rained out the day before the scheduled game with Carolina.

While Earl Bass and Greg Ward were numbers one and two in South Carolina's pitching rotation, they had pitched the doubleheader two days earlier at Florida State, and Richardson's starter against Clemson was sophomore Tim Lewis, a tall lefthander from Norristown, Pa., who quietly would win two more career games than either Bass or Ward while toiling his first three seasons in the shadows of the two ace righthanders.

Lewis mastered every Clemson hitter that day except the number eight batter in the lineup. Shortstop Pat Fitzsimmons reached him for singles in the third and fifth innings and a double in the

Coach Bobby Richardson flanked by his two All-America players, pitcher Earl Bass and first baseman/outfielder Hank Small.—*USC Sports Information*

seventh. The only other Clemson batter with a hit was designated hitter Brett Terrell, who singled with one out in the sixth.

Lewis struck out seven batters, walked two and hit one, and the only Clemson batter to reach third base was left fielder Charlie Ing who walked in the seventh and advanced two bases on Fitzsimmon's two out double. Second baseman Billy Wingo popped to Gamecock third baseman Jim Pankovits to end that threat.

The Tigers had two base runners in the fifth when catcher Lin Hamilton was hit by a pitch, with two out, and Fitzsimmons followed with a base hit. Wingo flied out to Mike Johnson in right field to end the inning.

Earl Bass, playing first base, reached on an error, moved to third on center fielder John Gambrell's double, and scored on a wild pitch in the South Carolina fourth inning. Shortstop Eddie Ford tripled to lead off the sixth and scored on left fielder Hank Small's double to make the score 2-0. Second baseman Jeff Grantz singled, stole second base, and scored on Small's single in the eighth inning to wrap up the day's scoring.

The headline in *The State* told the story: Lewis' Four Hitter Guns Gamecocks by Tigers.

"Tim Lewis fired a nifty four hit shutout and Hank Small knocked in two runs as South Carolina blanked Clemson, 3-0, here Thursday afternoon," Teddy Heffner wrote under a Clemson dateline.

During the ride back to Columbia, plate umpire Bill Cummings commented that Tim Lewis "had the best stuff" of any pitcher he had seen recently from his vantage point behind the plate. Lewis would go on to win a school record 36 games while losing only 6 during his 4 year career at South Carolina. Professionally he would rise as high as AAA in the New York Yankee organization.

South Carolina and Clemson in 1975 would again meet only once, the Gamecocks taking a 6-2 decision April 16 at Columbia behind the three hit pitching of Earl Bass. Clemson's two runs came on a high fly ball home run by Billy Wingo that hit the left field foul pole following a walk.

In 1976, at the suggestion of Bill Wilhelm, the teams played each other three times and have had multiple game series each year since, except 1984 when a dispute resulted in a one year break.

The 1974 Gamecocks would compile a 48-8 record and would earn the school's first bid to the NCAA baseball playoffs. Clemson would rally from its 7-10 record after losing to South Carolina to finish with 23 wins and 15 losses, thus preserving coach Bill Wilhelm's record of never having a losing season. He would retire after the 1993 season with 1,161 wins in 36 years.

The Tigers would finish first in the Atlantic Coast Conference race with a 10-1 league record but would lose the first game of the ACC tournament to Virginia before reaching the title game with wins over North Carolina, Virginia and N. C. State. However, N. C. State would win the showdown game of the double elimination tournament, defeating Clemson 8-6 to earn the ACC's automatic bid to the NCAA District III tournament at Starkville, Miss.

There, the Wolfpack would meet Carolina in the opening round.

South Carolina

vs

North Carolina State

May 23, 1974—South Carolina 9, North Carolina State 0
At Starkville, Miss. (NCAA District III Tournament)

As the bus taking the University of South Carolina baseball team to Starkville neared the end of a 12 hour journey, it passed through Columbus, Miss., and Earl Bass pointed out the ball park, where as a 12-year-old, he had pitched the Cayce-West Columbia, South Carolina team to the Dixie Youth World Series championship.

Ten years later, Bass was the ace of a South Carolina pitching staff that had won 44 of 50 games during the regular season, was ranked among the nation's top ten teams, and had earned the school's first ever invitation to the NCAA playoffs, the District III double elimination tournament at Starkville, Miss., with the winner to advance to the College World Series in Omaha, Neb.

Through fifty games Bass had a 10-1 record to lead a pitching staff that would lead the nation in strikeouts and compile a school record 1.60 staff earned run average that also led the nation, with five of its nine pitchers finishing with earned run averages of less than 2.00.

The Gamecocks boasted excellent fielding with a .966 team average. The .274 team batting average wasn't outstanding but three Gamecocks finished with double digit home runs—17 by outfielder-first baseman Hank Small, 12 by catcher Drew Choate, and 10 by second baseman Jeff Grantz—and the team stole a record 152 bases. Small drove in a record 65 runs, and they used wooden bats in 1974.

Small finished the season with a .360 batting average. Center fielder John Gambrell batted .400 in the regular season but was hitless in 21 at bats in the playoffs to finish at .355. They were the only Gamecocks to bat above .300 in 1974. Earl Bass hit .291, Eddie Ford .288, and Jeff Grantz .287.

The 1974 playoffs were the last year the NCAA used the district format, switching to regional play in 1975. Mississippi State hosted the district tournament but didn't win the Southeastern Conference and Vanderbilt was there as SEC champion. East Carolina was the champion of the Southern Conference and North Carolina State defeated regular season Atlantic Coast Conference winner Clemson in the ACC tournament to win the ACC's automatic bid.

The three at-large entrants were South Carolina, Miami of Florida and Georgia Southern.

The head coaches in the six team field were all outstanding. Half of them were former major league infielders. The other half built highly successful careers in baseball.

South Carolina's Bobby Richardson played 12 seasons with the New York Yankees and appeared in 7 World Series. Richardson in 1995 still held the record for starting 30 consecutive World Series games. Coach Sam Esposito of N. C. State spent 10 years in the American League, mostly with the Chicago White Sox. East Carolina Coach George Williams played parts of 3 major league seasons with the Phillies, Astros and Kansas City.

Coach Ron Fraser of Miami would win more than 1,000 collegiate games and two College World Series titles in his long career. Ron Polk of Georgia Southern would soon move to Mississippi State and become one of the top names in collegiate coaching. Coach Larry Schmittou of Vanderbilt would leave the college ranks to become a highly successful owner of several minor league baseball clubs.

The guest of honor and banquet speaker at the 1974 NCAA District III championship playoffs was Starkville native James "Cool Papa" Bell who left segregated Mississippi as a youth to become one of the greatest players in the Negro League.

A base stealing star of the 1920s and '30s, stories about Bell's speed on the base paths were legend. His supporters insisted "Cool Papa was so fast he could turn out the light, jump into bed and be asleep before the room got dark."

Another story said he once hit a ground ball up the middle and was hit in the buttocks by the baseball as he slid into second base.

Two months after his return to Starkville, Bell was inducted into the Baseball Hall of Fame, Aug. 12, 1974, along with Mickey Mantle, Whitey Ford, Jim Bottomley, Sam Thompson and umpire Jocko Conlon.

For the first time, University of South Carolina baseball would be broadcast over a statewide radio network. As sports information director I had managed to line up nine stations with WIS in Columbia the originating and flagship radio station. Bob Fulton, long time "Voice of the Gamecocks," and I were the announcers.

South Carolina's opening opponent in its first venture into NCAA playoff competition was Atlantic Coast Conference champion North Carolina State. The Wolfpack and Gamecocks hadn't met during the 1974 season, but South Carolina was 6-0 against members of the ACC, having defeated Virginia 2-0 and 6-3; Duke 8-4 and 9-1; Clemson 3-0; and Wake Forest 5-1 in compiling a 44-6 record.

N.C. State's record entering the playoffs was 22-10. The only team in the six team field that South Carolina had played during the 1974 season was Georgia Southern, which had won three of five to inflict half of the Gamecocks' six losses. The only loss suffered by Earl Bass was a 6-4 decision at Georgia Southern in which Bass didn't surrender an earned run but the Gamecock defense committed a modern school record nine errors. Carolina also lost to Georgia Southern 2-0 and 4-1, and defeated the Eagles 9-1 and 9-2.

Other Gamecock defeats included two to South Alabama and one to Central Michigan.

"The University of South Carolina seeks to attain its second goal of the season," sportswriter Teddy Heffner wrote in his advance story in *The State*.

"Coach Bobby Richardson's club, 44-6 and ranked fourth in the nation by *Collegiate Baseball*, accomplished its first goal by receiving a bid to the district playoffs," Heffner added.

Heffner predicted South Carolina's stiffest competition would likely come from two other at large southeastern independents, Georgia Southern and Miami.

Heffner was of the opinion, "The Gamecocks received one break before boarding a bus for the long trek to Mississippi State. The pairings, determined by lot, have USC tackling the 30th ranked Wolfpack while Miami, Ranked sixth, and Georgia Southern, ranked seventh, clash opening day."

Heffner's advance went on to say, "The Wolfpack's top man is towering Tim Stoddard. Stoddard missed much of the first half of the season while helping N. C. State to the national basketball title, but is 5-0 with a 1.26 earned run average in 28 innings." Stoddard, at 6 feet 7 inches tall and 245 pounds, was the strong forward on N.C. State's NCAA championship 1974 team.

"Gamecock ace Earl Bass is 10-1 with an identical 1.26 ERA, but the Cayce product has worked 92 innings this season, striking out a school record 120 batters," the advance story added.

N.C. State managed base runners in each of the first six innings but couldn't push across a run and South Carolina built a 9-0 lead. Coach Bobby Richardson gave Bass the remainder of the day off and brought in righthander Allen Johnson who completed the shutout although N.C. State continued to manage at least one base runner every inning.

Here's the way Teddy Heffner described it in *The State*:

"South Carolina got steady pitching from Earl Bass and Allen Johnson, four runs batted in from Hank Small and three hits from Eddie Ford and the Gamecocks pounded N. C. State 9-0 in the opening round of the NCAA District III tournament."

The Gamecocks scored one run in the first inning, two in the third and broke the game open with three runs each in the fourth and sixth innings.

Second baseman Jeff Grantz opened the game with an infield hit, stole second, moved to third on a wild pitch, and scored on a single by first baseman Hank Small. In the third, Grantz walked, shortstop Eddie Ford singled, and Small walked to load the bases. Grantz and Ford scored on a single by cleanup batter and pitcher Bass.

Right fielder Ray Lavigne walked to open the Gamecock fourth. With one out, left fielder Jim Fleming singled, sending Lavigne to third. Grantz reached on a fielder's choice with Lavigne out at the plate. Ford doubled, scoring Fleming and Grantz and Ford scored on a single by Small to increase the Gamecock lead to 6-0.

South Carolina closed out the scoring with three sixth inning runs. Catcher Drew Choate and Fleming opened the inning with back-to-back doubles, Choate scoring. Grantz grounded out but Ford tripled to drive in Fleming. Ford scored on Small's sacrifice fly, his fourth run batted in of the game.

Bass gave up an infield single and a walk in the first inning, a walk in the second, a single in the third, two singles in the fourth, and singles in the fifth and sixth innings. Johnson allowed an infield hit and a walk in the seventh, a double and a walk in the eighth, and two Wolfpack batters reached in the ninth, Buddy Green on an error and Don Zagorski on a walk.

In a sidebar story, Teddy Heffner said, "There was never really any doubt about Thursday's first round NCAA District III clash between South Carolina and N.C. State—the Wolfpack never had a chance.

"Earl Bass wasn't as sharp as usual and the Gamecocks really didn't hit the hard line drives they usually come up with but Bass shut State out for six innings and Allen Johnson came on and hung goose eggs on the board the rest of the way and enough of USC's softly hit balls found holes to score nine runs."

Bass struck out 7, walked 2 and allowed 6 hits, all singles. Johnson struck out 2, walked 3 and gave up 2 hits, including a double, in his 3 innings of work.

N.C. State coach Sam Esposito said, in his post game comments, "We got as many hits as we could have reasonably expected

An All-America quarterback in football, Jeff Grantz set defensive records as a Gamecock infielder in baseball.—*Larry Cagle, The State*

against the type of pitching we were facing, but we didn't hit when it counted.

Bass said he was looking forward to another start in the tournament.

"That's one of the reasons I was taken out," he said. " Now I can pitch if needed Sunday" with two days rest.

The day after South Carolina shut out N.C. State, 9-0, Greg Ward pitched a three hit complete game as the Gamecocks advanced by eliminating East Carolina, 5-1. Mike Hogan led off the ECU second inning with a home run for the only score off Ward. East Carolina's only other hits were a single by Bobby Harrison followed by a double by Ron Staggs in the fourth. Harrison was out at the plate, center fielder John Gambrell to shortstop Eddie Ford to catcher Drew Choate attempting to score on Staggs' double.

Ward retired 17 of the final 18 East Carolina batters, walking only Staggs with two out in the sixth. Four consecutive two out singles by Grantz, Ford, Small and Bass plated three Gamecock runs in the third inning and single runs in the fourth and fifth closed out the scoring. Bass, playing first base, and Grantz had three hits apiece to account for more than half of South Carolina's eleven hits.

In the third round, South Carolina ran afoul of Jerry Brust, a six foot six inch, 205 pound sidearm throwing righthander who shut the Gamecocks out on two hits, 5-0. Both South Carolina hits, by Bass and freshman third baseman Jim Pankovits, came in the fifth inning. Lefthander Tim Lewis, the first of four Gamecock pitchers, took the loss.

Faced with elimination, Bobby Richardson sent junior righthander Ray Lavigne to the mound against Georgia Southern, a team that had inflicted three losses on South Carolina in five 1974 meetings. Lavigne and Georgia Southern starter Bob Gerdes were locked in a classic scoreless pitching duel through eight innings.

The Eagles managed only two hits off Lavigne, a sixth inning two out infield single by right fielder John Butler and a one out single to right field by catcher Bob Salter after a walk to give the Eagles an eighth inning threat with two base runners. Steve Garcia, the DH, opened the inning with a walk and was forced at second by Rich Toth who moved to third on Salter's single. Lavigne pitched out of the jam by coaxing infield pop ups from Keithel Chauncey and Butler.

South Carolina had only three hits off Gerdes in the first eight innings, a two out first inning single by Hank Small, a two out bunt single by Earl Bass in the fourth, and a two out single by Jim Pankovits in the seventh.

Eddie Ford doubled for South Carolina's fourth hit and the game's first extra base blow, to lead off the bottom of the ninth. Small was walked intentionally and Bass flied to right field for the first out.

Ken Kruppa replaced Gerdes on the mound for Georgia Southern. He walked John Gambrell on a three and one count to load the bases. Freshman Jim Pankovits lifted a fly ball to medium deep center field and Chauncey's strong throw after the catch was too late to retire Ford who scored on the sacrifice fly to give the Gamecocks a 1-0 victory.

Georgia Southern, which finished with a 47-14 record, was eliminated and South Carolina remained alive but was faced with the task of trying to defeat Miami twice to win the district championship and a trip to the World Series in Omaha. Both teams got a day of rest as rain washed out the showdown for twenty four hours.

Earl Bass, on three day's rest, got the call in the first game and, although reached for nine hits, held the Hurricanes to a single run in a 3-1 South Carolina victory. Wayne Krenchicki singled in the first but was caught stealing and Jeff Grantz started a double play after Rich Reichle's leadoff single in the second. A single and a walk gave Miami two base hits but Bass pitched out of that jam.

Miami got a runner to third but couldn't score in the sixth and had two base runners without scoring in the seventh. The Hurricane's lone run of the game, in the eighth inning, was unearned. Orlando Gonzales and Krenchicki singled and Gonzales scored on an error by Gamecock shortstop Eddie Ford.

South Carolina broke a scoreless tie in the pitching duel between Bass and Miami's Stan Jakubowski, with three two out unearned runs in the top of the eighth inning. After Ray Lavigne and Jim Pankovits were retired, Drew Choate reached on Krenchicki's error at shortstop. Jim Fleming singled and Jeff Grantz drove in Choate with a single. Eddie Ford walked and Hank Small singled to drive in Fleming and Grantz.

Miami got the tying runs on base in the bottom of the ninth on Manny Trujillo's infield single and a two out walk to Jim Crosta. Bass retired Orlando Gonzales on a fly to left field to end the game and preserve the 3-1 victory, the 12th of the season for the pitching ace.

Half an hour after the first game ended, the showdown game began and Miami coach Ron Fraser trotted out lanky side arming Jerry Brust to pitch with only one day's rest. Greg Ward was on the mound for the Gamecocks, pitching with two days rest.

Crosta led off the game for Miami with a single and stole second base. Gonzales coaxed a walk and Krenchicki moved both runners up with a sacrifice. Rich Reicle grounded to Jeff Grantz at

A Gamecock freshman in 1974, Jim Pankovits became a major league infielder.—*USC Sports Information*

second base with Crosta scoring and Gonzales taking third from where he scored on Greg Ward's only wild pitch of the season, in 103 2/3 innings. Miami led 2-0 before the Gamecocks came to bat.

In the bottom of the first, Jeff Grantz hit Brust's fourth pitch out of the park for a home run. South Carolina's only hits the remainder of the game were a one out eighth inning single by Drew Choate and a one out ninth inning single by Hank Small.

Ward shut Miami out over the next eight innings but the 2-1 Miami lead held up. In a three day period, Jerry Brust had pitched a two hitter and a three hitter against the Gamecocks and had allowed one run—Grantz's homer—in 18 innings. The Miami victory sent the Hurricanes to Omaha with a 48-9 record, and the Gamecocks, 48-8, home to Columbia.

The final tally for South Carolina's 1974 baseball season showed a 48-8 record, breaking the school record of 26 wins set the season before by 22 games. However, that record would last just one year because the Gamecock baseball program under Coach Bobby Richardson was loaded.

Earl Bass finished the season with a 12-1 record, a 1.10 earned run average and 129 strikeouts in 106 innings. In winning two games in the district playoffs, Bass allowed only one unearned run in 15 innings. He won his final six decisions in 1974, starting a string that would result the following year in a national collegiate record for consecutive victories.

Bass was named a first team All-America by the American Baseball Coaches Association. Hank Small batted .360 with 17 home runs, 68 hits and 65 runs batted in, all school records, and was a second team All-America choice.

Both of them would be back in 1975 along with the entire pitching staff except for relief pitcher Allen Johnson, who contributed a 5-0 record, eight saves and a 1.35 ERA in 1974. Ray Lavigne's record was 5-0 with a 1.15 ERA. Tim Lewis was 11-2, 2.29; and Greg Ward's record was 10-4 with an ERA of 1.30. Relief pitchers Mike Cromer and Scott Thomas, both lefthanders, had 2-0 and 1-0 records, respectively, and righthanded reliever Tom Luckstone was 2-1.

A freshman righthander who would later pitch eight major league seasons with the New York Mets and Chicago Cubs and become general manager of the Cubs appeared in one 1974 game with no record. His name was Ed Lynch.

Shortstop Eddie Ford, a junior, would be drafted in the first round by the Boston Red Sox and would not return for his senior collegiate season. All of the other regular position players would return plus outfielder-first baseman Steve King, a slugger who missed his sophomore year with a broken leg after batting .315 in 1973 as a freshman.

March 25, 1975—South Carolina 10, Old Dominion 0

March 26, 1975—South Carolina 8, George Mason 0
At Columbia (No-Hit Games)

Back-to-back no-hit, no-run baseball games are almost as rare as a snowstorm at the equator but the 1975 University of South Carolina baseball team matched Cincinnati Reds lefthander Johnny Vander Meer in accomplishing that feat.

Vander Meer pitched no-hitters in consecutive starts during the 1938 National League season, beating the Boston Bees 3-0 on June 11, and on June 15, in the first night game played at Ebbetts Field, he set the Brooklyn Dodgers down without a hit in a 6-0 victory.

The Gamecocks did it as a team, no-hitting Old Dominion University 10-0 March 25, 1975 in the seven inning second game of a doubleheader and following with a nine inning no-hitter the next day in an 8-0 win over another team from Virginia, George Mason University.

Lefthander Tim Lewis was the South Carolina pitcher in the first no-hitter and righthander Ray Lavigne did the honors the following day. They were the numbers three and four starters on the South Carolina pitching staff behind All-America Earl Bass and Greg Ward, but for two days in March Lewis and Lavigne grabbed the spotlight.

On most teams Lewis, a junior, and Lavigne, a senior, would have been recognized as super stars. Neither lost a game in 1975, Lewis compiling an 11-0 record and Lavigne going 8-0. In fact, Lavigne never lost a game at South Carolina, recording a 13-0 record in two seasons after two years in junior college.

Bass, however, was on his way to winning an NCAA record 23 consecutive games over two seasons, a 17-1 record for 1975 and All-America recognition for the second time. Ward would be 14-3 as the Gamecocks ran up a 51-6-1 record and a second place finish in the College World Series.

Going into the 1975 schedule, the general consensus was, "South Carolina is loaded." The Gamecocks had compiled a 48-8 record in 1974 and most of that team was back.

Sportswriter Teddy Heffner, in a pre-season story in Columbia's morning newspaper, *The State*, wrote, "South Carolina's baseball team, one that is thought to be as good as ever fielded by the Gamecocks, gets a chance to show what it can do on the field."

Heffner noted that Coach Bobby Richardson's team, "returns veterans at every position, has promising newcomers and potentially one of the best pitching staffs in the college game."

Shortstop Eddie Ford and center fielder John Gambrell were the only everyday players missing from 1974 and relief pitcher Allen Johnson was the only loss from the pitching staff. Outfielder Steve King, who missed 1974 with a broken leg, was back, along with the addition of four junior college stars, outfielders Garry Hancock and Steve Cook, catcher Greg Keatley, and second baseman Mark Van Bever.

"Its hard to compare this team with last year," Richardson said in assessing prospects. "We've got more depth this season and I think that's going to be a big difference."

Richardson added the team's goal was to make the College World Series in Omaha. "We came close last year," when South Carolina lost to Miami, Fla., 2-1, in the District III championship game at Starkville, Miss.

Heffner wrote that the pitching staff "looms as the strength of the Gamecocks although the hitting also looks formidable."

He quoted Richardson, "We've got more lefthanded hitting (King and Hancock) this year and we've got more overall speed. we'll still be aggressive on the bases. Our whole infield can run. We have a good team and we have a good schedule to play. It should be a good year."

With Ford gone to professional baseball, Jeff Grantz moved from second base to shortstop with Van Bever, a speedy base stealer, taking over at second. Sophomore Jim Pankovits was at third base with senior Hank Small, a second team All-America in 1974, at first base. Newcomer Greg Keatley was the catcher.

The outfield included newcomers Garry Hancock in right and Steve Cook in center, and Steve King—back from the injured list— in left field. However, with the new designated hitter rule, Don Repsher, Chuck McLean and Johnny Hinkel logged considerable playing time, as did third baseman David Small.

The Gamecocks got a scare in their season opener, finding themselves tied 5-5 in the top of the ninth inning at Charleston against Baptist College. Jim Pankovits stole home and Jeff Grantz scored on a wild pitch and the Gamecocks survived a one run rally by the Buccaneers in the bottom of the ninth to win 7-6.

The next four games weren't as tough as the Gamecocks scored in double digits to beat Wofford 16-1, West Virginia 19-2 and 13-1, and Richmond 10-1. South Carolina won the second game of the Richmond series 6-3.

The Gamecocks went to Florence to dedicate Francis Marion's new baseball park with its AstroTurf infield. In the first inning, Hancock singled, stole second, and scored on a single by Steve King for the Game's only run. Ray Lavigne allowed only one hit before the game was called after six innings due to heavy rain.

South Carolina swept a home series from Atlantic Coast Conference member Virginia, 6-0 and 5-4, to take a 9-0 record on a spring trip to the Stetson University tournament in Deland, Fla. The Gamecocks won the first four games there, 9-2 over Miami, Ohio, 4-2 over host Stetson, 6-5 over Seton Hall and 3-1 over Miami, to stretch their winning streak to 13 games before dropping 2 close decisions, 7-6 to Stetson and 4-3 to Seton Hall.

The 4-2 record was the best in the tournament field and South Carolina brought the championship tournament and a 13-2 record home to Columbia. South Carolina would see Seton Hall and its All-America catcher, Rick Cerone, later in Omaha.

While the Gamecocks were in Florida, athletics director Harold "Bo" Hagan announced a new contract for baseball coach Bobby Richardson.

"Bobby has agreed, verbally," Hagan announced. "His signature is just a technicality. His team is 10-0 so far. That should speak for itself on the fine program he has built here."

Terms of the new contract were not revealed.

The Gamecocks returned home to meet Old Dominion University in a doubleheader, two seven inning games, March 25, 1975.

Bobby Richardson and Old Dominion coach Bud Metheny had something in common. Both played for the New York Yankees. Richardson starred at second base for the Yankees, 1955-66, and Metheny was the Yankee's wartime (1943-46) right fielder. He started the baseball program at Old Dominion and was in his 27th season as head coach at the Norfolk, Va., institution.

South Carolina almost had two no-hitters that day. Earl Bass didn't allow a hit until the sixth inning when Old Dominion third baseman Mark Potter, the ninth hitter in the batting order, dragged a one out bunt. South Carolina led 19-0 and Richardson had emptied his bench. David Small, at third base in place of Jim Pankovits, was playing deep and Potter beat out an infield hit.

Bass promptly struck out the next two batters, his 11th and 12th strikeouts in six innings, and turned the final inning over to sophomore Ed Lynch who gave up three hits and two runs to make the final score 19-2.

In the second game, Tim Lewis struck out ten and walked four in holding the Monarchs hitless.

The headline in *The State* the next morning told the story: Gem By Lewis Aids Gamecocks In Doubleheader.

"South Carolina's Timmy Lewis hurled the first Gamecock no-hitter in eight years and USC pounded seven home runs in a 19-2, 10-0 doubleheader sweep of Old Dominion," Teddy Heffner wrote.

"Earl Bass narrowly missed a no-hitter in the first game, surrendering a bunt single with one out in the sixth inning."

The story added, "Lewis had good stuff during the windy day, and all three hard hit balls by the Monarchs were fielded by his teammates. He walked four and struck out ten.

"Lewis' closest call came in the final inning when John Mamoudis lined a pitch just foul along the right field line. It was USCs first gem since Billy Reitmeier baffled Georgia in 1967.

"Bass was also superb, striking out twelve in the six innings he worked."

Hank Small hit a grand slam home run in the first game and Jeff Grantz, who had six hits in the doubleheader, lined a grand slam in the nightcap.

Steve Cook hit a solo homer in the second inning of the opener and South Carolina broke it open with a four run third. Greg Keatley homered, Grantz singled, Garry Hancock doubled, Hank Small doubled, Jim Pankovits doubled and Don Repsher singled.

In the fourth inning the Gamecocks added five runs and Small's grand slam highlighted a nine run fifth. Reserve catcher Donnie Branham also homered.

In Lewis' no-hit game, the Gamecocks wasted no time, scoring

Tim Lewis (L) and Ray Lavigne pitched no-hit games on consecutive days for South Carolina in 1975.—*USC Sports Information*

four runs in the first inning on an Old Dominion error and singles by Hancock, Small, Pankovits and Jim Fleming. They added a pair on Don Repsher's two run homer in the third, and four on Grantz's fifth inning grand slam.

Old Dominion never advanced a runner beyond first base against Lewis. He walked Mamoudis with two out in the second, Jim Sanzo with one out in the fourth, Dan McCarthy to lead off the sixth, and Don Hauck with one out in the seventh.

The headline in *The State* on March 27, 1975, was an echo of the previous day, an overline shouting, "USC Gets 2nd Gem in a Row," over the main head which read: Lavigne Fires No-Hitter.

"Raymond Lavigne hurled a no-hitter and South Carolina exploded for six runs in the second inning as the Gamecocks blanked George Mason 8-0 Wednesday afternoon at the Roost," Teddy Heffner's lead paragraph said.

"Lavigne's gem was the second straight for Gamecock pitching. Timmy Lewis no-hit Old Dominion Tuesday."

Heffner added Lavigne, "was in complete control in gaining his fourth straight win of the season and ninth against no losses in his two years at USC.

"The Gamecocks took advantage of a wild streak by George Mason starter Kevin Carr in the second inning. Carr hit Jim Fleming and Don Repsher to open the inning and then consecutive singles by Steve Cook and Greg Keatley provided a 2-0 USC lead.

"Johnny Hinkel then walked to load the bases and Jeff Grantz made it 4-0 with a single through the middle. Garry Hancock and Hank Small got two more runs in with infield outs.

"USC lost its hitting after the second as reliever Craig Burlingame went three innings without surrendering a hit. Small broke that in the eighth against relief pitcher Pete Sausville with his seventh home run of the season, a line drive to left."

Lavigne walked four and struck out seven. Joe Anderson hit a deep fly ball to left fielder Don Repsher in the first inning, David Miller hit a long fly ball to center fielder Steve Cook in the fifth, and Dave Marion lined out to Repsher in the seventh. Cook made a running catch of Randy Russell's pop fly to short center field to end the eighth.

Collegiate Baseball released its first poll of the season on the day of South Carolina's second straight no-hitter and the Gamecocks, with a 15-2 record, were ranked eighth behind Arizona State, Miami, Texas, Southern California, Arizona, Florida State and Santa Clara. South Alabama was ninth and Pan American tenth.

In June, only Arizona State and Texas from that top ten would join the Gamecocks in Omaha for the 1975 College World Series.

South Carolina

vs

North Carolina State

May 25, 1975—South Carolina 4, N. C. State 3
At Columbia
(NCAA South Atlantic Regional Championship)

South Carolina ran up a seventeen game win streak in the middle of the 1975 season, beginning with a two game sweep of Old Dominion University. The second game of that series was the first of consecutive game no-hitters by the Gamecock pitching staff.

After losing the final two games of a spring break trip to Florida, 7-6 to Stetson and 4-3 to Seton Hall in the Stetson tournament, South Carolina wouldn't taste defeat again for nearly a month when the Gamecocks dropped the first of a three game series to Georgia Southern, 6-2, at Statesboro. South Carolina won the final two games of the series, 8-2 and 7-4, to start a four game streak before being upset at home by Davidson, 4-3, on April 22.

They wouldn't taste defeat again until the College World Series. South Carolina would win ten more regular season games and play an 8-8 tie with Western Carolina at Asheville, a contest added to the original schedule that was called after six innings due to a rain and hail storm.

With a 44-4-1 record and ranked second in the nation by *Collegiate Baseball*, South Carolina was selected to host the NCAA South Atlantic Regional tournament that would send its winner to the College World Series in Omaha. Independent South Carolina was an at-large entry. Others in the four team regional included Atlantic Coast Conference champion North Carolina State, Southern Conference champion The Citadel, and East Coast Conference champion Temple.

Sportswriter Teddy Heffner of *The State* credited South Carolina's outstanding pitching staff with leading the Gamecocks to their second consecutive NCAA playoff berth and built a story around an interview with righthander Greg Ward.

"South Carolina led the nation in pitching last season and ranks very high in that statistic this year," Heffner wrote. "Pitching and USC have gone hand in hand the last few years. Most people can tell you that Earl Bass is the main reason for the glowing record, but one pitcher does not a staff make."

Heffner quoted Ward as saying, "I'm used to being behind Earl. But if I have to be rated behind someone, I guess he's the best choice in the country."

Up to that point in their careers, Ward had actually won more games than Bass, 31 to 30, and each would compile 34 wins, Bass finishing his career with a 34-3 record while Ward would finish 34-13. Bass missed almost an entire sophomore season with an arm injury.

"I don't compare myself with anyone," Ward told Heffner. "I just try to do my best. My statistics aren't as impressive as last year, but I've had tougher assignments. Beating Georgia Southern and Pete Manos was a big game for me. I'd like to be undefeated now, but I lost to good teams. Seton Hall and Georgia Southern are tough and I pitched against Stetson."

Ward and Bass were roommates throughout their four years at South Carolina and Ward said, "I pull for him and he pulls for me. We've talked a lot about pitching and our goals."

When he was being recruited, Ward said, "I envisioned the program being where it is now. I'd heard about Earl Bass and Hank Small and Eddie Ford and I knew we could have a good team.

"I couldn't be happier with my college career. I've gotten good exposure here. The first thing is to win and the second is to get good exposure."

On the eve of the NCAA regional tournament in Columbia it was announced that Earl Bass, Hank Small and Clemson outfielder Denny Walling were among nineteen final nominees for the Lefty Gomez Plate, awarded to the nation's top collegiate player and baseball's equivalent of the Heisman Trophy.

It was also announced that Clemson, runnerup to N. C. State for the Atlantic Coast Conference championship with a 33-8 record, had been awarded an at-large bid to the NCAA Mideast Regional at Ypsilanti, Mich. Newberry College received a bid to the NAIA playoffs, giving the state of South Carolina four teams competing for national baseball championships.

N.C. State came into the regional with a nine game win streak, a 25-5 record, and the nation's second best pitching staff earned run average, 1.56. The Wolfpack was in the playoffs for the third consecutive year and shared favorite billing with South Carolina, although Temple was ranked higher in the national poll.

"Our pitching has been outstanding," N.C. State coach Sam Esposito said in assessing his team.

The N.C. State pitching staff included six foot eight inch lefthander Mike Dempsey, who had a 5-1 record and a miniscule 0.63 earned run average; 6-7 basketball star Tim Stoddard, 3-0, 5 saves, 1.13 ERA; Tom Hayes, 5-1, 2.05; Richard Spanton, 4-1, 1.76; and reliever Lewis Hardy, 3-0, 0.79.

Dempsey, a high school teammate of Greg Ward at Greensboro, N.C., had originally signed with South Carolina but begged out of his scholarship commitment to attend N.C. State.

"That's our strength and that's the best place to be strong," Esposito declared. "Nobody ever had too much pitching."

Temple, with a 31-10-1 record, was the only team in the regional field with a pitching staff earned run average above 3.00. The Owls were batting .294 as a team with a 3.77 ERA. South Carolina was .292, 1.80; The Citadel .292, 2.82; and N. C. State .275, 1.56.

The Citadel's record was 21-7 and the Bulldogs drew the host Gamecocks in the regional's opening round after N.C. State and Temple opened the tournament. South Carolina was ranked second nationally behind Arizona State in the *Collegiate Baseball* poll. Temple was ranked 13th and N. C. State 20th while The Citadel was unranked.

John Sandoz drew a bases loaded walk to force in a run and Steve Yost followed with a single as Temple rallied for three runs in the bottom of the ninth to upset N.C. State, 4-3, in the double elimination tournament's first game.

With more than 4,000 fans overflowing the Gamecock home field that night, South Carolina cruised past The Citadel 11-3. Earl Bass allowed 6 hits, 2 runs, struck out 5, and walked none in 6 innings before turning the mound over to Chuck McLean.

In the winners bracket game the next day, South Carolina crushed Temple 15-0, while in the loser's bracket N.C. State remained alive by eliminating The Citadel, 16-3.

"South Carolina continued its torrid hitting and Greg Ward turned in a superb pitching performance as the Gamecocks moved into control of the South Atlantic Regional baseball tournament with a 15-0 lacing of Temple," Teddy Heffner wrote in *The State*.

Greg Keatley, Steve King and Jim Pankovits homered against the Owls and Pankovits, Steve Cook and Jim Fleming had 2 hits each. Hank Small had 1 hit and 2 RBI as Coach Bobby Richardson used 19 of his 22 players in the rout.

South Carolina had rapped out 28 hits and scored 26 runs in two NCAA playoff games, prompting Richardson to comment, "All year long we've seemed to play just good enough to win but our fellows are obviously fired up for this tournament."

N.C. State continued its battle back through the loser's bracket by edging Temple 4-2 to advance to the finals against South Carolina. However, the Wolfpack would have to defeat the Gamecocks twice on Sunday to advance to the World Series in Omaha. South Carolina needed just one win.

Lefthander Tim Lewis was on the mound for the Gamecocks and Hank Small staked him to a first inning lead with a two run home run. Lewis shut the Wolfpack out over the first three innings, yielding only a second inning single to Dick Chappell.

In the fourth inning, however, Dan Moore clouted a one out double and Bill Smodic followed with a home run over the left centerfield fence to tie the score at 2-2.

South Carolina, the visiting team, regained the lead with two runs in the top of the sixth. Jim Pankovits walked, Steve Cook laid down a sacrifice bunt which N.C. State pitcher Rich Spanton threw away for an error, putting runners at the corners with no outs.

Cook stole second base and Greg Keatley singled, scoring Pankovits. Cook moved to third and scored on an infield hit by Mark Van Bever. Lewis walked Dan Moore with one out in the bottom of the sixth and Bill Smodic and Dick Chappell followed with singles to score Moore and reduce South Carolina's lead to 4-3, with two runners on base.

Bobby Richardson signaled to the bullpen for his ace righthander, Earl Bass, who was making his only relief appearance of the season, with just one day's rest after his six inning stint against The Citadel.

Bass struck out Roy Dixon and got Gerry Feldkamp on a pop to Van Bever at second base to end that threat. He retired the next eight Wolfpack batters before walking Feldkamp with two out in the bottom of the ninth. He struck out pinch hitter David Moody on three pitches to end the game and send the Gamecocks to Omaha.

Meanwhile, at Ypsilanti, Mich., Clemson was going out in two games, losing to Eastern Michigan 5-3, and Penn State 5-4. Eastern Michigan won that regional and would join the Gamecocks in Omaha.

"Second ranked South Carolina, completing a furious charge through the NCAA South Atlantic Regional baseball tournament, rode the sensational relief pitching of Earl Bass to a 4-3 decision over N.C. State in Sunday afternoon's championship game at the Roost," Herman Helms wrote in *The State.*

"The victory sends Coach Bobby Richardson's Gamecocks into the College World Series at Omaha, Neb. They will meet Seton Hall, winner of the Northeast Regional, in the second day of the double elimination tournament June 7.

"Bass, coming on in relief of starter Tim Lewis in the sixth inning, saved the game and the title with three and two thirds innings of hitless relief pitching which thrilled the overflow crowd of 4,000 looking on in blistering heat.

"The ace righthander retired 11 of the 12 batters he faced, mowing down the first 10 in order before issuing a walk to Gerry Feldkamp after two outs in the ninth. He then struck out pinch hitter Dave Moody to end the game."

Bass Struck out five of the twelve batters he faced.

"Carolina jumped out front in the first inning on a two run homer by Hank Small," Helms related. "The Hammer, college baseball's all time home run king, ripped into a delivery from State's starting pitcher, Rich Spanton, and sailed a blast over the left field fence which scored Garry Hancock ahead of him. Hancock had reached on a fielder's choice.

"It was Small's 18th home run of the season and 47th of his career.

Earl Bass and Hank Small celebrate South Carolina's first NCAA regional championship in 1975.—*Billy Deal (L); Vic Tutte, The State*

101

"The Gamecock lead held up until the fourth inning when Bill Smodic gunned a two run homer over the left field fence to pull the Wolfpack into a 2-2 tie. Dan Moore, who had doubled, scored ahead of Smodic.

"Carolina, actually the visiting team in Sunday's game, pushed across two decisive runs in the top of the sixth inning. Jim Pankovits walked to start the surge. Steve Cook then dumped a sacrifice bunt which was fielded cleanly by Spanton, but the State pitcher uncorked a wild throw to first, and the Gamecocks had runners at first and third with no outs.

"State coach Sam Exposito then went to his bullpen, calling on righthander Tim Stoddard to replace Spanton. Cook stole second, putting two Gamecocks in scoring position with Greg Keatley at the plate.

"Keatley singled to right, scoring Pankovits, Cook stopping at third. An infield hit by Van Bever sent Cook in with USC's fourth and final run of the game."

Helms' description continued, "State fought back in the bottom of the sixth, shoving over its third and final run after one out on a walk to Moore and singles by Smodic and Dick Chappell.

"Chappell's hit finished off Lewis and brought on Bass. The USC super star struck out Roy Dixon and retired Feldkamp on a soft fly which Van Bever caught in right center to end the inning and the Wolfpack was never to launch a threat after that."

A sidebar story by Teddy Heffner featured post-game interviews that dealt with the Gamecocks' upcoming trip to Omaha for their first College World Series.

"We have to go out there and play our type of game," was Hank Small's assessment.

"I think we have just as good a team as any in the country," a confident Earl Bass said. "The winner will be the one that gets the breaks. The tournament is just icing on the cake."

Richardson said "We achieved our first goal of making it into the series. But I think the goal now is to be the number one team in the country."

Heffner followed up with a second day story that credited "togetherness" for making the Gamecocks' banner season.

"That's the key. Everybody pulls together and we pick up each other," Heffner quoted shortstop Jeff Grantz. "This is a close team., Everybody hangs around together. One thing that has helped a lot is the group that doesn't get to play as much. They're always behind us, trying to help the starters and they do a good job when they get a chance to play."

June 7, 1975—South Carolina 3, Seton Hall 1

June 11, 1975—South Carolina 6, Arizona State 3
At Omaha, Neb. (College World Series)

The week between the 1975 NCAA regional tournaments and the beginning of the College World Series in Omaha was a period for all-star honors and the professional baseball free agent draft.

South Carolina first baseman Hank Small and righthanded pitcher Earl Bass were named to the first team NCAA District III team along with two others from South Carolina colleges, Clemson's Denny Walling and The Citadel's Paul Martin. South Carolina third baseman Jim Pankovits and outfielder Steve King were second team selections and South Carolina Coach Bobby Richardson was the District's Coach of the Year.

Richardson wasn't the Coach of the Year in the state of South Carolina, however. That honor went to Chal Port of The Citadel. The all-state team, selected by the state's nine collegiate coaches, included Earl Bass, Hank Small, Jim Pankovits and outfielder Garry Hancock of the Gamecocks.

Despite sweeping through the South Atlantic Regional in three games and raising its record to 47-4-1, South Carolina dropped from second to fourth in the *Collegiate Baseball* poll and Florida State ousted Arizona State as the nation's number one ranked team going into the College World Series.

Texas was ranked second, Arizona State third, South Carolina fourth, Oklahoma fifth, Cal. State-Fullerton sixth, Tulsa seventh, Eastern Michigan eighth, Seton Hall ninth and Pepperdine tenth.

The All-South Independent team was announced and Bass and Small were on the first team along with four Florida State players. Pankovits and King made the second team.

The primary phase of the professional free agent draft was held the day before the Gamecocks departed for Omaha. Small was drafted in the fourth round by the Atlanta Braves, King in the 11th by the California Angels, and Greg Ward in the 13th by the Baltimore Orioles.

The secondary phase—involving players previously drafted but unsigned—was held the following day and the Gamecocks were changing planes in Chicago enroute to Omaha when Earl Bass learned the St. Louis Cardinals had chosen him with the second pick in the first round. Another South Carolina college player, Clemson outfielder Denny Walling, was chosen by the Oakland Athletics as the first pick in the secondary phase.

Gamecock outfielder Garry Hancock was a first round secondary phase pick of the Cleveland Indians, the third time he had been a first round draft choice.

Bobby Richardson lamented the distraction caused by the draft, saying, "In fairness to the players, I feel the draft should be held after the World Series."

The Coaches' All-America team was announced in Omaha. Earl Bass was a first team selection for the second consecutive year and Hank Small moved up from the second team in 1974 to the first. Clemson's Denny Walling was also a first team choice and Davidson's George Weicker, whose home run helped beat the Gamecocks in their last loss, fifteen games earlier, was the All-America designated hitter, although he had played the entire season at first base.

Rinky Dink and his owner, retired army sergeant Benny Estes, flew to Omaha with the Gamecocks. Rinky Dink was a springer spaniel trained by Estes to retrieve foul balls and was a regular at Gamecock practices and home games. Team trainer Jim Price gave Rinky Dink a couple of tranqualizers before he in his dog carrier was stowed aboard the Delta Airlines flight out of Columbia.

"We would have lost fifty baseballs or more this season if it hadn't been for Rinky Dink," Bobby Richardson said.

The only team in the World Series field that South Carolina had met during the 1975 regular season was Seton Hall and, by coincidence, that's who the Gamecocks were paired against in the first round.

The Gamecocks and Seton Hall had met twice in the Stetson tournament at Deland, Fla., South Carolina winning the first game, 6-5, behind Earl Bass and reliever Scott Thomas, with Bass getting the win, and Seton Hall taking the second game, 4-2, with Greg Ward taking the loss.

Seton Hall was in the World Series for the second consecutive year and brought a 14 game win streak and a 31-8 record to Omaha.

Coach Mike Shepherd said, "We've got two pretty good pitchers and our catcher—Rick Cerone—is one of the best players in the country."

Cerone had a .405 batting average, 13 home runs and 57 runs batted in. The team had a .300 average and center fielder Ted Schoenhaus was batting .331 with 42 RBI. The Seton Hall pitching staff included Lynn Glowzenski, whose 10-1 record and 3.78 ERA included a win over South Carolina. Todd Heimer had a 7-0 record and a 2.21 ERA.

South Carolina defeated Seton Hall 3-1 and Earl Bass got the win to raise his season record to 16-0, but the hero of the victory was journeyman relief pitcher Mike Cromer who relieved the faltering Bass in the eighth inning and choked off a rally to save the victory.

Bass was near flawless for seven innings, allowing only three hits—singles in the third inning to Tony Roselle, in the fourth to Ricco Bellini, and the fifth to Ed Blankmeyer. Rick Sposta reached on a fifth inning error by Hank Small and Tom Kober walked in the seventh.

Those were Seton Hall's only base runners in the first seven innings. However, Bass recorded only three strikeouts, far below his average, and none after the second inning.

South Carolina built a 3-0 lead with single runs in the second, third and eighth innings.

Jim Pankovits reached on an error in the second. Steve Cook's sacrifice bunt was thrown away, putting runners at the corners with no outs. Greg Keatley walked to load the bases and Pankovits scored on Mark Van Bever's sacrifice fly.

Jeff Grantz opened the third inning with an infield hit and continued to second on second baseman Ed Blankmeyer's bad throw. Grantz scored on a base hit by Garry Hancock.

The third Gamecock run scored with two outs in the eighth when Cook was hit by a pitch and scored on consecutive singles by Keatley and Van Bever.

Bass suddenly lost it in the bottom of the eighth, surrendering consecutive singles to Rick Sposta, pinch hitter Todd Heimer and leadoff batter Ricco Bellini, Sposta scoring. That's when Richardson summoned Cromer from the bullpen. The lefthander, who had a 1-2 record, 3 saves and a 4.00 earned run average for the season, was brilliant in his first World Series opportunity.

Greg Jemison attempted to sacrifice but Cromer fielded the bunt and forced Heimer at third base for the first out. Cerone popped to Grantz at shortstop and Ted Schoenhaus grounded to second baseman Van Bever to snuff out the threat.

In the bottom of the ninth, Cromer got Tom Kober on a bouncer back to the mound, walked Mike O'Connor, struck out Ed Blankmeyer, and Rick Sposta ended the game with another bouncer back to the mound. Seton Hall ace Len Glowzenski was the losing pitcher, his record dropping to 10-2.

Herman Helms, writing the lead story for *The State,* said, "Senior lefthander Mike Cromer sparkled in a relief role as South

Carolina's Gamecocks polished off an error-plagued Seton Hall."
Helms said Cromer, "walked from the bullpen in an ugly situation
in the eighth inning. There were no outs and three successive singles
had produced a Seton Hall run and finished off the Gamecock ace
righthander, Earl Bass.

"Cromer, razor sharp in the pressure moment, proceeded to
retire the Pirates without further damage and mowed them down in
the ninth to preserve the victory."

South Carolina had its first ever College World Series victory,
but the road ahead was strewn with outstanding talent.

Eastern Michigan, behind lefthander Bob Owchinko, shut out
top-ranked Florida State, 1-0, and had another future major league
star named Bob in freshman righthander Bob Welch to throw at the
Gamecocks. His record was 7-3. A third future major leaguer, Glenn
Gulliver, was the Eastern Michigan shortstop.

In the loser's bracket the next day, Seton Hall rebounded to
clobber Florida State 11-0 and the top-ranked Seminoles went home
to Tallahassee without having scored a run in Omaha. Cerone, who
was hitless in four at bats against South Carolina, hit two home
runs against Florida State.

The South Carolina-Eastern Michigan game lasted only six innings before being called due to heavy rain with South Carolina
leading 5-1. In later years the rules were changed to require that
all games be played through the full nine innings. But in 1975, it
went into the books as a Gamecock victory rather than a suspended
game.

"South Carolina's Gamecocks combined the two hit pitching of
Greg Ward with some timely hitting of their own to shatter Eastern
Michigan 5-1 in a rain shortened second round game of the Col-
lege World Series," Herman Helms wrote.

"The Gamecocks had scored two runs and had the bases loaded
with no outs when play was halted in the bottom of the sixth inning."

The Gamecocks moved undefeated into the third round against
Arizona State, also 2-0. The Sun Devils were gunning for their fourth
World Series championship, and—with Florida State gone—were
the tournament favorite after knocking Texas into the loser's bracket,
5-2. Future long time major leaguer Floyd Bannister was Coach
Jim Brock's starting pitcher against South Carolina.

Lefthander Tim Lewis, with a 10-0 record, was South Carolina's
scheduled third game starter, but the game was postponed a day
due to rain and Coach Bobby Richardson by-passed Lewis in favor
of Bass, who had three days rest after working six innings in the
win over Seton Hall.

"South Carolina's Gamecocks bombed out Arizona State's ace

lefthander, Floyd Bannister, and rolled behind Earl Bass to a 6 to 3 decision over the Sun Devils," Herman Helms wrote.

"Bass recovered from a shaky start and spread eight hits in racking up his 17th victory of the season against no losses.

"Catcher Greg Keatley swung the hot bat for the Gamecocks, ripping two singles and a triple and driving in three runs."

The Gamecocks fell behind, 2-0, in the first inning when Tom Sain doubled with one out, Ken Landreaux walked, and after Clay Westlake struck out, Ken Phelps singled to drive in two runs.

A crowd of 10,902 saw Carolina take charge of the game with a four run outburst in the fourth inning. Hank Small singled, Steve King walked but Small was picked off second base for the first out. Jim Pankovits singled but Steve Cook struck out. Keatley then tripled, driving in King and Pankovits.

Van Bever surprised the Arizona State infield with a two out squeeze bunt and beat it out for a hit with Keatley scoring. Van Bever stole second base and scored when Sun Devil second baseman Tom Sain dropped Jim Fleming's pop fly down the right field line.

In the fifth inning, Cook doubled with one out and scored on Keatley's single. In the eighth, King walked, stole second, moved to third on Cook's ground out, and scored on a passed ball to make the final score 6-3.

Arizona State had gotten its third run in the sixth on a solo home run by Ken Phelps. Bass struck out nine Sun Devil batters and walked only one, Landreaux, who scored in the first.

After three games, South Carolina was the only undefeated team remaining, but that bubble would burst at the hands of the Texas Longhorns, who pounded out 18 hits—including 3 home runs— against Greg Ward, Ray Lavigne and Mike Cromer to down the Gamecocks 17-6.

Jim Gideon, Texas' All-America righthander, was the winning pitcher to improve his record to 17-0. First baseman Mickey Reichenbach, who would emerge as the tournament's Most Valuable Player, had two doubles, a single, walked twice, struck out once, and scored three runs against the Gamecocks.

The rules were changed the following year to grant the last unbeaten team a bye to the championship game if three teams with one loss each remained in the double elimination tournament. That team would have been South Carolina, but under the rule in force in 1975, there was a drawing and Texas drew the lucky envelope.

South Carolina would have to get by Arizona State a second time to meet the Longhorns for the national championship.

South Carolina

vs

Arizona State

June 13, 1975—South Carolina 4, Arizona State 1
At Omaha, Neb. (College World Series)

While in Omaha for the 1975 College World Series, Herman Helms, executive sports editor of *The State*, sat down with South Carolina coach Bobby Richardson and asked him how he had assembled a baseball squad strong enough to win fifty games, including three wins in four College World Series games.

Richardson's answers appeared in a column by Helms as the Gamecocks prepared for a second meeting with Arizona State, the winner to advance to the national championship game against Texas.

All-America righthanded pitcher Earl Bass of Cayce, S.C.—*"I've known and watched him since he was in the Little League playoffs."*

Righthanded pitcher Greg Ward of Greensboro, N.C.—*"Mace Brown, Red Sox scout, told me that Greg was one of the best prospects in North Carolina."*

Lefthanded pitcher Tim Lewis of Norristown, Pa.—*"Robin Roberts, the former Phillie pitcher, brought four guys down from Pennsylvania for me to look over. Robin's son was one of them and Curt Simmons' (another Phillie pitcher) son was another. I took Timmy because I liked the way he threw the ball and he was the best student of the four. I advised the other three to go to junior college and they did."*

Righthanded pitcher-outfielder Ray Lavigne of Columbia—*"I watched him in high school and saw potential in him, but I felt he needed a couple of years in junior college."* Lavigne enrolled at South Carolina after two years at Spartanburg Junior College (later renamed Spartanburg Methodist College).

Catcher Greg Keatley and outfielder Steve Cook—*"Sam Supplizzo (former pro player) sent me rave notices about them. Sam's word was good enough for me."* Keatley and Cook, both of Miami, Fla., came to South Carolina from Miami Dade North Junior College.

First baseman Hank Small of Atlanta—*"I received numerous reports that Small was the best player in the Atlanta area. I went to see him play and couldn't believe that a big guy who hit the ball so hard struck out as few times as he did. One game convinced me."*

Second baseman Mark Van Bever of Melbourne, Fla.—*"Johnny Hunton (assistant coach) and I go to the junior college all-star game at Orlando each year. I saw Mark there and was impressed with his speed."* Van Bever, a dean's list student and first team Academic All-America, enrolled at South Carolina after a freshman season at Brevard Community College.

Shortstop Jeff Grantz of Bel Air, Md.—*"John Bridgers, who was then on the football coaching staff at Carolina, told me about this great football player who was a super infielder...One day Whitey Ford was in Columbia with his son, Eddie. We were having lunch and got a call from Bridgers at the Grantz home in Bel Air, Md. He wanted me to talk to Jeff and I also got Whitey to talk to him. Bridgers always felt that Whitey telling Jeff his own son was coming to Carolina helped swing Grantz our way."* Grantz was an All-America quarterback at South Carolina in addition to becoming a record setting infielder.

Jim Pankovits of Richmond, Va. — *"I got a letter from his pastor in Richmond telling me that Jim was a tremendous athlete. I sent Johnny Hunton to see him play. His report was so good that I flew to Richmond and offered Jim on the spot a full scholarship."*

Outfielder Garry Hancock of Tampa, Fla.—*"We got a lot of help from big league scouts. We needed an outfielder so we asked the scouts who was the best in junior college. He (Hancock) was a first round draft choice, picked by the Texas Rangers. I found out he was getting married and called to offer congratulations. He visited at my invitation when we were having a cookout at Johnny's house. I think the closeness of our team impressed him. He turned down the pro offer and signed with us."* Hancock came to Carolina from Hillsborough College in Tampa.

Outfielder Steve King of Wilmington, N. C. — *"June Raines was on my coaching staff and scouts told him that there was a boy in Wilmington who was just terrific. June went to see him play and he wasn't by himself that night. Thirty two scouts and one major league general manager (Al Campanis of the Los Angeles Dodgers) were on hand. King hit three home runs. He was drafted and offered pretty good money, but turned it down to come with us."*

Infielder Jim Fleming of New Brunswick, N.J. — *"Jim was drafted by the Los Angeles Dodgers (fourth round) and offered $25,000 to sign. But his father called me and said that Jim didn't want to turn pro. He wanted to come to Carolina. I told him the only way I could take him was if he would consider coming on his own. He paid his own way and hit .305 as a freshman. I gave him a full scholarship after that."*

Tim Lewis, passed over in favor of Earl Bass when South Carolina's first game against Arizona State was delayed a day by rain, finally got his chance to pitch in the College World Series when he opposed Arizona State righthander Greg Cochran in a showdown battle at Omaha. Lewis had been idle for nineteen days., having last pitched in the final game of the South Atlantic Regional tournament May 25.

The winner would play Texas for the national championship. The loser would go home.

It shaped up as a classic battle and it was every bit of that. For seven and a half innings the pitchers dominated and the game was scoreless.

Lewis retired the first five Sun Devils before yielding a two out, second inning single to Gary Allenson and a walk to Clay Westlake. Chris Nyman popped up to second baseman Mark Van Bever to snuff out that threat. R.J. Harrison led off the third with a single but, after Ken Landreaux flied to Steve Cook in center field, Tom Sain hit into a double play, Jeff Grantz to Mark Van Bever to Hank Small.

Jerry Maddox hit a pop fly that fell for a single with one out in the fourth. Mike Colbern forced him at second but Allenson drew a walk to give the Sun Devils two base runners. Westlake grounded to Small and he flipped to Lewis, covering first, to retire the side.

In the sixth inning, with one out, Bob Pate beat out an infield hit and stole second base but Lewis retired the next two Arizona State batters on easy fly balls.

Allenson led off the Sun Devil seventh with an infield hit and advanced to third base on Nyman's one out single. Catcher Greg Keatley picked Nyman off first base and Harrison popped up to Jim Pankovits at third base to end the threat.

Meanwhile, Cochran was equally effective against the Gamecock batting order.

Jeff Grantz led off the game with a single and reached third with two outs on an infield out and a wild pitch, but was left stranded when designated hitter Steve King struck out. The Gamecocks went out in order in the second, third and fourth innings

Steve Cook reached on an error in the fifth but was out trying to advance. The Gamecocks went down one-two-three in the sixth. Pankovits singled with two out in the seventh but was out attempting to steal. Cochran retired the Gamecocks in order in the top of the eighth and the game was still scoreless.

In the bottom of the eighth, Landreaux grounded to Van Bever and Sain's foul pop up was caught by the Gamecock second baseman for two quick outs. Bob Pate singled up the middle and Jerry Maddox hit a soft fly ball down the right field round that hit a few feet fair and kicked off into foul territory for a triple. Pate scored to break the tie.

Lewis struck out Mike Colburn but it appeared the damage had been done as the Gamecocks batted in the top of the ninth inning.

Van Bever bounced a double down the left field line and Jeff Grantz bunted the tying run to third. Hancock, who had been described as having a "slow bat" by Arizona State coach Jim Brock in a television interview, pulled Cochran's fast ball into right field for a single to drive in Van Bever and tie the game at 1-1.

Lewis, who thought the fly ball triple by Maddox had cost South Carolina the game, had retreated into the tunnel between the dugout and Gamecock dressing room and was throwing a temper tantrum when the rally started. The roar of the crowd brought him back to the dugout with the score tied.

Hank Small singled, advancing Hancock to second base with the potential go ahead run. Brock called lefthander Rick Bethke from the bullpen to relieve Cochran, but he walked Steve King to load the bases. Pinch runner Chuck McLean replaced King and Tom Van Der Meerche came in to pitch for Arizona State.

Hancock scored on a fielder's choice grounder by Pankovits that was thrown away by Sun Devil shortstop Maddox. Cook's squeeze bunt single drove in Small with the third run and McLean scored, Pankovits moving to third, when third baseman Allenson threw the ball away.

As Greg Keatley struck out, Cook attempted to steal second but was out for a double play that ended the rally. However, South Carolina—on the brink of elimination minutes earlier—held a 4-1 lead.

Rejuvenated by the rally, Lewis forgot his temper tantrum and was sensational in the bottom of the ninth inning. Allenson fouled out to first baseman Small. Westlake took a called third strike. Nyman ended the game with a weak ground ball to Small at first.

The Gamecocks were in the championship game and Arizona State was eliminated.

"South Carolina, in a back to the wall situation, spurted for four runs in the top of the ninth inning to come from behind and topple Arizona State 4-1 Friday night and gain the finals of the College World Series," Herman Helms wrote in *The State*.

"The thrilling last ditch victory, Carolina's second of the series over the Sun Devils, puts the Gamecocks against Texas in tonight's championship game. A victory tonight would not only give USC the title, but it would also give the Gamecocks the distinction of being the only team from the state to ever win an NCAA championship."

Helms went on to say, "Friday night's ninth inning fireworks earned a well deserved win for Carolina lefthander Tim Lewis. Lewis,

111

razor sharp despite a nineteen day layoff, held the Sun Devils to eight hits in gaining his 11th victory against no defeats."

Cochran, who also had been undefeated in 1975, took the loss to drop his final record to 14-1.

Lewis pitched his masterpiece on his mother's birthday and with future Hall of Fame pitcher Robin Roberts, who was responsible for sending him to South Carolina, watching. Roberts and Brent Musberger were in Omaha preparing a television special on the College World Series for CBS.

Alas, South Carolina's national championship was not to be. The Gamecocks lost to Texas, 5-1, to finish second behind the Longhorns. Earl Bass, pitching with two days rest, struggled in the early innings, giving up a run in the second, two in the third and one in the fourth. He then shut the Longhorns out until the eighth when they scored their final run.

South Carolina could manage only four hits off Texas lefthander Richard Wortham who struck out nine and walked only one. The Gamecocks averted a shutout when Hank Small hit a 390 foot home run in the fourth inning. It was the 19th of the season for the Hammer and 47th of his career, at that time an all time collegiate high.

Bass, who had won his final 6 decisions in 1974 and his first 17 in 1975 to establish a national record of 23 consecutive victories, lost his final game as a Gamecock to finish with a career record of 34-3. Arizona State shortstop Jerry Maddox won the Lefty Gomez Plate as the nation's best collegiate player with Earl Bass a close second.

He, Hank Small, Garry Hancock and Greg Ward would sign professional contracts but most of the others from the Gamecocks' greatest team would be back in 1976.

One who wouldn't was senior Ray Lavigne who didn't get to pitch in the College World Series despite his undefeated collegiate record. He finished his baseball career with a 13-0 record at South Carolina, 8-0 in his senior season. Lavigne did play left field in two of the six CWS games, collecting one single in three at bats in each game.

The 1975 Gamecock defense committed only 54 errors in 58 games for a .975 fielding percentage, second best in the NCAA. The team batting average was .297, led by Small's .390. Hancock hit .351, King .341, Pankovits .315 and Cook .302.

The pitching staff's earned run average was 2.00 with 465 strikeouts in 503 innings. Bass struck out a school record 168 in 148 innings with a 1.40 ERA. Lewis had a 1.82 ERA in 94 innings with an 11-0 record. Ward's ERA in 119 1/3 innings was 1.88 to go with his 14-3 record. He struck out 102. Lavigne's 8-0 record in 66 2/3 innings accompanied a 2.16 earned run average.

Gamecock pitchers pitched 26 complete games in 58 starts, including 13 shutouts. The final 1975 record showed 51 victories, 6 defeats, 1 tie and a second place finish in the College World Series.

In 1985, Teddy Heffner wrote a tenth anniversary nostalgia piece for *The State.*

"The 1975 South Carolina team, coached by former Yankees great Bobby Richardson, was one of the finest collections of college baseball players in history," Heffner wrote. "They were the best to ever play at the school, even better than the 1977 outfit which featured college player of the year Randy Martz and future big leaguers Mookie Wilson, Jim Lewis and Ed Lynch.

"And they're the best that will ever be at Carolina, unless the rules are changed. That club had 21 players on scholarship. The current rules allow baseball only 13 (since reduced to 11.7).

"The 1975 team, which finished 51-6-1 and second in the nation, featured Earl Bass and Hank Small, both All-Americans. Bass is the best college pitcher I ever saw and I covered a lot of college baseball in my time. I also think he's the best all-around player in USC's history.

"And Small is the second best college hitter I ever saw, second only to Bob Horner, now with the Atlanta Braves. Of course, baseball players can be judged only by seeing them over a long period, and I saw South Carolina a lot, which surely colors my judgment."

Heffner noted that South Carolina twice defeated an Arizona State team that included nine future major leaguers—Ken Phelps, Rick Peters, Gary Allenson, Jerry Maddox, Floyd Bannister, Ken Landreaux, Mike Colbern, Chris Nyman and Bob Pate.

"The also beat Rick Cerone's Seton Hall club and the Bob Welch-Bob Owchinko-Glenn Gulliver Eastern Michigan team," Heffner added.

The writer noted that twelve members of South Carolina's 1975 team eventually signed professional contracts and Garry Hancock, Hank Small, Greg Keatley and Jim Pankovits made it to the big leagues. He left out pitcher Ed Lynch who played sparingly in 1975 but developed into a star the following two seasons. Lynch pitched eight seasons in the National League and became general manager of the Chicago Cubs.

"King in left, Cook in center and Hancock in right did not make an error in the regular season," Heffner marveled. "And who can forget Cook's outstanding catch of Landreaux's deep drive to right center in the College World Series?"

Any Gamecock teams since 1975, said Heffner, "would have trouble winning many games against the '75 outfit."

South Carolina

vs

Clemson

March 28, 1977—South Carolina 2, Clemson 1
At Clemson, S.C.

Twenty games into the 1977 baseball schedule under new head coach June Raines, the South Carolina Gamecocks were struggling by comparison with recent seasons, although they had won sixty five per cent of their games.

Bobby Richardson, after seven seasons, had resigned to make a run for the U. S. House of Representatives and Raines, a catching instructor and manager in the Philadelphia Phillies organization the previous four years after serving as a student assistant coach under Richardson and his predecessor, Jack Powers, had returned to Carolina as Richardson's successor.

With a good nucleus from Richardson's 1976 team which had compiled a 38-14 record but had failed to win the NCAA regional that it hosted after going all the way to the championship game in the 1975 College World Series, Raines' career as a head coach had gotten off to a fast start before hitting a wall.

Raines added a couple of superb players in center fielder Mookie Wilson from Spartanburg Methodist Junior College and righthanded pitcher Randy Martz from the Gamecock football squad. South Carolina won 10 of its first 11 games, but in the 9 games since had lost 5 and tied 1 to show a 13-6-1 record after 20 games.

Clemson, on the other hand, was off to its fastest start in history. The Tigers won their first twenty six games. South Carolina was scheduled to play a two game series at Clemson March 28-29.

Mookie Wilson wasn't the first African American to play baseball at the University of South Carolina, but he was the first black star. He was one of eight Wilson brothers who had played at Bamberg-Ehrhardt High School during a period when the school won eight consecutive state championships.

I remember Coach Raines bringing Mookie to the sports information office and introducing him as "Willie Wilson." Mookie smiled and stated, "Back home they call me Mookie." He was never referred to as Willie again and it turned out to be a good thing because, when Mookie became a major league star with the New York Mets a few years later, another Wilson named Willie was starring with the Kansas City Royals.

Mookie, whose full name was William Hayward Wilson, couldn't explain why he was called Mookie except to say his grandmother had pinned the nickname on him.

When Wilson first enrolled at South Carolina he was a free swinger who seldom drew a base on balls because he tried to hit every pitch he could reach, and some he couldn't. When Raines urged him to be more selective, Wilson's reply was, "Coach, if it's white and moving, I'm going to swing at it."

His aggressiveness translated into a .357 batting average at Carolina and a twelve year major league career average of .274 in 1,403 games.

Martz, Raines' other new found star, had been buried in obscurity on the Gamecock football squad for three seasons. A six foot four inch, 210 pound drop back quarterback, Martz found his playing time non-existent on a squad that had switched to the veer offense.

Head football coach Jim Carlen, who normally frowned on his quarterbacks missing spring practice, decided to release Martz to the baseball squad in the spring of 1977. Martz had been a successful high school pitcher in addition to starring in football at his high school in Elizabethville, Pa., but hadn't been considered good enough to be drafted by professional baseball.

Jim Lewis, a senior righthander who had compiled an 8-5 record in 95 innings in 1976, was considered the pre-season ace of the 1977 Gamecock squad although righthander Ed Lynch, after not registering a decision his first two years, had posted a 9-1 record in 1976, and another righthander, junior Chuck McLean, was coming off a 6-1 mound season.

Perhaps the most versatile player on the squad, McLean as a sophomore had pitched 58 innings with a 2.79 earned run average in addition to playing the outfield, second base and third base. He had batted only .212 in 151 at bats, but had contributed 7 home runs, and 23 stolen bases.

Clemson had run up its 26-0 record against a schedule dotted with NAA Division II and small college NAIA opponents, but most of them had strong baseball programs despite their affiliations. For example, Lewis College—Clemson's victim, 3-0 and 9-8, in victories 25 and 26—had won the NAIA national championship the three previous seasons.

South Carolina's early schedule was also dotted with Division II opponents, including a couple of losses to Eckerd College during a spring trip to Florida, which prompted a derisive telephone call from a Clemson supporter declaring South Carolina had lost twice "to a drug store." Eckard, which would place second in the 1977 Division II World Series, was located in St. Petersburg, Fla., and supported by the Eckerd chain of drug stores family.

Two of the stars of the Eckerd team were future major leaguers Steve "Bye Bye" Balboni, a home run hitting first baseman, and outfielder-pitcher Joe Lefebvre.

In its last two games before the Clemson series, South Carolina dropped two home games to North Carolina, 3-2 and 9-6.

As the series with Clemson approached, Coach June Raines in a newspaper interview praised his senior second baseman, Mark Van Bever, calling him the Gamecock team leader. Van Bever had stolen a school record 56 bases while batting .314 as a junior and he and Mookie Wilson were the speed merchants of the 1977 squad.

"Mark typifies our team," Raines said of his second baseman. "We haven't had the long ball this season. We've had to rely on a single, a stolen base and a wild pitch or something. Mark is a real battler for us and he's been a good leader. He puts a lot of pressure on the other team's defense and forces them to make a mistake.

"Mark's done a real good job with Greg Jonson, our freshman shortstop. Greg's trying to fill some pretty big shoes in Jeff Grantz and Mark has helped him on attitude as well as positioning."

An academic All-America in the classroom, Van Bever's comments about Raines sounded like a mutual admiration society.

"I'd do anything to win for him," Van Bever said. "He's the best I've ever had. We don't have the raw talent we've had but we have some good players if we could just put it together. Early in the year we were getting great pitching and no hitting. When we hit we didn't get the pitching."

A pre-series advance story under a Clemson dateline by Teddy Heffner in *The State* set the stage for the battle between the Palmetto State arch rivals:

"Streaking Clemson and struggling South Carolina renew their long and intense rivalry on the baseball field at 3 o'clock with the Tigers seeking to keep a good thing going and USC battling to get back into the game.

"Freshman sensation Brian Snyder, a stylish lefthander with a 3-0 record and 0.32 earned run average, will pitch for Coach Bill Wilhelm's 26-0 Tigers while tall righthander Randy Martz is set to go for June Raines' Gamecocks.

"Ron Musselman, 6-0, will pitch Tuesday for Clemson against

South Carolina ace Jim Lewis, 3-2.

"The Tigers have done things right all season while South Carolina, owner of an early nine game winning skein, has struggled of late, losing five of its last seven games."

Heffner quoted Wilhelm, "We're looking forward to playing June's team. He's a good baseball man and that team will get better as he goes along with them."

Raines said of Clemson, "I hope its not a bad time to be playing them. We'll have to bounce back. We just haven't been making the plays, but I don't think we'll be down against Clemson. Clemson's something special to us. Its Clemson and they're undefeated."

Wilhelm, referring to a couple of injuries on his squad, said, "Everything's rosy up here. But if you find the roses you're going to find thorns in them. We're hot. We're making all the plays. Every time we need a hit the ball falls in. When the other team needs a hit they stroke it right at us. Our guys are playing with a lot of confidence. I don't think South Carolina can do anything to destroy that confidence."

Raines lamented, "Pitching depth is really hurting us. It's just a question of who wants to go out there and take charge. You've got to have four starters and a long and short man in the bullpen. We've had three starters and one (Scott Thomas) in the bullpen. With our bullpen we're going to have some wild and wooly games."

South Carolina wasted no time in jumping on Clemson starter Brian Snyder and would have scored more in the first inning but for an outstanding defense by the Tigers. After Mark Van Bever opened the game by popping out to Clemson second baseman Billy Wingo, Greg Jonson doubled down the left field line. However, the freshman shortstop attempted to stretch the hit into a triple and was out, left fielder Billy Weems to third baseman Pete Peltz.

Mookie Wilson tripled into the left center field gap and cleanup batter Don Repsher followed with a triple to right center, scoring Wilson. Steve King lined a single to center field to make the score 2-0. Johnny Hinkel ended the uprising with a strikeout and South Carolina's scoring for the day was ended.

Snyder shut the door on the Gamecocks into the ninth inning, giving up only a second inning single to Bart Murphy, a walk to Johnny Long in the fifth, and two infield singles in the sixth to Wilson and Repsher, after which he struck out Steve King, Hinkel and pinch hitter Chuck McLean to thwart that rally.

In the ninth inning, King doubled and Hinkel walked and, with one out, Wilhelm brought in reliever Dave Woessner, who retired Murphy and Long to take a 2-0 Clemson deficit in the ninth.

Martz allowed a one out first inning single to Neil Simons but

Robert Bonnette hit into a double play. Alan Hoover walked with one out in the second but Pete Peltz hit into a double play. Both twin killings were started by Gamecock freshman shortstop Greg Jonson.

Steve Nilsson led off the Clemson fourth with a double and held second when Simons beat out an infield roller. Both runners advanced on Bonnette's ground out to first baseman Hinkel but Martz struck out Bill Foley and Hoover to end the Tiger threat.

Martz hit Peltz with a pitch to open the Clemson fifth, but Bill Schroeder struck out and Jonson started his third double play of the game on Wingo's ground ball.

Weems led off the Clemson sixth with a single but Martz retired the next nine Tigers to take the Gamecocks into the ninth inning with a two run lead.

A steady rain had been falling since the fifth inning and it reached near downpour proportions by the ninth inning. Coach Wilhelm, determined to have the game continue with his Tigers trailing, took personal charge of the ground crew, raking the mound and spreading sand as the weather interrupted play three times.

Steve Nilsson singled on the ground into right field to open the bottom of the ninth inning. Martz twice slipped on the wet mound and uncorked wild pitches sending Nilsson to third base. Simons walked and Gamecock Coach Raines went to the mound and thought about signaling to his bullpen. Martz wanted to continue and Raines went along.

Robert Bonnette hit a sacrifice fly to Mookie Wilson in center field, Nilsson scoring after the catch to cut South Carolina's lead in half. The tying run was on first base in the person of Neil Simons and he moved into scoring position at second base as Bill Foley grounded out to first baseman Johnny Hinkel.

Alan Hoover hit a ground ball to second baseman Mark Van Bever and his throw to Hinkel retired the Tigers and ended Clemson's record breaking win streak.

"South Carolina jumped on Clemson starter Brian Snyder for two first inning runs and then relied on the strong right arm of Randy Martz to halt the Tigers' 26 game winning streak, 2-1," Teddy Heffner wrote in *The State*.

"Martz was just short of brilliant for the Gamecocks, limiting Clemson to just five hits and cruising until the ninth inning. The game was played amidst intermittent rain with the final inning contested in a steady downpour that forced two long delays and had Tiger Coach Bill Wilhelm working with a rake around the mound.

"Martz, obviously bothered by the muddy mound, uncorked a pair of wild pitches after an opening hit by Steve Nilsson and it appeared the Tiger magic might work again. But, after Neil Simons walked, Martz got Robert Bonnette on a sacrifice fly to center as Nilsson scored and then disposed of slugging Bill Foley on a slow roller to first. With Simons perched on second, Martz got Alan Hoover on a grounder to second."

Heffner said Martz, now 4-0 on the season, "was just too good for the Tigers. The tall junior mixed his pitches well, spotting a good slider with his fast ball and occasionally coming sidearm on the Tiger righthanded hitters. He fanned five and walked only two."

Heffner said the rain didn't play a major part in the game until the ninth inning when "Martz continually picked at his spikes and time was called three times to either clean his shoes or work on the mound. Finally, Wilhelm took charge, raking the mound and calling for sand when that didn't work."

The rain continued overnight, causing the second game of the series to be called off and rescheduled as part of an April 12 doubleheader at Columbia. The original 1975 schedule had called for three Carolina-Clemson games, two at Clemson and one at Columbia.

Immediately after losing 2-1 to South Carolina, Clemson dropped a 6-3 decision to NAIA member Newberry and then won six straight to bring a 32-2 record and a second national ranking to Columbia. South Carolina won seven of eight after the game at Clemson to face the Tigers with a 21-7-1 record.

Among those seven wins was a 3-0 shutout of North Carolina at Chapel Hill in which Martz allowed 7 hits, struck out 8 and walked only 1 in recording his sixth with of the season without a loss.

Just before the game at Chapel Hill, South Carolina swept a three game set against Mercer in Macon, Ga., 2-0, 4-3 in 10 innings, and 17-2. Mookie Wilson was the subject of some racial taunts by the Mercer crowd.

Black players were still rare on previously all white southern college rosters and Wilson was the subject of constant barbs from a group of Mercer students sunning themselves on the bank behind the center field fence.

The students called him "Spookie," and among other taunts, they invited Wilson to "come cut a watermelon with us."

With the score tied 3-3 in the 10th inning, Wilson hit a long home run which—almost as if it had been scripted—cleared the center field fence and landed among the taunting students, scattering them.

That provided the 4-3 extra inning win, and as we walked up the campus street to the Mercer athletic building where the players dressed, the ever smiling and good natured Mookie put his arm around me, the sports information director, and said, "Mr. Price. Let's go back and cut that watermelon."

In the rematch with Clemson, South Carolina won both of the seven inning games in Columbia, 7-6 and 7-2, to sweep the season series with Clemson.

Both South Carolina and Clemson would go on to win NCAA regional championships that would send both to the College World Series. However, they wouldn't face each other in Omaha.

Randy Martz compiled a 14-0 record in 1977 and was named National Collegiate Player of the Year.—*Tom Price Files*

May 21, 1977—South Carolina 4, East Carolina 1

May 22, 1977—South Carolina 11, South Alabama 2

May 22-23, 1977—South Carolina 5-6, Wake Forest 2-1
At Columbia (NCAA Atlantic Region Championship)

South Carolina qualified for the 1977 College World Series the hard way, battling back through the loser's bracket to win the NCAA Atlantic Region Championship in their home ball park.

The Gamecocks weren't sure until the last moment that they would host a regional although they felt their 33-9-1 record going into a season ending three game trip to Georgia and Georgia Tech would surely qualify them for an at large bid to play somewhere. South Carolina was ranked fourth nationally by *Collegiate Baseball*.

The 33 wins included a 3 game sweep of Clemson, 2-1 at Clemson when the Tigers were ranked number 1 with a record 26 game win streak, and 7-6, 7-2 at Columbia when Clemson was 32-2 and ranked second in the nation.

The regular season Atlantic Coast Conference leader, Clemson was upset by Wake Forest in the ACC tournament. The Deacons received the ACC's automatic bid and Clemson would go to the South regional at Coral Gables, Fla., as an at-large entry.

"I think these three games are very important," Coach June Raines said as the Gamecocks departed for a single game against Georgia at Athens and a two game series against Georgia Tech in Atlanta. Raines was worried over a growing injury list that showed righthanded pitcher Ed Lynch nursing a sore shoulder and center fielder Mookie Wilson slowed by a strained Achilles tendon.

Righthander Randy Martz improved his unbeaten record to 11-0 with a seven hit effort that downed Georgia 8-2.

In the first game of the Georgia Tech series, Atlanta native David Small's two run single highlighted a four run seventh inning and Jim Lewis picked up his ninth win and school record tenth complete game as South Carolina won 8-2.

The win the second day took a little longer, a 12th inning uprising producing a 9-8 decision with righthander Hal Hutchens, the fourth Gamecock pitcher, improving his record to 6-0.

South Carolina returned home to host the Atlantic Regional against independent South Alabama, Atlantic Coast Conference Champion Wake Forest and Southern Conference winner East Carolina.

Eddie Stanky, the crusty former major league infielder and manager, coached the South Alabama team and had some pointed comments about how the NCAA arrived at pairings for the double elimination tournament.

"We have Ben Martin who is 8-0 and South Carolina has Randy Martz who is 11-0 and who scouts tell me has the fastest fast ball in the country," Stanky declared.

"Its a strange coincidence that independents always wind up playing each other in the first round.

I'd like to get a representative up there to watch. I don't believe they draw them out of a hat. we're looking to play South Carolina Friday night. The way they do the pairings is the weakest part of the regionals. But, I'm not complaining. We're just glad to be here."

True to Stanky's prediction, when the pairings were announced, South Alabama was matched against host South Carolina after conference champions Wake Forest and East Carolina squared off in the first game.

Stanky described Martin as, "a good finesse pitcher who gets his fast ball up around 87 miles an hour. He's not an overpowering type like Martz. Martin has a good variety of pitches and he'll throw a knuckler in there every once in a while. We're going to have a good match up with those two teams; a real good match up."

South Alabama, with a 41-11 record, was ranked second nationally by *Collegiate Baseball* as the regionals got underway. South Carolina, 36-9-1, was ranked sixth. Miami, host of the South regional in which Clemson was participating, was ranked first. Clemson, ranked first and second when it met South Carolina during regular season play, had slipped to fourteenth.

June Raines expressed surprise at his team's record.

"If someone had told me at the first of the year that we would be 36-9-1, I would have had second thoughts about the individual I was talking to," he said. "We've come a long way and we've worked hard. We've matured into a pretty good club.

Wake Forest advanced into the winner's bracket by defeating East Carolina 6-3 as the Atlantic regional got underway.

In the night game, Randy Martz had limited South Alabama to three hits and nursed a 6-2 lead going into the ninth inning. Mookie Wilson's first inning home run and a three run homer by catcher Johnny Long in the second had staked South Carolina to an early 4-0 lead and had sent Ben Martin to an early shower.

After Jerry Poston's solo homer, his 21st of the season, had gotten South Alabama on the scoreboard in the sixth, Johnny Hinkel homered in the seventh for South Carolina. South Alabama scratched out a run in the seventh but South Carolina got one in the eighth to make it 6-2 South Carolina.

Mark Johnston led off the South Alabama eighth with a home run to cut South Carolina's lead to 6-3. When Martz walked Poston, Coach Raines summoned lefthander Scott Thomas from the bullpen. Steve Morrison singled, Greg Meier flied out to right fielder Don Repsher, but Ledell Lowe hit a three run homer to tie the game, 6-6.

Thomas retired Emeel Salem on a fly to Mookie Wilson in center field, but Mike Cullen blooped a double to center. Hal Hutchens replaced Thomas and gave up a single to Mike Jacobs that drove in Cullen with the go ahead run.

In the bottom of the ninth, Bart Murphy managed a one out single, but Johnny Long and Greg Jonson were retired and the Gamecocks found themselves on the short end of a 7-6 final score and in the loser's bracket. They would have to win four consecutive games to advance to the College World Series.

The Gamecocks, forced to fight for survival against East Carolina the next afternoon, got six hit pitching from righthander Jim Lewis and won 4-1.

Lewis gave up a solo home run to Sonny Wooten in the top of the fourth inning to fall behind 1-0, but quickly got that run back plus one in the bottom of the inning. Johnny Hinkel homered after Steve King had drawn a two out base on balls.

Johnny Long singled, stole second, moved to third on Greg Jonson's ground ball, and scored on Mookie Wilson's single to make it 3-1 after four innings. Wilson homered in the eighth for the game's final run.

The win was the tenth of the season for the workhorse Lewis, who would finish the year having pitched 149 innings in 20 appearances, including 17 starts and a school record 13 complete games. He would record 2 saves in 3 relief appearances and 145 strikeouts with a 2.17 earned run average.

Surprising Wake Forest survived a three run top of the first inning by tournament favorite South Alabama to come from behind and down the Jaguars, 9-6, knocking Eddie Stanky's club into the loser's bracket and a rematch with South Carolina. Wake Forest was in the driver's seat, needing just one more win to go to Omaha.

South Carolina was faced with having to defeat both South Alabama and Wake Forest on Sunday to survive and force a Monday night game.

Jim Lewis helped pitch the Gamecocks to the 1977 College World Series. Freshman shortstop Greg Jonson is in background.—*USC Sports Information*

Six-foot-five-inch former basketball player Ed Lynch got the starting assignment in the first Sunday game and stifled South Alabama, scattering seven hits.

Mark Van Bever doubled, Chuck McLean tripled, and Don Repsher singled in the third inning to give South Carolina a 2-0 lead., which South Alabama cut to 2-1 with a run in the fifth.

The lead widened to 6-1 with a four run Gamecock uprising in the bottom of the inning. With one out, Mookie Wilson singled. Chuck McLean was hit by a pitch but was retired for the second out on Don Repsher's fielder's choice. Steve King hit a three run home run and Johnny Hinkel followed with a solo shot.

South Alabama scored its second run in the top of the sixth but South Carolina countered with two in the bottom of the inning on singles by Long, Wilson and McLean wrapped around Jonson's sacrifice fly. The Gamecocks led 8-2 but they weren't finished.

In the bottom of the eighth, with one out, Van Bever singled, stole second and continued to third on an overthrow by South Alabama catcher Greg Meier. Wilson walked and Van Bever scored on

McLean's sacrifice fly. Don Repsher hit a two run homer to make the final score 11-2.

Sophomore righthander Hal Hutchens, undefeated but considered the fourth best pitcher in the South Carolina rotation, faced unbeaten Wake Forest. He almost gave Coach June Raines a heart attack but he was tough in the clutch and came out a winner.

Hutchens, from Wilmington, N. C., gave up 12 hits and walked 4 batters and the Gamecocks committed 1 error, giving the Demon Deacons 17 base runners. Only 2 of them scored. It seemed that in almost every inning Wake Forest had two runners on base with less than two out only to have Hutchens wriggle out of the jam.

In the first inning, John Zeglinski doubled and Ken Gerrity singled but Kenny Baker hit into a double play and Wake Forest didn't score. The Deacons got only one run in the second on three hits, and left two runners stranded in the third. Steve Hanson singled and Doug Henley reached on an error in the fourth but Zeglinski hit into an inning ending double play.

Hutchens retired the Deacons in order in the fifth and gave up a one out single to Al Zyskowski in the sixth. Back to back singles by Doug Henley and Zeglenski came to naught in the seventh. Ken Gerrity sacrificed the runners to second and third, but Hutchens struck out Kenny Baker and Stan Johnson popped up to the mound.

Hutchens again allowed two leadoff base runners in the eighth on a single by Bob Hely and a walk to Zyskowski. Johnny Pacer sacrificed and Hely scored on a passed ball. Hutchens opened the ninth inning by striking out Gerrity but he walked Baker and Johnson singled.

With the tying run on deck and the Gamecocks two outs away from forcing an extra game, June Raines summoned workhorse Jim Lewis from the bullpen, slightly more than 24 hours after he had pitched 9 innings against East Carolina.

Lewis struck out Bob Hely and got Al Zyskowski on a pop up to Van Bever at second base and the Gamecocks would live to play another day. Lewis recorded a save and Hutchens picked up his seventh win against no losses. The final score was 5-2 Carolina.

The Gamecocks had to come from behind to win. Trailing 1-0 in the sixth inning, South Carolina took the lead with two runs. Wilson reached on a three base error by Wake Forest third baseman Steve Hanson, racing all the way to third on Hanson's bad throw on Wilson's ground ball. Wilson scored on Chuck McLean's sacrifice fly. Steve King reached on a two out infield hit and scored on another error by Hanson who made a wild throw on King's infield hit.

Van Bever reached on a fielder's choice in the seventh, stole second and scored on Wilson's single. The Gamecocks added two insurance runs in the top of the ninth. Van Bever homered. Wilson reached on Hanson's third error, stole second, moved to third on McLean's sacrifice, and scored on a passed ball.

With two days rest, Randy Martz got the call in the showdown game before an overflow crowd of 6,300. He was magnificent. Although he allowed 10 hits, Martz walked only 2 and struck out 12. Wake Forest managed only 1 run. It came in the fifth inning when Hanson singled and came around to score on infield hits by Zeglinski and Kenny Baker.

Don Repsher homered for South Carolina's first run in the second inning and started a two run fourth inning rally with a single. Repsher scored ahead of Johnny Hinkel's fourth home run of the tournament. Bart Murphy reached on an error in the seventh and scored ahead of Van Bever's home run, which preceded Mookie Wilson's solo homer.

Final score, South Carolina 6, Wake Forest 1. The Gamecocks had a ticket to Omaha, their second in three years.

Martz, Homers Power USC to Regional Title read the headline in *The State*. The story under Herman Helms' byline began:

"South Carolina backed the steady pitching of Randy Martz with a power show of four home runs and muscled out a 6-1 victory over Wake Forest in the championship game of the NCAA Atlantic Regional Baseball Tournament at the Roost Monday night.

"The Gamecocks won the double elimination event the hard way, storming back from an opening loss to South Alabama to rack up four straight victories and earn a berth in the College World Series at Omaha, Neb. June 10-17.

"Martz carefully spaced 10 Deacon hits, 3 of them infield blows, in cruising to his 12th win against no losses. The hard throwing righthander struck out 12 and walked only 2.

"An estimated crowd of 6,300 which brought the tournament attendance for seven games to an unofficial 20,400, saw Don Repsher begin Monday night's home run fireworks with a leadoff swat over the center field fence in the second inning.

"It was Repsher's 11th homer of the season and second of the tournament. Johnny Hinkel blasted his fourth of the tournament and 15th of the year with Repsher, who had singled, on base in the fourth. Mark Van Bever and Mookie Wilson drilled back to back shots over the left field fence in the seventh inning. It was the fifth of the year for Van Bever and seventh for Wilson.

"Monday's four homers increased the Gamecocks' total for five tournament games to thirteen.

"The Deacons, who were absorbing their second straight loss at the hands of the Carolina club after reeling off eleven consecutive victories, got their only run off Martz on singles by Steve Hanson, John Zeglinski and Ken Baker in the fifth inning.

"The Gamecock ace, who was pitching after only two days of rest, had to pitch himself out of trouble in both the first and ninth innings."

In a post-game interview, Martz said, "The support has been there all year. They've scored runs for me like they did tonight. You're always going to have some doubts but the way we played against South Alabama (the second ranked team in the country) we knew we could play with anybody. When we beat them 11-2, it really helped our confidence."

First baseman Johnny Hinkel, who hit four home runs in the tournament, said of Martz and the remainder of the pitching staff, "Nothing he does surprises me. Our pitching staff really came through for us. We were sick after that first loss to South Alabama but we showed our character by coming back."

Wake Forest center fielder Ken Gerrity said Martz, "surprised us with his breaking stuff. We knew he could throw hard but we didn't realize he was that smart. He pitched a real smart game."

Wake Forest coach Marvin Crater said, "Martz is the best we have faced. He gave us the most trouble."

Of himself, Martz said, "I didn't pitch myself out like I did against South Alabama. I had good stuff, but I kept my emotion out of it. I didn't overthrow and I mixed my pitches well. My sidearm pitch was devastating tonight. That's the pitch that did it."

June Raines, delighted over advancing to the College World Series in his rookie year as head coach, said Martz, "pitched like Randy Martz. He's a power pitcher but he's also a rhythm pitcher. If he doesn't have that rhythm he doesn't have the power.

"I had confidence in the guys to come back. Until you're out of it you have a chance to win."

Raines added, "Jim Lewis came back and gave us a real big game Saturday against East Carolina. He gave our other pitchers the rest they needed. Our pitchers did a super job. We got complete games out of Lewis, Ed Lynch and Martz and eight and a third innings from Hal Hutchens.

"You can't ask for better pitching than that."

Meanwhile, at Coral Gables, Fla., Clemson defeated Mississippi 8-7 and Miami 7-2, lost to the Hurricanes 10-3, and in a third and showdown meeting, defeated Miami 10-9 to win the South regional championship.

The state of South Carolina would have two teams in the eight team field seeking the NCAA championship in the College World Series at Omaha.

South Carolina

vs

Baylor

June 11, 1977—South Carolina 3, Baylor 2
At Omaha, Neb. (College World Series)

In more than sixty years of watching baseball games, I have seen a number of inside the park home runs.

Only once, however, can I recall an inside the park home run that brought a team from the brink of defeat to victory in an extra inning game. It was the most thrilling single play that I can recall at any level of the game.

It happened in the opening round of the 1977 College World Series at Omaha, Neb.

South Carolina, with a roster stocked with unlikely heroes, including a first year head coach, had earned its second trip to the College World Series the hard way, by battling through the loser's bracket to win four consecutive games and the NCAA Atlantic Region tournament which the Gamecocks hosted in Columbia.

June Raines, a former minor league catcher who had worked four years as an instructor and manager in the Philadelphia Phillies organization after four seasons as a student assistant coach while attending South Carolina, returned to his alma mater as head coach before the 1977 season.

He recruited fleet footed outfielder Mookie Wilson and catcher Johnny Long, a hard nosed leader, from the junior college ranks and third string quarterback Randy Martz from the Gamecock football squad. He also brought in a slick fielding freshman shortstop named Greg Jonson.

Among the veterans the newcomers joined was righthanded pitcher Ed Lynch, who had blossomed to a 9-1 record in 1976 after not recording a decision in two seasons after coming over from the basketball squad.

Chuck McLean had batted only .212 as a sophomore utility man in 1976, but had recorded a 6-1 record and a 2.79 earned run average as a part-time pitcher. Senior righthanded pitcher Jim Lewis was coming off an 8-5 record and righthander Hal Hutchens had recorded a 3-2 record as a freshman.

Raines inherited some other proven performers from departed coach Bobby Richardson, including second baseman Mark Van Bever, whose 56 stolen bases in 1976 had set a school record, outfielder-designated hitter Steve King, who had batted above .300 three different seasons, and first baseman Johnny Hinkel, who produced seven home runs and a .306 average as a part-time player the year before.

King, who struggled through his senior season while playing with a sprained thumb that resulted in his batting average dropping more than a hundred points and his home run power slumping, credited Raines with keeping the Gamecocks focused through the season and regional championship which saw them go to Omaha with a 40-10-1 record.

"He had a pretty tough act to follow (succeeding Richardson) but he's proven himself and has been a steadying factor for us all season long," King said in a newspaper interview.

"Coach Raines never talks about winning," King added. "He says if we play and don't press, that'll take care of itself. We're down to eight teams now and I think the one that wins will be the one that stays loose and makes the fewest mistakes. We run the bases aggressively with Mark (Van Bever) and Mookie (Wilson) and everybody else. We've been thrown out by thirty feet a couple of times but more often we've taken the extra base."

South Carolina was joined in the eight team field at Omaha by another Palmetto State entry, the Clemson Tigers, who won the South Regional at Coral Gables, Fla., and brought a sparkling 41-8 record to Omaha. Three of the losses were to the Gamecocks.

We had started broadcasting South Carolina baseball on radio in 1974 and lined up a network of stations for the NCAA playoffs. At that time Clemson did not have regular broadcasts and Clemson was invited to participate in our network.

Twenty nine radio stations throughout South Carolina signed up with Clemson play-by-play announcer Jim Phillips and sports information director Bob Bradley participating along with Gamecock play-by-play announcer Bob Bradley and me.

When South Carolina played, Bob Fulton broadcast the first three and final three innings with Phillips doing the middle three and I served as analyst or color announcer. When Clemson played, Phillips did the first and last three innings, Fulton the middle three, and Bradley was the analyst. Fans of both schools were able to listen to the games.

There was one slight deviation from this format. Bradley, in an effort to break the cigarette habit, was into chewing tobacco. He left his spit cup on the radio booth counter and Bob Fulton—thinking it was a soft drink—picked it up and took a sip. Jim Phillips had to take over from the "Voice" for an inning.

The entire group from South Carolina was concerned over the condition of Clemson athletics director Frank Howard, who had undergone gall bladder surgery. When reports indicated the crusty old former football coach was recovering in an Anderson hospital, Bob Bradley send him a telegram that read, "By a vote of 11 to 10, the Clemson baseball team wishes you a speedy recovery."

The professional baseball free agent draft was held as the teams were arriving in Omaha. South Carolina's unbeaten junior righthanded pitcher, Randy Martz, was the 12th player selected, going in the first round to the Chicago Cubs. Junior outfielder Mookie Wilson was a second round pick by the New York Mets, senior second baseman Mark Van Bever was drafted in the seventh round by the Baltimore Orioles and senior righthanded pitcher Ed Lynch went to the Texas Rangers in the 22nd round.

Senior righthanded pitcher Jim Lewis, despite his 10-5 record and 2.17 earned run average, was not drafted, an omission that perplexed him and all the Gamecocks.

Martz took a 12-0 record and a 1.80 ERA to Omaha.

"I knew I would be picked but I'm surprised that I went 12th in the country," he told reporters. "Naturally, I'm pleased. It's really a good feeling to go so high."

Southern Illinois (38-10) met Temple (34-7) and Arizona State (52-11) played Clemson (41-8) on the first day of action. The second day's program matched California State-Los Angeles (40-20) against Minnesota (38-10) with the final game sending South Carolina (40-10-1) against Baylor (42-13).

Collegiate Baseball ranked Arizona State as the nation's number one team. Minnesota was ranked second, South Carolina and Southern Illinois were tied for third, Clemson was fifth, Cal State-Los Angeles sixth, Baylor seventh, and Temple eighth.

Arizona State beat Clemson 10-7 and Southern Illinois doubled up Temple, 10-5 as South Carolina awaited the second day of action. Clemson remained alive by eliminating Temple, 13-4, in a loser's bracket game.

In an advance story in *The State*, sports writer Teddy Heffner said "South Carolina seeks to add some trimming to a surprising season when the Gamecocks take on Southwest Conference power Baylor," adding, the Gamecocks had "turned a rebuilding year into a 40-10-1 record under first year head coach June Raines."

Heffner quoted Raines as saying, "We're really looking forward to playing here. We're loose and ready to play. We're always ready to play. I really expect us to play well."

Heffner was of the opinion that "Mark Van Bever and Mookie Wilson probably hold the offensive key for South Carolina."

Baylor coach Mickey Sullivan said he was glad 1977 was the year the Southwest Conference decided to end the season with a league tournament to decide the conference's automatic bid to the playoffs. Texas won its first thirty four games and Texas A & M emerged as the regular season SWC champion.

In the conference tournament, however, Baylor defeated Texas 3-2 and 7-0, and Texas A & M 2-1, to earn the automatic bid and then won its regional to advance to Omaha.

The Bears were led by shortstop Steve Macko, who led the SWC in batting with a .421 average, had 22 doubles, 7 triples, 8 home runs and 48 runs batted in. Center fielder Burl Coker had a .322 average, first baseman Luke Prestridge, .316, designated hitter Kenny Kolkhorst, .363 with 20 doubles, 6 home runs and 50 RBI, third baseman Fritz Connally, .316, left fielder Leonard Woods, .303, catcher Mike Czimskey, .283 with 9 homers, second baseman Duncan Shanklin, .294, and right fielder Shane Nolen, .258.

Coker and Nolen were also pitchers, Coker boasting a 10-4 record with a 2.25 earned run average while Nolen was 4-2, 3.39. Sandy Bickman had a 10-3 record and a 3.18 ERA, and Panamanian sophomore righthander Jaime Cocanower, Sullivan's starting pitcher against South Carolina, brought an 8-2 record and 3.07 ERA to Omaha.

"I don't think our kids will be awed," Sullivan said after calling South Carolina "one of the best teams in the country."

Cocanower and Martz locked up in a classic pitching duel through nine innings. Coker singled to lead off the second inning, moved to third on Mike Czimskey's hit and run single, and scored on Kenny Kolkhorst's hit to give the Bears a 1-0 lead.

The Gamecocks tied it in the eighth. Mookie Wilson led off the inning with a double. Chuck McLean was hit by a pitch. Don Repsher struck out and Steve King's fielder's choice forced McLean at second, Wilson taking third. Freshman Tom Williams ran for King and was caught in a rundown between first and second on a delayed double steal. Williams was tagged for the final out but Wilson scored the tying run before the tag was made.

In the top of the 10th inning, Martz retired Duncan Shanklin on a grounder to Bart Murphy at third base and Macko on a fly to Wilson in center field, but successive ground ball singles by Leonard Woods, Luke Prestridge and Fritz Connally gave Baylor a 2-1 lead before

Martz coaxed a ground ball to Jonson at shortstop from Burl Coker to end the uprising.

Things looked bleak for the Gamecocks who had managed seven hits and one run off Cocanower in nine innings. Wilson had two doubles, in the sixth and eighth, and had scored the only Gamecock run.

Van Bever renewed Gamecock hopes by lashing a double down the left field line to lead off the bottom of the 10th inning. Wilson grounded to deep shortstop and appeared to have beaten the throw for an infield hit but was called out by first base umpire C. J. Mitchell. Van Bever moved to third base with the potential tying run.

Chuck McLean hit a line drive on Cocanower's first pitch toward the right centerfield gap. The ball carried over Baylor center fielder Coker's head and rolled to the deepest part of Rosenblatt Stadium, some 420 feet from home plate.

June Raines said later if he had been at his customary spot coaching third base he would probably have stopped McLean at third. The superstitious Raines had turned the third base coaching box over to assistant Johnny Hunton in hopes of "changing our luck," and Hunton was waving his arms like a windmill as McLean approached third.

"Chuck's a fast man," Raines said after the game, "but I've never seen him move like that. He was running like someone was chasing him."

McLean beat the relay to the plate and defeat had been turned into victory by a one out inside the park home run.

While his home run won the game, a spectacular defensive play by McLean probably saved it. He robbed Luke Prestridge of a one out double or triple with a running, diving catch in the left center field gap in the eighth inning. A single by Fritz Connally that would have scored Prestridge followed.

"A two run inside the park home run by Chuck McLean in the bottom of the tenth inning swept South Carolina to a 3-2 victory over Baylor in a thrilling first round battle in the College World Series," Herman Helms' lead story in *The State* began.

"McLean's long blast into the right center field hole scored Mark Van Bever who had opened the inning with a double and took third on Mookie Wilson's ground out.

"Baylor had surged to a 2-1 lead in the top of the 10th when singles by Leonard Woods, Luke Prestridge and Fritz Connally produced a run with two outs.

"Randy Martz, unbeaten righthander of the Gamecocks, went the distance for USC, allowing the Bears 11 hits and stretching his victory string to 13 games. The big righthander struck out 8 and walked 2.

Chuck McLean, shown here against Clemson, hit a dramatic 10th inning inside the park home run to produce a College World Series win over Baylor in 1977.—*Bill Cain*

"Martz bested righthander Jaime Cocanower in a gutsy pitcher's duel. Cocanower, who also went the distance, was touched for nine hits by the Gamecocks in absorbing his third loss against eight wins."

Helms cited McLean's defensive play by writing, "In addition to furnishing the game winning homer, McLean also furnished the fielding gem of the night when he made a diving catch of a tremendous drive off the bat of Prestridge in deep left center in the eighth inning."

McLean noted that Cocanower's fast ball had been clocked at ninety four miles an hour and he got the pitch he was looking for.

"I guessed he would throw me a fast ball, one a little outside," McLean told reporters. "I felt that I hit it good, but when I saw the center fielder going for it I thought he might catch it."

"Nobody caught it and the relay to the plate was not in time to nip the flying McLean," Herman Helms noted.

McLean credited pre-season conditioning with making it possible for him to circle the bases.

"Coach Raines almost ran us to death before the season began," he said. "It was no fun then, but I know why he did it. Our legs are in a little better shape, I believe, than some of the teams we've played."

Sports writer Hamp Rogers of *The Columbia Record*, called the dramatic game ending, "Ecstasy for South Carolina, bitter disappointment for Baylor, and quoted McLean, "If I had been playing for a school that wasn't used to winning close games I never would have made it home. We have a winning tradition at South Carolina and that in itself is enough to make you win the close ones.

"I didn't break stride once. When I saw coach Hunton waving his arms at third base I knew I was heading home."

Hunton, a lay preacher scheduled for a church appearance the next morning, said "I had to preach at 11 o'clock Sunday and if I had to play that same afternoon (in the loser's bracket) I might have to cut my sermon short. I guess somebody was making sure that didn't happen."

Rain suspended the loser's bracket game between Baylor and Minnesota and the World Series, was delayed a day. When South Carolina next took the field, Jim Lewis, still smarting from being snubbed in the draft, was the Gamecock starting pitcher against Cal State-Los Angeles.

He struck out 14 and scattered 8 hits in a 6-2 victory. The Gamecocks scored four runs in the third inning on singles by Johnny Long and McLean, a walk, and Mookie Wilson's triple. Three walks, Wilson's single and Steve King's sacrifice fly plated two more runs in the seventh.

"I wanted to prove I wasn't as bad as they (pro scouts) seem to think," Lewis commented.

After losing to the Gamecocks, Cal State-Los Angeles defeated Clemson 1-0 as Mike Sutherland of Cal State and Clemson's Ron Musselman matched four hitters. The Tigers were eliminated before a rematch between the two South Carolina World Series entries could materialize.

Herman Helms wrote a column declaring, "The most outstanding player so far in the College World Series has been without question University of South Carolina center fielder Mookie Wilson."

Helms noted that in two games, Wilson had collected 5 hits in 10 at bats, including 2 doubles and a triple, and had thrown out a Baylor runner attempting to take an extra base. He was to make another spectacular defensive play in the championship game when he climbed the wall in deep center field to spear a drive off the bat of Arizona State's Steve Michael.

"He runs like an antelope, swings a tough bat and puts something on the ball when he throws it," Helms wrote.

Wilson, who had never been on an airplane until the trip to Omaha, was asked about his first flight.

"I just closed my eyes and let it take me with it," he replied. Wilson would experience a lot of air travel in the future during his twelve year major league career.

In third round action, South Carolina had to twice come from behind to edge Southern Illinois and emerge as the only undefeated team after three rounds in the double elimination College World Series.

Randy Martz pitched a complete game for his fourteenth win without a loss despite giving up a couple of solo home runs among nine hits.

Southern Illinois built a 2-0 lead on three hits that produced a first inning run and Jim Reeves' fourth inning home run. Chuck McLean singled, and Don Repsher tripled and scored on a balk by Saluki pitcher Rick Keeton to tie the score in the seventh.

In the bottom of the seventh, Southern Illinois scored twice to go ahead 4-2. Rick Murray homered. Jim Robinson singled, moved to third on Steve Stieb's double, and scored on Neil Fiala's squeeze bunt.

Three consecutive singles by Mark Van Bever, Mookie Wilson and Chuck McLean, a walk, a sacrifice fly and Bart Murphy's fielder's choice scored three runs in the eighth inning and South Carolina held on for a 5-4 victory.

First baseman Johnny Hinkel separated his right shoulder in a seventh inning collision with Southern Illinois catcher Steve Steib, an injury that possibly had a bearing on Gamecock chances in their remaining two games of the series.

Hinkel, who had fifteen home runs on the season, was replaced in the first Arizona State game by utility man David Small, a .176 hitter who had never played first base. The Gamecocks lost, 6-2, despite a creditable complete game pitching performance by Ed Lynch, who suffered his first defeat of the season after six wins.

As the last team to be defeated, South Carolina received a bye to the championship game while Arizona State and Southern Illinois fought for survival. Arizona State, the pre-tournament favorite and the nation's top ranked team, won 10-0 to advance to the national championship game against the Gamecocks.

Jim Lewis pitched a seven hitter, South Carolina's fifth complete game effort of the series, struck out seven, and walked only one, but the Gamecocks fell a run short.

Arizona State took a 1-0 lead in the third inning when Rick Peters singled with two out and stole second base. Mike Henderson singled to left field and Peters stopped at third due to a strong throw by Chuck McLean to cutoff man Bart Murphy.

Henderson was trapped between first and second and in the ensuing rundown, Hinkel—playing with a separated shoulder after sitting out one game— made a weak throw to second baseman Mark Van Bever. Van Bever recovered the ball in time to tag Henderson out to end the inning, but Peters crossed the plate a split second before the tag.

Steve King tied the game with a towering home run into the right center field light tower in the seventh inning, but Arizona State catcher Chris Bando hit one to the same spot in the Sun Devil seventh. Arizona State held on for a 2-1 victory and the national championship.

In a column, Herman Helms said, "June Raines and his University of South Carolina Gamecocks were frustrated, disappointed and hurt that they didn't win the national collegiate baseball championship."

Raines said, "I was so sure we were going to win. I was confident Jim Lewis was just the right kind of pitcher to beat Arizona State."

Helms commented, "Lewis didn't beat the Sun Devils but he pitched a beauty of a game...Arizona State's Jerry Vazquez was just a little better."

With 226 schools playing NCAA Division I baseball, Helms rationalized, "Second among 226—It's no small feat."

Final team statistics for 1977 showed Randy Martz with a perfect 14-0 record, a 1.98 earned run average and 106 strikeouts in 131 2/3 innings. Hal Hutchens also had a perfect record, 7-0, and a 2.20 ERA in 57 1/3 innings. Ed Lynch's record was 6-1 with a 2.32 ERA in 62 innings, and Jim Lewis compiled an 11-6 record, 2.17 ERA and 145 strikeouts in 149 innings. Relief pitcher Scott Thomas' record was 4-2 with 2 saves.

Mookie Wilson led the hitters with a .357 average, 8 home runs, 33 runs batted in, and stole 33 bases. Mark Van Bever batted .335, stole 46 bases, and hit 6 homers. Chuck McLean had 5 homers and a .311 average. Don Repsher batted .301 with 11 homers and led the team in runs batted in with 57. Bart Murphy batted .287. Johnny Hinkel led in homers with 15 and batted .278, catcher Johnny Long hit .270, freshman shortstop Greg Jonson .238, and Steve King closed out his career with a .220 average.

In addition to his offensive exploits, Mookie Wilson contributed one of the top defensive plays of the series. He climbed the center field wall near the 420 foot sign to spear a second inning drive off the bat of Arizona State's Steve Michael in the championship game. When the College World Series all-tournament team was announced, Wilson was the only unanimous choice. South Carolina also placed pitcher Randy Martz and outfielder Chuck McLean on the honor squad.

Martz was named the winner of the Lefty Gomez Plate, awarded annually to the best player in the nation by *Collegiate Baseball*. In the three year history of the award he was the first winner who didn't play for Arizona State. Shortstop Jerry Maddox and lefthanded pitcher Floyd Bannister of the Sun Devils won the first two.

Martz was also named to the All-America teams selected by the American Association of Baseball Coaches and *The Sporting News*. Wilson was a second team selection by *The Sporting News*. Martz and Mark Van Bever, both honor students, were named to the first team Academic All-America selected by the College Sports Information Directors of America.

Martz and Wilson, both juniors with collegiate eligibility remaining but drafted in the first two rounds, signed with the Chicago Cubs and New York Mets, respectively and both went on to major league careers.

Newspaper accounts speculated that Martz received a $60,000 signing bonus. He would only say, "It was a satisfactory amount of money, plus they agreed to pay for the rest of my schooling."

Pitchers Ed Lynch and Jim Lewis and second baseman Mark Van Bever would also sign professional contracts and Lewis and Lynch would make it to the major leagues. Lewis would have brief stints with the Seattle Mariners, Minnesota Twins and New York Yankees, while Lynch would fashion an eight year major league career with the Mets and Chicago Cubs and would become general manager of the Cubs.

While playing for the New York Mets, Mookie Wilson and his wife, Rose, lived in Lakewood, N. J., where they founded a girl's club for teen-agers from low income neighborhoods. "Mookie's Roses," were featured on a CBS Television weekend magazine program and in *USA Today*.

South Carolina

vs

Miami

April 4-5, 1980—South Carolina 15-8, Miami 5-1
At Coral Gables, Fla.

After four consecutive seasons in the NCAA playoffs, including second place finishes in the 1975 and 1977 College World Series, the University of South Carolina baseball teams of 1978 and 1979 were left at home.

The Gamecocks had winning teams both years, 31-14 in 1978 and 31-16 the following year but weren't considered quite good enough by the NCAA selection committee. Rosters of those teams contained some outstanding players, however.

Third baseman John Marquardt batted .381 with 16 home runs and 61 runs batted in and was a first team All-America choice in 1978. Pitchers Bill Landrum and Jeff Twitty would make to the major league level in professional baseball. A knee injury that side-lined Landrum the entire 1979 season didn't help. He came back in 1980 to lead the pitching staff with ten wins.

Left fielder Mark Boatwright set a school record with eight runs batted in against Georgia Tech, March 28, 1979, only to have team-mate Wes Westbrook, the center fielder, top it with a nine runs batted in night against Georgia Southern ten days later when the Gamecocks won 21-5. Boatwright's dream game included two home runs and two doubles while Westbrook's included two hom-ers, one a grand slam, a double and a single.

The 1979 roster also included South Carolina's first interna-tional player, junior Etienne Andrew Angelo Farquharson, a native of the Bahamas who came to the Gamecocks after two years at Chipola Junior College in Florida. "Farkie"—who played any in-field or outfield position—led the 1979 team with a .331 batting average and raised his average to .354 in 1980 when the Game-cocks were back in the NCAA playoff field.

The 1980 Gamecocks were off to a 13-0 start before dropping both ends of a doubleheader at Statesboro to Georgia Southern.

South Carolina then won four straight to take a 17-2 record to Coral Gables for a four game series in the University of Miami's back yard.

Among the 6 shutouts fashioned by the pitching staff during the first half of the 1980 season was a 3 hit, 1-0, win by senior righthander Bill Landrum over Ohio State and 2 games in which sophomore lefthander Dennis Lubert flirted with the single game school strikeout record of 17. Lubert fanned 15 in a 6 hit, 9-0 win over UNC Charlotte and 16 in a 2 hit, 8-0, shutout of Furman.

Miami had played more than twice as many games as South Carolina and was ranked number one in the nation with a 34-5 record. The Gamecocks were ranked third.

Jeff Morrison shut South Carolina out, 9-0, in the series opener before a Mark Light Stadium record crowd of 4,266. The next night, a crowd of 4,738 broke the record and future major leaguer Neal Heaton held the Gamecocks to three hits in a 5-0 Miami victory.

South Carolina had been embarrassed by two consecutive shut-outs and the Gamecocks had their backs to the wall. A superstitious June Raines, in a bid to change his luck, sent shortstop and captain Greg Jonson to home plate with the lineup card and assistant Johnny Hunton to the third base coaching box, two duties he usually reserved for himself.

Raines also dressed his team out in their white home uniforms. The change of luck ploys didn't seem to work at first. South Carolina took a 1-0 lead in the top of the first inning on Robby Vollmer's home run but Miami's Paul Hundhammer led off the bottom of the first with a homer and the Hurricane added two runs in the second to go ahead, 3-1

South Carolina starting pitcher Don Gordon was touched for five hits and two walks in two plus innings and was replaced by lefthander Martin Small who held Miami in check, giving up only one run despite five walks and three Hurricane hits in four innings.

In the fourth inning, the Gamecocks began to take charge. With one out, Paul Hollins singled, Jim Curl walked and Greg Jonson singled to load the bases with the top of the batting order coming up. Joe McCarthy and Vollmer walked to force in two runs, and Etienne Farquharson singled to drive in two more and send Miami starter Bob Bastian to the showers.

Matt Tyner homered for Miami's only run off Small in the fourth, but the Gamecocks widened their lead to 8-4 with a three run fifth. Rod Carraway and Paul Hollins led off the inning with singles, followed by Jim Curl's double which scored Carraway. Greg Jonson bounced out to the pitcher, both runners holding, but Joe McCarthy doubled to drive in Hollins and Curl.

A five run seventh inning put the game out of reach, extending

South Carolina's lead to 13-4. Hollins walked and scored ahead of Curl's home run. With one out, McCarthy homered, Vollmer walked, stole second and advanced to third on an error. Farquharson singled, driving in Vollmer, stole second, moved to third on an error, and scored on Mark Boatwright's ground ball.

Miami pushed across an eighth inning run but South Carolina countered with two in the ninth to take a 15-5 victory, a morale booster after the Gamecocks had been shut out twice by the nation's top ranked team. Small, who had compiled a 4-0 record as a spot assignment freshman in 1979, picked up his first 1980 victory and fifth of his career without a loss.

Versatile Etienne Farquharson, from the Bahamas, shown here playing second base, was South Carolina's first international baseball player.—*Johnny Drummings, The Columbia Record*

Richard Chesley, who covered the series for *The State*, wrote "June Raines denied he was superstitious, but superstition or not, this much was certain: the results were different."

News reports after the first two games of the series described South Carolina as "shell shocked," but after the third game, Chesley reported, "USC erupted for 15 hits and roughed up 4 Miami pitchers to win its first game in the 4 game series.

"Led by Joe McCarthy, who had two hits—including a home run —and four runs batted in, and Jim Curl, who rapped three hits—including his seventh homer of the season—while driving home three runs, USC improved its record to 18-4."

Farquharson also had three hits and three RBI.

Chesley added the South Carolina win also ended 2 strings, Miami's 13 game winning streak and the Hurricane's 7 straight over the Gamecocks.

There was another game to play, and June Raines sent sophomore lefthander Dennis Lubert to the mound in search of a split in the back yard of the nation's top ranked team. The third game drew 4,630, just shy of the Mark Light Stadium record set the night before, but—after the South Carolina win and possibly influenced by threatening weather—only 3,521 showed up for the final game.

The four game series attracted 17,155, an average of 4,289 per game.

First inning singles by Joe McCarthy, Etienne Farquharson and Jim Curl staked South Carolina to a quick 1-0 lead, but Lubert walked Paul Hundhammer and Mike Kutner, Miami's first two batters in the bottom of the first, then retired two batters before walking Alex DeJesus and Ross Jones to give the Hurricane a tying run without a hit.

The Gamecock lefthander remained rather wild through the first 3 innings, walking 1 in the second and 2 in the third for 7 bases on balls over the first 3 innings. He didn't walk anyone after the third and limited the heavy hitting Miami team to 4 hits in shutting Coach Ron Fraser's team out over the final 8 innings. He struck out 8.

Tony Barquin singled to lead off the Miami second. Kutner and DeJesus singled in the eighth, and Leigh Gullette singled with two outs in the ninth inning.

South Carolina missed a chance to take the lead when Paul Hollins was left stranded after tripling with one out in the second inning, but the Gamecocks broke the 1-1 tie with a four run fifth inning.

Keith Taylor singled, Greg Jonson reached on an error and Joe McCarthy walked to load the bases with no outs. Robby Vollmer drove in three runs with a double and scored on Rod Carraway's two out bloop single.

The Gamecocks made it 7-1 in the sixth. Taylor singled, took second on Jonson's sacrifice and scored ahead of McCarthy's home run. McCarthy drove in the game's final run—his third RBI of the game—in the eighth inning. Taylor doubled and scored on McCarthy's single.

After being shut out twice, South Carolina had fought back to gain a split on the home field of the nation's top ranked team, and actually outscored Miami in the four games, 23-20. Lubert improved his record to 4-0.

Henry Seiden wrote the following lead in *The Miami Herald:*

"Rainy skies prompted a flood of telephone calls to the University of Miami baseball office late Saturday afternoon.

"'No, it never rains on the Light,' said UM coach Ron Fraser, manning the phones and urging callers to attend the game at Mark Light Stadium.

"True, not a drop of rain fell at Mark Light Saturday night. But misfortune poured on the Hurricanes in an 8-1 loss to third ranked South Carolina...

"'This is the big one,' Fraser said before the game. 'We need this to remain ranked No. 1. If we lose it could knock us down to fourth or fifth'."

Seiden wrote that Fraser had hoped to win three of four but had to settle for a split.

"We're still 36-7. We've got a hell of a thing going," Seiden quoted Fraser.

Seiden blamed "shoddy play and absence of timely hits" for the Miami losses.

""Besides being handcuffed on a four hitter by South Carolina starter Dennis Lubert Saturday night, the Hurricanes, who stranded eight, consistently managed to handcuff themselves."

He did concede, however, that South Carolina "battered Hurricane pitching for 14 hits in the finale." Gamecock bats collected 29 hits in the final 2 games of the series.

Richard Chesley's story in *The State* began:

"Given up on by some and written off by others, the University of South Carolina baseball team showed what it was made of by downing top-ranked Miami 8-1 in the final game of the four game series Saturday night at Mark Light Stadium

"The win earned the third-ranked Gamecocks, now 19-4, a split in the crucial showdown between the two college baseball powers."

Chesley added, "The keys were many as the Gamecocks combined superb pitching, clutch hitting and a sparkling defense in taking their second straight one-sided win over Miami after suffering shutout losses in the first two games."

The writer said, "If one individual stands out, it would be sopho-more lefthander Dennis Lubert, who held Miami to just four hits."

South Carolina came home from the Miami series to defeat North Carolina 8-5, but then the Gamecocks were upset, 2-1, by Winthrop which was in its initial season of collegiate baseball. Winthrop had recently become coeducational after many years as the South Carolina College for Women.

The loss prompted derisive phone calls from Clemson fans about losing "to a girl's school." Two years later, Clemson would also lose a one run decision to that "girl's school." Winthrop defeated the Tigers March 28, 1982, 7-6, as Coach Horace Turbeville quickly built a competitive program at the former state college for women.

The Gamecocks won a couple, then lost 3 including a 2 game series at Clemson, before running off a 12 game win streak and 15 wins in the final 16 regular season games. South Carolina closed out the regular schedule by sweeping Clemson 6-1 and 4-1, at Columbia to split the season's 4 game series with the Tigers.

The first game of the home series with Clemson drew a record crowd estimated at 8,500 with more than 6,000 on hand for the second game.

In a ceremony preceding the second home game with Clemson, South Carolina's baseball stadium was named "Sarge Frye Field," in honor of the Gamecocks' long time supervisor of facilities who had been South Carolina's groundskeeper since 1954. He joined the University staff after a 23 year career in the U. S. Army.

Although he officially retired in 1977, Frye stayed on to main-tain the University of South Carolina's athletic fields, and entering the 1995-96 academic year he was still going strong, in his 43rd year.

South Carolina returned to the NCAA playoffs after a two year absence, and was assigned to the Atlantic Region tournament hosted by Clemson. The first round opponent was Georgia South-ern with whom the Gamecocks had split four regular season games, dropping a doubleheader at Statesboro but winning twice at Co-lumbia.

South Carolina defeated Georgia Southern 7-2, but then fell into the loser's bracket with a 6-2 loss to Clemson. The Game-cocks bounced back to eliminate East Tennessee State, 8-5, but lost a slugfest to Clemson, 17-12, to finish the 1980 season with a 39-11 record.

Future major leaguer Bill Landrum led the pitching staff with a 10-2 record and a 2.91 earned run average. Lefthanders Dennis Lubert and Bret Baynham were each 6-2. Lubert's ERA was 1.89, Baynham's 2.93. Righthander Mark Calvert had a 5-0 record with a

Dennis Lubert won 31 games in his South Carolina career, including an 8-1 decision at Miami.—*USC Sports Information*

4.40 ERA. Martin Small and Ross Bledsoe were each 2-0, with ERAs of 1.53 and 1.96. Righthanders Bobby Kish and Joe Kucharski each had a record of 4-2.

Senior shortstop and captain Greg Jonson led the hitters with a .367 average, followed by third baseman Rod Carraway, .355, handyman Etienne Farquharson, .354; right fielder Paul Hollins, .335; first baseman Jim Curl, .326; catcher Keith Taylor, .303; center fielder Robby Vollmer, .297; left fielder Joe McCarthy, .290; and right fielder Mark Boatwright, .279.

Curl hit 12 home runs and drove in 47. McCarthy stole 36 bases and Jonson had 26 steals. The team batting average was .308 and the Gamecocks fielded at a .965 clip.

South Carolina was ranked eighth in the final *Collegiate Baseball* poll.

June 2, 1981—South Carolina 12, Maine 7

June 4, 1981—South Carolina 6, Mississippi State 5

At Omaha, Neb. (College World Series)

After returning to the NCAA playoff field in 1980 following a two year absence, University of South Carolina baseball coach June Raines felt good about his team's prospects in 1981.

"We're expecting good things this year," Raines told Richard Chesley of Columbia's morning newspaper in a pre-season interview. "We're a senior dominated ball club. We have an experienced team. We're looking forward to the coming season."

Chesley warned that Raines, "always has the optimism of a sailor on a three-day pass, but acknowledged there was reason for the head coach's optimism.

Academic All-America Jim Curl, who batted .326 with 12 home runs in 1980, was back at first base. Veterans Jamey Thaw and Tom Williams were competing at second base.

When the everyday lineup evolved, Williams—a fifth year player coming back from a serious knee injury—would wind up at third base with senior Rod Carraway moving to shortstop. Carraway would .hit .372 and perform outstandingly on defense. Williams would hit .298 and do equally as well at third base. Thaw would hit .305, have defensive problems, but would contribute eight home runs.

For the first time, South Carolina would have two .400 hitters. Senior catcher-designated hitter Rob Lowery batted .404 and senior right fielder Paul Hollins hit an even .400. Curl hit .347 and drove in 75 runs. Freshman catcher-DH Chris Boyle batted .289, senior left fielder Joe McCarthy .266 with 51 stolen bases, and senior center fielder Robby Vollmer .235.

The 1981 Gamecocks were a power team with a composite batting average of .316 and 83 home runs with four double digit homer hitters. Curl hit 17, Hollins 14, Lowery 13 and freshman Boyle 10.

Defensively, the Gamecocks were just average and the composite pitching staff earned run average was a so-so 3.58, but the Gamecocks knew how to win. Dennis Lubert pitched 10 complete games, Don Gordon 8, Bret Baynham 3, and Joe Kucharski 2. Baynham posted a 10-1 record, Lubert 12-2, Gordon 8-3, and Kucharski 6-2. Reliever Bobby Kish contributed seven saves.

145

South Carolina ended regular season play with a 41-13 record including three of four over in-state rival Clemson.

Both South Carolina and Clemson were selected to host NCAA regional tournaments, leading veteran Tiger coach Bill Wilhelm to comment, "I think that's mighty fine for the state of South Carolina."

June Raines, who had to sweat out the at large bid as well as the host site, said, "I feel like a 300 pound weight has been lifted off me. Sure I was worried. We haven't been playing well lately and I just didn't know what the selection committee might do."

The regional tournament at Sarge Frye Field was designated the East with South Carolina paired against East Coast Conference champion Temple (27-11-1) while Metro Conference runner-up Memphis State (46-9) met Eastern Collegiate Athletic Conference champion James Madison (40-16-1).

The first two games of the East regionals were mismatches. Memphis State clobbered James Madison 16-3, and South Carolina clubbed Temple 15-6. Jim Curl hit two home runs with Rob Lowery and Jamey Thaw collecting one each.

Dennis Lubert wasn't sharp, allowing 11 hits and 6 runs, 5 earned, in 6 innings but picked up the win to improve his record to 12-1. Bobby Kish pitched three innings of shutout relief.

James Madison eliminated Temple 10-2 in the loser's bracket game before South Carolina and Memphis State squared off in second day action. The Gamecocks prevailed, 8-5, with Bret Baynham working six innings to get the win and Kish going the final three.

Lowery homered again and South Carolina also got home runs from the bats of Rod Carraway and little Robby Vollmer who was about 5 feet 7 inches tall and weighed about 150 pounds. Carraway and Curl had 3 hits and 3 runs batted in apiece.

Memphis State remained alive by eliminating James Madison and faced off against the Gamecocks a second time. South Carolina won 11-5 to earn its third trip to the College World Series in Omaha. Lowery homered for the third time, Vollmer and Thaw clouted their second of the tournament, and Chris Boyle also homered.

Don Gordon pitched a complete game and easily won his eighth game of the season despite giving up 15 hits before an overflow crowd of 4,700 at Sarge Frye Field. Despite allowing 15 hits, Gordon threw only 93 pitches in the complete game. He struck out only 2 but walked none and never had a 3 ball count.

Future major leaguer Dave Anderson, the Memphis State shortstop, homered and was one of 2 Tigers to get 3 hits. Anderson had 12 hits in 19 at bats, including 2 homers, in the regional tournament.

In 3 games, South Carolina scored 34 runs on 41 hits, including 11 home runs. The team batting average for the 3 games was .380.

Jim Curl was named the tournament's most valuable player. He batted .583 with 7 hits in 12 at bats, and drove in 9 runs, 6 of them in the Temple game. Other Gamecocks joining the first baseman on the all-tournament team were catcher Rob Lowery, outfielder Robby Vollmer and pitcher Bobby Kish, who earned saves with three innings of work in each of the three games the Gamecock played.

Meanwhile, Mississippi State was winning the Atlantic regional at Clemson and would join South Carolina in the world series. Host Clemson lost its first game to Wichita State 7-2, and then was eliminated by East Tennessee State 2-1.

South Carolina's opening round opponent in Omaha would be Oklahoma State, winner of the Midwest regional. *Collegiate Baseball*, in its final national poll of the season, jumped the Gamecocks on the strength of their strong regional from 18th to 8th.

Texas was in the College World Series for the 20th time. Oklahoma State and Arizona State were making their 11th trips. Top ranked Arizona State was considered the favorite on the strength of its .359 team batting average and 50-12 record.

However, second ranked Miami was close behind and brought the best overall record, 60-8. Texas had a 58-9-1 record. Oklahoma State was 49-15, Mississippi State 45-15, South Carolina 44-13, Michigan 41-18, and Maine 32-12.

The only player on the South Carolina roster who had been to Omaha before was third baseman Tom "Termite" Williams. A freshman on the 1977 team that finished second to Arizona State, Williams had been granted a fifth year of eligibility after suffering a severe knee injury early in the 1979 season. He also missed part of 1978 with a shoulder injury.

"I want to win real bad but whatever we do I will be satisfied personally because of my injury situation," Williams said in an interview with Richard Chesley of *The State*. "I was able to come back and play 53 games this year and now with Omaha, that's personally satisfying."

Things didn't start out well for South Carolina in the College World Series. Oklahoma State scored 3 runs in the bottom of the first inning and 2 more in the fifth to jump out to a 5-0 lead by the time starter Dennis Lubert was replaced by reliever Bobby Kish at the beginning of the seventh inning.

Kish shut the Cowboys out for three innings and the Gamecocks battled back with a run in the seventh, 3 in the eighth and 1 in the ninth to tie the score on Rod Carraway's 2 out RBI double. In the first extra inning, however, Stan Baughn's three run home run knocked South Carolina into the loser's bracket, 8-5.

It was the first time in three trips to Omaha that South Carolina

Joe Kucharski (left) starred as a sophomore in the 1981 College World Series and was an All-America pitcher as a junior. Rod Carraway (top) was named to the 1981 CWS All-Tournament team, and Rob Lowery (right) hit two home runs against Maine in the CWS.—*USC Sports Information*

had lost in the first round. In 1975 and 1977, the Gamecocks had won their first three games enroute to a second place finish.

"If its any consolation," Barry Magnus wrote in *The Columbia Record*, "there may not be a better game in this year's College World Series that Oklahoma State's first round, 10 inning, 8-5 win over South Carolina."

Miami defeated Maine 6-1 and the Black Bears faced South Carolina in a battle for survival in the loser's bracket. Rain postponed the showdown from a Monday night to a 3:10 p. m., Tuesday start.

The overnight postponement and a long rain delay with South Carolina trailing 5-2 in the third inning, didn't do a lot for the Gamecocks confidence and they committed 5 errors and allowed 7 unearned runs, all of them charged to starter Don Gordon who was replaced after 4 2/3 innings by Joe Kucharski.

The hefty (6-3, 225) sophomore handcuffed the Black Bears on 2 singles over the final 4 1/3 innings. South Carolina scored twice in the bottom of the third to pull within a run, took a 6-5 lead with 2 in the fourth only to see Maine take a 7-6 lead in the fifth, and then took control of the game behind Kucharski's shutout relief pitching with a tying run in the fifth, 1 in the sixth, and 2 each in the seventh and eighth.

"South Carolina is still alive in the College World Series because of its ability to outslug an opponent and certainly not because of its defense," Mike Hunt wrote of the five error performance in *The Greenville News*.

"The Gamecocks got by Maine 12-7 in a game interrupted by an 82 minute rain delay Monday afternoon with a defensive performance that could only be described as a comedy of errors. But, thanks to a 17 hit attack, including 2 monstrous home runs by catcher Rob Lowery, USC is still in the fight for the national championship."

Both of Lowery's home runs came after a single by Paul Hollins, in the second and eighth innings. He was the sixth player to homer twice in a College World Series game but the first in twenty five years.

Maine, which committed six errors in its loss to Miami, matched South Carolina's five error defense on the wet diamond at Rosenblatt Stadium.

Hunt noted that all seven runs off Gordon were unearned and said the righthander from Woodhaven, N. Y., "pitched well enough to help USC to the victory as he forced Maine to hit ground balls with his effective sinker."

Coach June Raines said he called on Kucharski because, "I wanted to bring in a fastball pitcher to make them hit some pop ups to improve our defense and get our confidence back. I didn't make the change because Gordon wasn't doing the job. I was very proud of Donnie Gordon because he kept his composure."

Maine scored in the first inning when Dick Whiten rached on an error, stole second and scored on Kevin Buckley's single. Lowery's 400 foot 2 run blast in the second gave the Gamecocks a 2-1 lead, but Maine batted around in the top of the third and scored 4 runs on just 2 hits, 1 of them an infield dribbler. Two Gamecock errors and a passed ball contributed to Maine's inning.

In an effort to shore up the defense, Raines moved Tom Williams to second base replacing Jamey Thaw whose 2 errors in the inning raised his season total to 28. Freshman John Sullivan went to third base and contributed 2 singles, a run and an RBI, to South Carolina's 17 hit attack.

Curl's two run home run in the bottom of the third started the South Carolina comeback after the nightmare Maine half of the inning. Sullivan's RBI single in the fifth inning tied the score at 7-7, and South Carolina took the lead for good on Rod Carraway's run-scoring single in the sixth.

Kucharski explained his strategy that silenced the Brown Bear bats. "I saw Maine play against Miami and they were hitting (Miami starter Neal) Heaton's fastball to right field, so I decided to try and get inside and make them pull it. Once we got the lead I went with my fastball all the way and made them go after it."

Sportswriter Barry Magnus of *The Columbia Record* noted, "The sophomore from Clinton, Md., was so successful that Maine never had more than one runner on base against him."

Meanwhile, wrote Magnus, "USC's assault on Black Bear relief pitchers Don DeWolfe and Kevin Buckley continued."

"In the seventh, Chris Boyle doubled, went to third on Sullivan's fielder's choice and scored on Robby Vollmer's grounder to second. Sullivan later scored on Carraway's sacrifice fly to center.

"USC completed its scoring when Hollins led off the eighth with his third hit of the game, a single to left field, and Lowery ripped a monstrous homer to right center against the wind."

The senior catcher from Tampa, Fla., said in post-game comments, "The ball is coming up to the place looking real big and I'm swinging the bat as well as I have all year. It's never good to play any game poorly, but I'm glad we could still win and hang in there."

"Neither wind nor rain nor Maine's baseball team could stop South Carolina's Rob Lowery," Bill Neff reported in *The Charlotte Observer*.

Veteran Maine Coach John Winkin paid tribute to South Carolina's hitters.

"They're as good a hitting team as we've faced his year," Winkin declared. "Other than Arizona State, I'd rank this South Carolina club as the next best hitting team I've seen. They're strong in power through the seventh spot and (designated hitter Chris) Boyle in the seventh spot can really sting the ball."

In a second day story Mike Hunt of *The Greenville News* was of the opinion, "Watching the South Carolina Gamecocks play baseball can be a painful experience, comparable only to a disaster movie in which somehow, some way, the Phoenix rises from the ashes."

Hunt said June Raines hadn't seen anything like it in his five years at South Carolina.

"We don't look pretty but somehow they get the job done," Raines told Hunt. "They get themselves into a lot of hot water but they get themselves out of it. They're quite unique in that way."

Mississippi State lost to Arizona State, 4-3, and became South Carolina's third round opponent in the battle for survival in the double elimination world series.

On the day off before meeting the Bulldogs, South Carolina practiced at the Creighton University field and Paul Hollins hit a towering drive onto a bridge that crossed the right field edge of the ball park. An irate motorist and a policeman holding a somewhat battered and blackened baseball appeared at the practice site a few minutes later.

"Is this your baseball?" the officer asked June Raines.

The coach took a look and replied, "No, we play with new ones."

It seems the Hollins drive had crashed through a windshield. College World Series insurance took care of the problem.

South Carolina jumped to a 6-0 lead after three innings and held on to eliminate Mississippi State 6-5 and live to play another day.

"Chris Boyle and Rob Lowery rapped home runs and Bobby Kish earned his third post-season save as the University of South Carolina, with a heads-up defensive play, outlasted Mississippi State 6-5 Thursday night to stay alive in the 35th annual College World Series," is the way Richard Chesley reported it in *The State*.

"USC packed all its scoring into the first 3 innings and moved to a 6-0 lead. But the Bulldogs erupted for 3 runs in the seventh to cut the gap to 6-5 and still had the bases loaded with one out and slugging Bruce Castoria at the plate.

"Earlier, Castoria had reduced USC's lead to 6-2 with his 29th home run of the season following a double by Pete White. The blast gave the slugger a share of the NCAA's all time record for homers in a single season.

"But Kish, the third Carolina pitcher of the inning, took over and responded by striking out Castoria on three pitches and retiring Terry Loe on a pop to second baseman Tommy Williams."

Kish gave up a leadoff triple to Tony Gage in the eighth inning. Brad Winkler popped to first baseman Jim Curl for the first out. Sensing a suicide squeeze, Gamecock catcher Rob Lowery called for a pitchout.

Steve D'Ercole wasn't able to bunt the ball and Gage was an easy out in a rundown between third and home.

"Robby and I talked about that," Kish said in a postgame interview. "We sensed they might try something like that. Robby is a smart catcher. He and I think alike. We had decided I was going to throw whatever pitch he had called for—even if it was a curve ball. He did the rest."

Mississippi State Coach Ron Polk defended his squeeze play call, saying "We have tried the squeeze play three times this season and we were successful twice."

South Carolina's June Raines said, "I wish I could take credit for calling a pitchout but I can't. Thank goodness my catcher is smart enough to call for a pitchout in that situation. We kind of sensed it in the dugout but he called it on the field."

Raines also commented, "Thank goodness for Bobby Kish. He's the man we want in that situation and he did the job for us."

However, Kish and Raines had a confrontation before the game was safely won.

After retiring the first two Mississippi State batters in the ninth inning, Kish gave up a single to Pete White and walked All-America outfielder Mark Gillaspie. A wild pitch moved the tying run to third and Gillaspie, the winning run, to second with Castoria due up.

Raines ordered Kish to intentionally walk Castoria. Kish protested, pointing out he had struck out the nation's leading home run hitter with the bases loaded. Raines persisted, not wanting to play with fire, and four wide pitches loaded the bases for Terry Loe.

He hit a ground ball to shortstop and Rod Carraway flipped to Tommy Williams covering second to force Castoria. The Gamecocks had advanced to the semi-finals. Lefthander Bret Baynham, the South Carolina starter, was the winning pitcher, raising his record to 10-1. Kish earned his seventh save with 2 2/3 innings of shutout relief.

Richard Chesley noted Baynham was helped throughout the game by fine defensive plays, including a running one-handed catch by right fielder Paul Hollins of a warning track drive by Castoria, and "the revamped infield played almost flawlessly and turned three double plays."

Richard Chesley wrote that Arizona State, ranked number one

in the nation, owned a reputation that made others shake their heads in awe and the Sun Devils "consistently produce major league baseball players."

However, Chesley added, South Carolina was "a team with some tradition of its own."

Arizona State was in the College World Series for the 11th time and had claimed 4 national championships, including a 2-1 final game victory over South Carolina in 1977. The Gamecocks were in the world series for the third time in the past 7 years.

"Their alumni include Bob Horner, Reggie Jackson, Rick Monday, Bump Wills, Sal Bando, Craig Swan, Ken Landreaux, Larry Gura and Hubie Brooks," Chesley said of the Sun Devils' heritage.

"That's all I've heard during my four years," South Carolina first baseman Jim Curl said. "Arizona State this, Arizona State that. I think we surprised a lot of people. We were ranked eighth in an eight team tournament and I don't think many people gave us much of a chance."

He pointed out, however, there were only four teams left and, "If this were basketball, it would be considered the final four."

For the third time in 4 world series games the Gamecocks fell behind early, giving up 4 runs to Arizona State in the top of the first inning, and once again the Gamecocks would battle back from a 7-1 deficit, scoring 4 of their own in the third and rallying for 2 runs in the ninth, but it was too little too late and South Carolina lost to the Sun Devils 10-7.

"Alvin Davis collected 3 hits and drove home 3 runs including 2 in a 4 run first inning and Arizona State never looked back," Richard Chesley wrote in *The State.*

South Carolina managed 11 hits, 3 of them by Curl who hit his 17th home run of the season, but Arizona State starter Kendall Carter, 9-1, hung on to pitch a complete game for the victory. Dennis Lubert, the first of four South Carolina pitchers, took the loss to drop his final 1981 record to 12-2.

Arizona State advanced to the finals and defeated Oklahoma State 7-4 to win its fifth College World Series championship.

South Carolina shortstop Rod Carraway, who had 8 hits in 17 at bats for a .471 world series average, was named to the all-tournament team. Rob Lowery was the All-America catcher on the team selected by *Baseball Bulletin*, and outfielder Paul Hollins was named second team by both *Baseball Bulletin* and the American Baseball Coaches Association.

South Carolina

vs

West Virginia

May 27, 30, 1982—South Carolina 7-2, West Virginia 0-1
At Columbia (NCAA East Region Championship)

I was about 12,000 miles away in late May 1982 when the University of South Carolina Gamecocks won the NCAA East Region baseball championship to advance to the College World Series for the second year in a row and fourth time in school history.

But I was with them in spirit and by long distance telephone from the far east.

Coach Bill Foster's Gamecock basketball team had been scheduled for a seventeen day summer exhibition tour of Asia and I went along to handle sports information duties. We visited Manila, Hong Kong, Beijing, Seoul and Tokyo while Coach June Raines' baseball Gamecocks were winding up the regular season and hosting the regional tournament at Sarge Frye Field.

Raines entered the 1982 season needing replacements for his four top hitters from the 1981 team that compiled a 46-15 record and placed fourth in the College World Series. On the plus side, he had three starting pitchers returning who had combined for twenty six wins the year before.

Lefthander Dennis Lubert had compiled a 12-2 record in 1981, while righthanders Joe Kucharskski and Don Gordon were 6-2, 8-3.

With such a veteran pitching staff, Raines expected good things in 1982 provided he could fill the gaps left by .404 hitting catcher Rob Lowery, right fielder Paul Hollins, who hit .400, shortstop Rod Carraway, .372, and first baseman Jim Curl, .347.

Sophomore Chris Boyle, who had batted .289 with 10 home runs and 55 runs batted in as a freshman designated hitter and backup catcher, moved into Lowery's spot behind the plate. Larry Hernandez from Valencia Junior College in Florida took over in right field, freshman Kent Anderson, a future major leaguer, was the shortstop, and another freshman, Greg Morhardt, took Curl's spot at first base.

Phillip Wilson, another freshman and younger brother of former Gamecock All America Mookie Wilson, replaced graduated Joe McCarthy in left field and sophomore John Sullivan took over for the departed Tom Williams at third base. Senior Robby Vollmer in center field and junior Jamey Thaw at second base were the only veteran everyday starters.

It took eleven innings, but the season opener—on the road—was a success. After scoring two runs in the top of the eleventh, the Gamecocks survived a one run Georgia Tech rally in the bottom of the inning to take a 9-8 victory.

South Carolina used the extra inning win at Georgia Tech to build a nine game win streak to open the season but crashed down to reality when the Gamecocks lost four consecutive close games to Miami at Coral Gables. The scores were 2-1, 4-3 in 12 innings, 8-6, and 4-1.

The disaster at Miami was followed by two seven game win streaks wrapped around a single loss and at midseason the record was 23-5. The Gamecocks split a pair with Clemson but lost three of four when Miami visited Sarge Frye Field. Seven of ten losses up to that point were to the Hurricanes.

The Gamecocks wound up the regular season by winning 15 of their final 16 games to take a 41-11 record into post season play.

The basketball team left The Roost while the fourth inning of the May 15 game against Georgia State was being played. Telephone calls from Columbia Metropolitan Airport and Atlanta's Hartsfield International kept us abreast of the action as the Gamecocks pounded out an 11-1 victory.

Subsequent calls from Manila revealed the Gamecocks had swept a season ending two game series from Clemson, 11-5, 4-1, giving South Carolina the season series, three games to one.

Junior righthander Joe Kucharski pitched a three hitter in the 4-1 win over the Tigers, with a dozen strikeouts without a walk to raise his record to 10-2. It was the type of performance that would make Kucharski a first team All-America and the first round draft choice of the Baltimore Orioles.

"Overpowering. Intimidating. Awesome. Choose your favorite adjective, because University of South Carolina righthander Joe Kucharski was all of these last night," Barry Magnus wrote in *The Columbia Record*.

"Joe threw the hardest of any time I've got him in the last two years," said catcher Chris Boyle. "That includes the playoffs and the College World Series."

A pre-medicine major with a 4.0 grade point average the previous semester, Kucharski was willing to put his further education on hold for a chance to pitch in the big leagues.

Mike Hunt, in *The Greenville News*, wrote that the first thing you notice about Joe Kucharski is his size.

"He's 6-foot-3 and weighs about 230 pounds, which helps him throw a 95-mph fastball, which in turn has helped him to a 10-2 record..." Hunt declared, adding, "The second thing you notice about Joe Kucharski is his intelligence. He made a perfect 4.0 in the classroom this semester, which helps him with his major, which happens to be pre-medicine. All of which leads to a problem of sorts.

"Joe Kucharski is a junior, but he wants to turn professional next season. Chances are that he will be selected high in the draft. But unlike the talented athlete who prematurely leaves school with no intentions of returning, Kucharski places a high value on completing his education. He has to. He wants to be a dentist."

Hunt quoted the pitcher, "I've always liked baseball and that's what I want to give my first shot to. I got into pre-med in case something didn't work with baseball. I definitely want to get these four years in one way or another and then worry about med school. If I happen to get lucky and go in the draft, I'll try to come back as soon as I can, maybe one semester at a time."

Kucharski's only mistake against Clemson was a "curve ball that didn't get down" that Jim McCollom hit over the left center field fence to give the Tigers a 1-0 lead in the fifth inning.

Back to back two out doubles by Kent Anderson and Phillip Wilson and a wild throw attempting to get Wilson at second turned into a 2-1 South Carolina lead in the seventh inning. The speedy outfielder from Ehrhardt scored from second base on the overthrow.

Chris Boyle's two run home run, his eleventh of the season, iced the game in the eighth inning.

Besides at large South Carolina and West Virginia, champion of the Eastern Eight Conference, the field included Atlantic Coast Conference champion North Carolina, ECAC South Champion East Carolina, Southern Conference champion The Citadel, and at large entry Old Dominion.

South Carolina entered the playoffs with a 41-11 record. The Citadel was 38-6, Old Dominion 37-1-21, and East Carolina 33-12. North Carolina and West Virginia, who qualified by winning conference tournaments, were just above .500, the Tar Heels at 29-25 and the Mountaineers 22-21.

Coach June Raines, interviewed by writer Barry Magnus of *The Columbia Record*, called the 1982 Gamecock team, "one of my favorites. They've battled long odds—three freshmen starting, the injuries—to get where they are. I have to give a lot of credit to the pitching."

Magnus said, "Indeed, this Gamecock team did little to dispel the notion that pitching is at least 75 per cent of baseball. In compiling a 41-11 record, USC has 8 shutouts, 16 complete games, a 3.23 earned run average, and the 4 starters—Joe Kucharski (10-2), Don Gordon (9-3), Dennis Lubert (8-3) and Mark Calvert (7-1)—have combined for a 34-9 mark.

"The bullpen, with Jeb Babel (3-0, 2.88 ERA), Mike Werner (3-2, 2 saves), and Mark Ridgik (1-0, 2.63) isn't bad either."

Despite a triple play turned by West Virginia, the Gamecocks shut out the Mountaineers 7-0 behind Kucharski's 7 hit pitching in the opening round of the regional. All of the hits off Kucharski were singles and he struck out 10 and walked 2 in 8 innings. Lefthander Jeb Babel pitched the ninth, retiring the Mountaineers in order.

"West Virginia hung on courageously and even turned a triple play, but it was only a matter of time before the combination of a high team ERA and low batting average caught up with the Mountaineers, especially with Joe Kucharski on the mound," Mike Hunt wrote in *The Greenville News*.

"South Carolina's ace struck out 10 and pitched 8 shutout innings in the Gamecocks' 7-0 victory over West Virginia in the first round of the NCAA East Regional Thursday night.

Greg Morhardt was an outstanding hitter and first baseman for the Gamecocks, 1982-84.—*USC Sports Information*

"Other tournament action saw The Citadel pound North Carolina 9-4 and Old Dominion beat East Carolina 2-1 in the day's best game."

Hunt was of the opinion, "Although Kucharski wasn't nearly as sharp as he was in his last outing when he struck out 12 in a 3 hitter against Clemson, he came up with the big strikeout when the Gamecocks needed it. Twice with a one run lead in the fourth and fifth innings with two men on, Kucharski came up with strikeouts to end the inning.."

After giving up an unearned run in the first inning on an error and a wild pitch, West Virginia's John Holsey held the Gamecocks at bay until the sixth when a two run home run by Chris Boyle, Neil Fox's single, an RBI double by Greg Morhardt and an infield out RBI by Jamey Thaw produced four runs and a 5-0 South Carolina lead.

"That homer took the wind out of our sails," West Virginia Coach Dale Ramsburg said. "It deflated us real quickly. Up until then we played about as good as we can play."

Ramsburg was impressed by Kucharski, saying "He was striking out people that haven't struck out all year."

West Virginia's triple play occurred in the third inning. With no outs and Kent Anderson on second base and Phillip Wilson on first, Robby Vollmer hit a line drive to Mountaineer shortstop Tom Croftcheck. He doubled Anderson off second and threw to first baseman Roger Hohlrein to catch Wilson before he could scramble back to the bag.

South Carolina, designated the visiting team, added single runs in the top of the seventh and ninth innings before 5,900 fans that overflowed Sarge Frye Field.

Boyle told reporters after the game he was looking for a fast ball but Holsey threw him a curve on the home run swing.

"He'd been throwing me curve balls all night so I was looking for his fastball," Boyle said. "But I was on the curve. I felt comfortable. It was one of the few times I really knew I could hit it out. He threw me the curve and I picked it up real good. I knew it was gone as soon as I hit it."

Kucharski said his job became "a lot easier" after Boyle's home run which triggered the four run inning.

"With a one run lead you have to think about every pitch," he said. "You can't make a mistake like I almost did twice when they hit long foul balls. I think I pitched a lot better after we got the (big) lead."

East Carolina eliminated North Carolina 1-0, and West Virginia stayed alive in the loser's bracket with a 7-6, 10 inning win that sent Old Dominion home and The Citadel-South Carolina game was suspended by rain and lightning with the Gamecocks leading 6-2 after 3 1/2 innings. before a crowd estimated at 6,100.

A bases loaded home run by little Robby Vollmer after an RBI single by Kent Anderson highlighted a five run Gamecock top of the fourth as South Carolina was again designated the visiting team.

When the suspended game was resumed the following morning, Mike Cherry—the victim of all six Gamecock runs the night before—was still on the mound for The Citadel. He shut the Gamecocks out the remainder of the game, striking out eleven.

The Citadel closed the gap to 6-4 with two unearned runs scored without a hit in the fifth inning, but got no closer. West Virginia continued its battle back through the loser's bracket with a 4-1 win that eliminated East Carolina.

The Citadel stayed alive and earned the right to meet South Carolina again by pounding Old Dominion 15-1.

Dennis Lubert scattered 6 hits and South Carolina pounded out 17 off 3 Citadel pitchers as the Gamecocks remained unbeaten and advanced to the championship game with an 11-2 win. Phillip Wilson homered for the Gamecocks and both Bulldog runs came on solo homers by Marty Blair and Bill White.

West Virginia, the ragamuffin long shot that entered the regional with a 22-21 record after becoming the surprise winner of the Eastern Eight tournament, found itself in the finals against tournament favorite and host South Carolina. However, the Mountaineers would have to defeat the Gamecocks twice to get to the College World Series in Omaha.

The South Carolina basketball team was in Tokyo on the last leg of its exhibition trip to Asia. With an eleven hour time differential, I tried to figure out a time the game should be over and called the Sarge Frye Field press box from Japan. The game was in the seventh inning and South Carolina was leading 2-1, not exactly a safe lead.

When I called back, there was no answer. The game was over and the press box was deserted.

That evening in Tokyo, early morning in Columbia, my roommate, trainer Jim Price, called home to wish his stepdaughter, Elizabeth Ward, a happy birthday.

"Ask her who won the ball game," I told Jim.

"What ball game?" was Elizabeth's reply.

"Get her mother on the phone," I instructed Jim.

Harriet Price's answer was, "I don't know."

"Look in the newspaper," I told Jim to ask her.

"We haven't brought the paper in," Harriet informed.

"Go get it," I pleaded.

She did and reported the Gamecocks had held on for a 2-1 win and would be making their second consecutive trip to the College World Series and fourth trip to Omaha since 1975.

Junior lefthander Mark Calvert held West Virginia to four hits and one run over seven innings to earn the win and improve his record to 8-1. Two other lefthanders, Mike Werner and Jeb Babel each pitched a hitless inning, although they walked three between them, with Babel earning his third save of the season.

Babel delighted the crowd of 5,800 by picking a runner off first base immediately after relieving Werner, who had opened the ninth inning by walking the first West Virginia batter.

West Virginia scored first to take a 1-0 lead in the top of the third inning. Larry Kumor walked, moved to second on Greg Van Zant's sacrifice, to third on an infield out, and scored on Vic Rabbits' single to left field.

The Mountaineer lead was short lived as the Gamecocks completed the day's scoring with two runs in the bottom of the third.

Freshman Scott Mackie, starting in left field because Phillip Wilson had a slight muscle pull, led off the Gamecock inning with a single. He moved to second on a sacrifice and Robby Vollmer drew a base on balls. John Sullivan's single to left scored Mackie and sent the speedy Vollmer to third base, Sullivan taking second on the throw to the plate.

Vollmer was out attempting to score on Larry Hernanez's ground ball. Sullivan moved to third and scored what turned out to be the winning run on a wild pitch.

"I'm very proud," June Raines said of his team qualifying for its third world series in his six year tenure as head coach. "The first one is always the one you remember but this one was special.

"We started the season with three freshmen (Kent Anderson, Greg Morhardt and Phillip Wilson) and three sophomores (Chris Boyle, Neil Fox and John Sullivan) in the lineup. We were down after the Miami series, but after a team meeting, everyone continued to work. I'm very, very proud of all the players."

Morhardt, who had six hits including four doubles and drove in four runs, was named the tournament's most valuable player. Joining the Gamecock first baseman on the all-tournament team were teammates Kent Anderson, the shortstop, third baseman John Sullivan, outfielder Phillip Wilson and pitcher Joe Kucharski.

Unfortunately, the Cinderella season ended for the Gamecocks. For the first time they failed to win at least two games in the world series. They were drubbed 15-4 by Stanford and lost a high scoring 10-8 decision to Oklahoma State to finish with a record of 45-13.

The 1982 Gamecock team featured a balanced attack with five

starters hitting above .300, topped by right fielder Larry Hernandez at .344. Third baseman John Sullivan hit .341, first baseman Greg Morhardt, .330; catcher Chris Boyle .306; and left fielder Phillip Wilson .305. Designated hitter-catcher Neil Fox just missed the .300 mark at .299, second baseman Jeff Swindell hit .298, center fielder Robby Vollmer .285; outfielder Harvey Heise .271, shortstop Kent Anderson .255, and second baseman Jamey Thaw .234.

Boyle hit 12 home runs, giving him 22 for his first two collegiate seasons, and drove in 59 runs. Hernandez homered 10 times and had 52 RBI. The Gamecocks stole an even 100 bases with Vollmer collecting 23, Wilson 21 and Anderson and Hernandez 10 apiece.

The most amazing statistic of the season, however, was the fielding of freshman Greg Morhardt at first base. Recruited as an outfielder, he played 50 games at first base and committed only one error in 457 fielding chances for a .998 average. His error was a bad throw on a potential 3-6-3 double play ball.

Joe Kucharski's final record was 11-3 with a 2.97 earned run average over 112 innings. Don Gordon pitched 102 innings and compiled a 10-3 record with a 3.53 ERA. Mark Calvert's record was 8-1, his ERA 2.78. Dennis Lubert was 9-4, 3.26. Jeb Babel out of the bullpen had a 3-0 record with 3 saves and Mike Werner was 3-2 with 2 saves.

May 18, 1984—South Carolina 4, Mississippi State 1

May 19, 1984—South Carolina 5, North Carolina 4
At Starkville, Miss. (NCAA South II Regional)

The 1984 baseball season found South Carolina affiliated with a conference for the first time in thirteen years, but it was an unusual affiliation.

The Gamecocks, who withdrew from the Atlantic Coast Conference in 1971, joined the Metro but the first year that South Carolina was associated with the Metro, the conference did not require a structured league schedule in baseball. The official conference championship and automatic bid to the NCAA playoffs would go to the winner of the conference tournament.

South Carolina finished regular season play with a 36-14 record but Coach June Raines felt the Gamecocks would have to win the Metro tournament or at least finish second to advance to the NCAA playoffs.

"If the University of South Carolina baseball team is to make the NCAA playoffs for their ninth time in eleven years, the Gamecocks must win their first Metro Conference tournament, or at least finish second. That's the opinion of head coach June Raines," Mike Hunt wrote in *The Greenville News*.

The tournament was to be played in Florida State's home ball park at Tallahassee and tournament seeding was based on overall winning percentage against Division I opposition.

The Gamecocks were seeded fourth and were paired against host FSU, which had played 73 games but was seeded fifth on the basis of its 48-25, .658 record. Tulane, 42-14, .750, was seeded first and paired against eighth seed Southern Mississippi, 12-34-1. Second seed Louisville, 31-9, .775 but with several wins over non-division I opponents, met seventh seed Cincinnati, 11-27-1. Third seed Virginia Tech, 38-15, met sixth seed Memphis State, 25-13.

On the eve of the tournament's first round, coaches elected the All-Metro Conference team which included two South Carolina players, first baseman Greg Morhardt and shortstop Kent Anderson.

South Carolina and Florida State had not met during the regular season. The Gamecocks' Metro wins included three each over Cincinnati and Virginia Tech and one over Louisville. South Carolina lost two games at Tulane and one to Virginia Tech and Louisville.

Despite its fifth seeding, Florida State was regarded as the overwhelming favorite and the matchup with South Carolina was the marquee game of the tournament's first round. The weakness of basing seeding on overall record, since some teams played weak schedules, was quickly demonstrated as the three top seeds, Tulane, Louisville and Virginia Tech all lost their opening games.

Florida State led South Carolina 3-1 going to the bottom of the ninth inning. The Gamecocks, by virtue of their higher seeding, were the home team and rallied for three runs to win 4-3 and relegate the host Seminoles to the loser's bracket. Larry Price pitched seven innings but Glenn Jenkins worked the final two to get the win, boosting his record to 3-1.

First baseman Greg Morhardt started the rally with a single. After pinch hitter Neil Fox popped out, Scott Mackie singled with Morhardt stopping at second. John Sullivan singled and two runs scored, Sullivan reaching third, when the ball got past Florida State left fielder Frank Fazzini for an error. The score was tied.

Chris Boyle grounded to second base for the second out, but walk on second baseman Pete Fisher lined a single to center field to score Sullivan with the winning run.

Southern Mississippi, winless in twenty two consecutive games before upsetting Tulane 7-5, was the Gamecocks' second round opponent and gave South Carolina a tough battle before bowing 8-5. Fisher and Morhardt homered for the Gamecocks.

Morhardt homered again as the Gamecocks downed Cincinnati 4-3 to become the only unbeaten team in the tournament. However, in a second game the same day, South Carolina lost to Virginia Tech 6-3 on a grand slam home run by Shaun Sullivan in the bottom of the ninth inning.

The Hokies then lost to Florida State, which battled back through the loser's bracket to meet the Gamecocks in a showdown for the championship. It was a humdinger, but a pitcher's duel it was not. Sports writer Thom Fladung of *The Columbia Record* said "It was more a Pier Six brawl than a baseball game."

When the smoke had cleared, "and the carcasses of several pitchers had been carted off, the two teams had combined for 21 runs and 31 hits," Fladung reported. South Carolina used five pitchers, Florida State four, with the home town Seminoles outlasting the Gamecocks 11-10.

South Carolina jumped to a 4-0 first inning lead on singles by Rob Rinehart, Jim St. Laurent and Kent Anderson and a three run home run by Greg Morhardt. Morhardt and John Sullivan homered in the third inning as the lead grew to 6-1.

Things went downhill after that and Vince Calandra's grand slam home run for Florida State tied the score at 6-6, but the Seminoles weren't through, scoring two more times in a seven run fifth inning and FSU went on to win 11-10 and take the championship.

South Carolina with its 39-16 record, awaited an at large call from the NCAA. With more than a week before the bids would be tendered, the team disbanded and went home subject to a call from Coach June Raines.

First baseman Greg Morhardt, who hit four home runs and drove in nine runs in the Metro tournament, was named to the all-tournament team along with Gamecock outfielders Rob Rinehart and Jim St. Laurent. St. Laurent batted .409 in the tournament and twice threw out opposing runners at the plate.

The call came on Wednesday, May 16. The Gamecocks were invited but had to wait five more days to learn where they would play. They were assigned to the South II regional at Mississippi State's Dudy Noble Field in Starkville, the same site where they played in their first NCAA tournament ten years earlier.

Rudy Jones, writing in *The Greenville Piedmont*, was of the opinion the Gamecocks faced a difficult road in the regionals.

"If South Carolina should advance to the College World Series for the fifth time, it's unlikely Coach June Raines and the Gamecocks will have an easy path to Omaha, Neb.," Jones wrote.

"Despite a 39-16 record, the Gamecocks were seeded fourth among six teams for the South II regional which begins Thursday at Starkville, Miss.

"USC has drawn host team Mississippi State for its first round game...The Bulldogs (42-14) are the third seed in the tournament. If that task isn't difficult enough, the Gamecocks are assured of playing a first round winner in the second round."

Atlantic Coast Conference champion North Carolina (43-11) was seeded first and matched against Ohio Valley winner Eastern Kentucky (29-17). Second seeded New Orleans (41-23), an at large entry, was matched against Southern Conference champion Appalachian State (35-5).

Sophomore righthander Mike Cook, who had gotten off to a 5-1 start in 1984 before battling a sore arm, was June Raines' choice as a starting pitcher against Mississippi State's Jeff Brantley, a future major league star.

Cook, scheduled for post-season surgery to remove bone chips from his pitching elbow, hadn't won a game in two months, suffering two losses and numerous no decisions to enter the playoffs with a 5-3 record. He said he had lived with the bone chips, thinking the ailment was tendinitis, for four years and didn't think the injury curtailed his effectiveness.

"It has nothing to do with my pitching as far as throwing harder or slower," he told reporters. "Psychologically it could be a factor, but not physically."

The sophomore, who would earn All-America honors and become a first round draft choice the following year, was brilliant in Starkville. He held the potent Mississippi State batting order to 6 hits and struck out 10 in a 4-1 Gamecock win. Mississippi State first baseman Will Clark entered the tournament with 25 home runs and center fielder Rafael Palmeiro had 24.

In addition to Brantley, Clark and Palmeiro, the Mississippi State roster boasted a fourth future major leaguer, pitcher-outfielder Bobby Thigpen.

The famous Dudy Noble left field lounge, where fans park their pickup trucks and cook hamburgers, hot dogs and steaks on charcoal grills atop the bank beyond the left field fence, came into play in the first inning. Additional smoke was created by a pre-game fireworks display.

With two outs, Cook hit Palmeiro with a pitch and Clark lifted a high fly ball to right center field. Gamecock center fielder Scott Mackie and right fielder Jim St. Laurent lost the ball in the smoke that had drifted over from the left field lounge and the ball fell for a triple, scoring Palmeiro. That finished Mississippi State's scoring for the day, but the Gamecocks trailed 1-0.

South Carolina packed all of its scoring into the bottom of the third inning, rocking Brantley for six hits and four runs. Chris Boyle and Pete Fisher hit back-to-back doubles, tying the score. St. Laurent, Kent Anderson, Greg Morhardt and Harvey Heise singled and by the time Brantley retired the side, the Gamecocks led 4-1.

Boyle thought his double was the turning point in the game.

"That double was our first extra base hit and it pumped up everyone on the bench," he said during post game interviews. "We hit the ball hard and it happened to go through for hits a couple of times. We knew we would be facing Brantley and we knew he threw strikes. He doesn't walk many."

Both pitchers threw shutout innings for the remainder of the game with Cook improving his record to 6-3; Brantley dropped to 13-2.

Cook said the key to the game was when the Gamecocks got into trouble they were able to get Palmeiro and Clark, Mississippi State's two sluggers, out. Neither super star or the overflow crowd of 5,635 was a factor after the first inning although Palmeiro did register one single in four at bats. After his smoke aided triple, Clark reached once on a base on balls.

In the top of the third inning, when Mississippi State threatened to increase its 1-0 lead, Cook rose to the occasion. Dan Van Cleve led off the inning with a single and advanced when Rob Reinhardt booted the ball in left field. Bob Parker reached on an error by second baseman Pete Fisher and Mississippi State had runners at the corners with no outs.

Palmeiro popped to first baseman Greg Morhardt and Clark hit into a double play to end the threat.

North Carolina advanced in the winners bracket with a 4-2 win over Eastern Kentucky and was South Carolina's second round opponent. Tar Heel Coach Mike Roberts, who anticipated meeting Mississippi State in the second round action, had held back his All-America pitcher, Scott Bankhead to start the second round game. The North Carolina lineup was loaded with two other future major league stars in catcher B.J. Surhoff and shortstop Walt Weiss.

Bankhead had not lost a game in two seasons and had a 20 decision streak going. His record was 9-0 in 1983, followed by 11-0 in 1984. He stymied the Gamecocks on six hits and one un-earned run, but was lifted after six innings, apparently with the thought of bringing him back on short rest later in the tournament. North Carolina led 4-1 when Bankhead left the game.

Lefthander Tim Kirk, who relieved Bankhead, retired the first five Gamecocks he faced, but—with two out in the eighth—he walked Chris Boyle and pinch-hitter Keith Killian. Rob Rinehart, who had hit only one home run during the regular season—swung and missed two sliders before hitting a hanging curve ball over the scoreboard in right center field for a three run homer that tied the score at 4-4.

"It was the biggest hit of my life," Rinehart said afterwards. "I flew around the bases."

Rinehart said Kirk, "threw me two sliders and made me look bad." Then he threw the curve.

"I think he made a mistake there," Rinehart said. "He wants that back bad, I think."

"If so," wrote Thom Fladung in *The Columbia Record*, "Kirk will have to go to the parking area beyond the right center field fence."

South Carolina righthander Larry Price, who had held the potent Tar Heel bats to five hits but had given up four runs, only three earned, retired North Carolina in order in the bottom of the eighth inning.

Kent Anderson beat out an infield hit that Tar Heel shortstop Walt Weiss threw away, sending Anderson to second base with no outs in the top of the ninth. South Carolina's top long ball threat, first baseman Greg Morhardt, struck out and Coach June Raines called on his pitcher, Larry Price, to pinch hit for designated hitter Harvey Heise.

Price lined a double off the top of the left center field fence, scoring Anderson, to give the Gamecocks a 5-4 lead.

"Larry is a pretty good hitter," Raines told reporters after the game. "He gets up there and takes his swings. I made the decision to pinch hit Price when Mo struck out."

Price said, "As a pinch hitter, I was looking for a dead fast ball. I was fooled a little at first but I hung with it."

North Carolina Coach Mike Roberts said, "They got the right hit at the right time."

However, the game wasn't over. South Carolina still had to re-

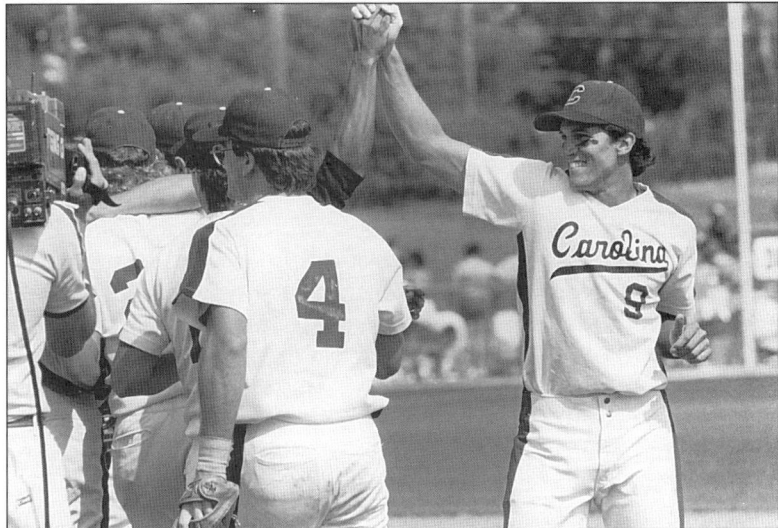

Larry Price's (top) pitching and pinch-hit double and Rob Rinehart's home run (bottom) produced an NCAA playoff win over North Carolina in 1984.
—USC Sports Information; Chris Hildreth

tire the Tar Heels in the bottom of the ninth. The hyperactive Price promptly hit the first batter to put the potential tying run on first base.

June Raines called in Robby Coker from the bull pen. Scott Johnson attempted a sacrifice bunt but the alert Gamecock defense got a force at second for the first out. Johnson broke for second on a hit and run sign as John O'Leary smashed a line drive at third baseman John Sullivan. He speared the ball and lobbed to Morhardt at first for a game ending double play.

Larry Price was the winning pitcher to improve his record to 9-3. Coker recorded his fifth save.

Greenville News writer Mike Hunt said of the six teams in the South II regional, none had a tougher draw than South Carolina.

"On Thursday, the Gamecocks faced ninth ranked and host team Mississippi State and pitcher Jeff Brantley, the best the Southeastern Conference has to offer, and won. And they won with Mike Cook, a hard luck, sore-armed pitcher who hadn't won in two months," Hunt wrote.

"On Friday, USC faced fifth ranked and top seeded North Carolina and pitcher Scott Bankhead, the best the ACC—and possibly the nation—has to offer, and won. And the Gamecocks won in highly dramatic fashion, with a three run homer from a player who had one homer all year, and a double by winning pitcher Larry Price, who was pinch-hitting for the designated hitter."

New Orleans sent North Carolina packing, 13-6 and was South Carolina's third round opponent. The Privateers scored in each of the first four innings and held on to edge the Gamecocks 6-5 and leave the double elimination tournament with three once beaten teams.

In the bottom of the ninth inning with two out, Chris Boyle doubled off the top of the right center field fence to drive in a run and narrow the New Orleans lead to one. A couple of inches higher and the final result might have been different but Boyle was left stranded. Greg Morhardt hit his 15th home run of the season for the Gamecocks.

South Carolina met Mississippi State in a rematch for survival and the right to play New Orleans for the right to advance to Omaha. Both teams had run out of pitching and the battle turned into a slugfest. In the final analysis, Mississippi State had more fire power than the Gamecocks.

Greg Morhardt's two run first inning home run staked South Carolina to a 2-0 lead over Bulldog starting pitcher Harold Myles but Dan Van Cleve led off the bottom of the first with a homer and before the side was retired Mississippi State led 4-2 and Gamecock starter Chris Norman was out of the game.

Morhardt hit his second homer of the game and 17th of the season but Mississippi State wound up with a school record six homers —two each by Will Clark and Rafael Palmeiro—and when the smoke had cleared, South Carolina was eliminated 18-9.

"You could tell it was going to be a hitter's day," June Raines said. "The wind was blowing out and the teams start running out of pitchers at this stage. There's nothing like the long ball. Babe Ruth started it and its the best thing in baseball. State has got two guys who can hit it out of anywhere."

New Orleans beat Mississippi State 6-3 to win the regional and move on to Omaha and the College World Series while the Bulldogs stayed home and the Gamecocks went home.

Greg Morhardt was chosen for the U. S. Olympic team trials but once again came in second best to Mississippi State's Will Clark. Among 3,000 Olympic tryouts, Morhardt survived to the final 44 when he was one of three first basemen left. Clark and Mark McGwire of Southern California were Morhardt's competition for two spots on the final 20 player roster.

The 1984 South II NCAA regional was loaded with Olympic talent as two North Carolina players—catcher B. J. Surhoff and pitcher Scott Bankhead—also made the team that represented the United States.

Morhardt, the Olympic odd man out, was selected in the second round of the June draft by the Minnesota Twins and signed after his junior year. Junior shortstop Kent Anderson was a fourth round pick by the California Angels and made it to the major leagues for 135 games with the Angels in 1989-90.

Pitcher Chris Norman, a punter on the South Carolina football team, was a 14th round pick by the Cleveland Indians but opted for the National Football League and punted four seasons for the Denver Broncos. Outfielder Jim St. Laurent was drafted in the 18th round by the Texas Rangers and played as high as AAA in professional baseball.

Apr 26-28, 1985—South Carolina 14-11-6, Clemson 2-6-5,
At Columbia

May 14-16—South Carolina 12-8-8, Clemson 6-6-3
At Clemson, S. C.

South Carolina and Clemson were scheduled to play each other in baseball again during the 1985 season after a one year hiatus, the first break in the series in forty years.

There was a difference of opinion as to what caused the cancellation of the rivalry in 1984. Mike Hunt wrote in *The Greenville News* Aug. 15, 1984:

"Last season's two game series was canceled on Oct. 27 when Clemson athletic director Bill McLellan accused South Carolina athletic director Bob Marcum of demanding that the teams play four games or none at all. Marcum countered that Clemson was trying to dictate to USC when the game in Columbia was to be played."

Hunt quoted Marcum as saying Clemson wanted the Columbia game to be played on a week day afternoon when the Gamecock home crowd would be smaller.

"Clemson coach Bill Wilhelm has been critical of the treatment he says he and his team has received from the crowd at Sarge Frye Field. USC wanted at least two weekend games in Columbia," Hunt reported.

During a meeting involving the two athletic directors and associate athletic directors Bobby Robinson of Clemson and Bobby Foster of South Carolina, Hunt said "the problems were apparently ironed out."

Wilhelm and South Carolina coach June Raines were given the option of scheduling two, four or six games and they agreed to resume the rivalry with six games, three in Columbia and three at Clemson, but Wilhelm groused about the agreement.

"At South Carolina they have very poor crowd control," Wilhelm was quoted by Teddy Heffner of *The State.* We have six games scheduled; sort of on a trial basis. We'll have to wait and see about 1986."

Wilhelm claimed Clemson had insisted upon several conditions, among them umpires assigned from another area, no mascots allowed on the field while the game was in progress, and a specified number of seats behind the Clemson dugout at Sarge Frye Field reserved for Clemson fans.

Clemson associate AD Bobby Robinson disagreed with his coach that USC had acquiesced to Tiger demands.

"We didn't make any ultimatums and they didn't make any ultimatums," Robinson declared. "We're satisfied. We're glad to be back in the series. We're going to play baseball."

"The two schools ought to play," South Carolina athletic director Bob Marcum commented. "They had some concerns and we had some concerns. We thought we should have some say-so in when the games should be played down here. They talked about crowd control and we agreed we'd do our part. Nothing such as roping off an area behind their dugout or anything like that. We gave Clemson our word we'd do a good job of supervision and I'm sure our fans will respond."

June Raines was delighted the series would be resumed, saying, "We're thrilled to death because it's six games. We think it's a plus for college baseball. I can't see anything but good happening. I think it's one of the great series in college baseball."

Wilhelm wasn't so sure, saying, "We're in the same state, but that's about all we have in common. It'd be great if we could play but they have determined we can't play in a fair situation. It's good for their fans but not for ours."

Clemson held a large lead in the series that dated back to 1899, 102-70-2, but South Carolina had won 8 of the past 12 games. In their personal rivalry since June Raines became South Carolina's head coach in 1977, he held a 3 game advantage, 15-12, over Wilhelm.

The 1984 break was not the first time that Wilhelm had sought to end the rivalry with South Carolina. He attempted to break off the series in 1974, resulted in a compromise in which the two teams played each other only once in 1974 and 1975, South Carolina winning both under Coach Bobby Richardson, 3-0 at Clemson in '74, and 6-2 at Columbia in '75.

The season was in its latter stages when Clemson came to Columbia to resume the South Carolina series, April 24-26. The Tigers had played 53 games and brought a 32-20-1 record to Sarge Frye Field. The Atlantic Coast Conference tournament had already been played, Clemson finishing second to Georgia Tech.

South Carolina, in 52 games, had a 34-18 record and had clinched the northern division championship in the Metro Conference. The Gamecocks still had to play in the Metro tournament at Tallahassee.

"If this series doesn't fire us up, nothing will," June Raines declared. "It comes at a good time for us and it is a big motivational plus. We won a big ball game Wednesday night (7-6) against Virginia Tech and had to hit a home run in the last inning to win, so our guys are really fired up."

Mike Cook was an All-America pitcher for the Gamecocks in 1985.
—Chris Hildreth

Clemson called on righthander John Pawlowski, who had a 7-2 record, to start against South Carolina ace righthander Mike Cook in the first game. Cook's record was 11-1 with an earned run average of 1.49.

The South Carolina lineup was loaded with power hitters. The Gamecocks came into the series with 101 home runs, 18 more than the previous school record for an entire season. First baseman Joe Datin had hit 16 homers, outfielders Keith Killian and Charlie Aldrich had 10 each, while shortstop Jeff Barns and third baseman Lewis Jenkins had each hit 9.

Outfielder Rob Rinehart was South Carolina's leading hitter with a .396 average on 72 hits.

Scott Peterson's evaluation was, "Clemson can match Carolina's hitting but is erratic when it comes to pitching and fielding."

"We have a team that is capable of playing good baseball, but we've had so many down moments that we can also play very bad baseball," Wilhelm said. "Cook is going to be tough, we know that. But if we can keep things like fielding and pitching together, we'll be all right."

Mike Cook held Clemson to 2 hits, struck out 14 and the Gamecocks hit 6 home runs as the series began with a 14-2 Gamecock rout before an overflow Sarge Frye Field crowd of 5,800.

"Now I know how those folks in London and Berlin felt during World War II," Bill Wilhelm commented. "The game was over early and it was just a matter of playing it out. Tomorrow is another day."

First baseman Joe Datin and designated hitter Charlie Aldrich each homered twice, giving Datin 18 and Aldrich 11 on the season. Left fielder Rob Rinehart hit his eighth and catcher Jeff Churchich his fourth.

Clemson actually led 2-0 in the top of the first inning when Cook walked Steve Williams and gave up a home run to designated hitter John Jay. The only other hit off Cook was a sixth inning single by Clemson shortstop Chuck Baldwin. Cook walked four.

"I didn't have my fast ball working as good as I wanted it, although my curve ball was making up the difference," Cook—who had come back from off season elbow surgery to remove bone chips —commented after the game. "I was throwing it for strikes consistently."

South Carolina quickly erased the Clemson lead with a school record tying four home runs in a six run bottom of the first inning and the Gamecocks never looked back. Rinehart, Datin and Aldrich hit bases empty homers and Churchich homered with two teammates on base.

"That was unbelievable," Joe Datin said of the four homer inning. He and Aldrich hit back to back homers in the third as the lead grew to 11-2. Datin's four runs batted in for the evening raised his team leading total to 71 for the season.

Raines said the key to the game was the four homer first inning and he thought Cook pitched his best since a sixteen strikeout performance in a 3-1 win over New Orleans early in the season.

The crowd wasn't as large for the second game of the series but 4,900 still overflowed 4,000 capacity Sarge Frye Field.

Keith Killians' first inning grand slam and three solo home runs by Rob Rinehart powered South Carolina to an 11-6 victory. Second baseman Riley Polk, who transferred to South Carolina after very little playing time in two seasons at Clemson, hit his second home run of the season.

After Killian's grand slam staked South Carolina to a 4-0 lead, Clemson knocked out Gamecock starter Brian Currie and tied the score with a four run second inning. Three of the runs were unearned.

Righthander Glenn Jenkins pitched six strong innings in relief, despite allowing 10 hits, 1 of which was an eighth inning line drive off Jenkins' rib cage for Jim McCollom's 82nd hit of the season, a Clemson record. Bo Taylor relieved the stunned Jenkins with the bases loaded and pitched 1 1/3 shutout innings to earn his first save while Jenkins picked up the win and some sore ribs to raise his record to 5-2.

"It looks like we are having a real tough weekend and they're having a great weekend," Bill Wilhelm stated after the second game. Wilhelm missed the first two innings, arriving late from his son's graduation from Winthrop College.

"Now we've got to come back tomorrow and see if there's anything at all left. I just have to apologize for the way we have looked. It's been very poor. But I'll remind you we can play a lot worse than this."

Wilhelm had one ace in the hole. Columbia native George Stone, Clemson's top pitcher with a 9-3 record and a 2.99 earned run average, was scheduled to start the third game against South Carolina freshman Scott Bailey whose record was 1-0 with a balloon-like ERA of 9.28.

Bailey lasted only one third of an inning, giving up three hits, a walk, and two runs before June Raines summoned righthander Steve Boley from the bullpen to halt the bleeding. Consecutive one out home runs by Steve Williams and Jim McCollom accounted for the Clemson lead.

Boley pitched 7 1/3 strong innings—allowing three third inning runs—before turning the mound over the freshman lefthander Clint Sawyer with two out in the eighth inning and the score tied 5-5 and the crowd of 6,500 restless.

The third standing room only crowd brought attendance for the series to 17,200.

South Carolina tied the score with two unearned runs in the bottom of the first. The Gamecocks took a 3-2 lead on Jeff Barns' RBI single in the second, but fell behind, 5-3, when Clemson tallied three times in the third. The Tiger rally featured the 271st career hit by Jim McCollom, an Atlantic Coast Conference record.

Boley walked a batter with the bases loaded and Clemson scored on a fielder's choice and a sacrifice fly to take the lead.

Scott Mackie hit his second home run of the season for South Carolina in the bottom of the third to pull the Gamecocks to within a run. Lewis Jenkins hit his 10th home run and South Carolina's 13th of the series, to tie it in the fifth.

Clemson starter George Stone wild pitched across the go ahead run in the bottom of the eighth inning and Sawyer retired the Tigers in the ninth to earn credit for the 6-5 victory which improved the freshman's record to 2-1.

Raines had high praise for the relief pitching of Steve Boley, calling him "definitely the difference. He threw an outstanding game.

I know Clint Sawyer will get credit for the win, but Steve sure deserved one too."

"I have very little to say," was Bill Wilhelm's opening comment. "We gave them the game. We played dead. I've seen lots of Clemson teams over the years. We have played worse. But we embarrassed ourselves out here. We have played our poorest baseball at the most important part of the season."

Sports writer David Newton of *The State* said the final game was "almost an anticlimactic ending to a series in which USC blasted Clemson pitching for 11 home runs and 25 runs in the first 2 games.

After the first inning, June Raines said, "I thought it was going to be a long ball day for them. I'm glad it wasn't."

After sweeping three games from Clemson, South Carolina won its first three starts in the Metro Conference tournament at Tallahassee. The Gamecocks defeated Southern Mississippi 13-1, Memphis State 19-8 and Virginia Tech 9-6, but then lost back to back decisions to host Florida State, 7-5, 11-5.

The Seminoles again won the Metro's automatic bid to the NCAA playoffs while South Carolina had to await an at large bid. But first, there was some unfinished business at Clemson May 14-16.

South Carolina's starting pitching was depleted from five games in four days at the Metro tournament and Steve Boley, on the strength of his strong relief effort in the third Clemson game at Columbia, earned the starting nod in the series opener.

June Raines was worried that the runner up battle for the Metro championship had taken too much out of his team.

"Sure, we're a tired ball club," he said. "We've just played five games in four days. But we've got to get up. Our entire season depends on this series."

South Carolina had a 40-20 record and Raines felt the Gamecocks could earn an at large bid to the NCAA playoffs by winning two of three at Clemson.

"There are a lot of good teams in the country with 15 to 20 losses," he said. "If we do well at Clemson, I think we still have a shot."

Boley was rocked for 9 hits and 6 earned runs in 6 plus innings but the Gamecock bats overcame that performance with a 15 hit attack and a seven run top of the first inning for a 12-6 victory. Ten different players, all of those used except for pitchers Boley and Clint Sawyer who didn't bat, collected at least one hit apiece. Five players had two hits with designated hitter Larry Price contributing the only home run.

Price was in the batting order because regular DH Charlie Aldrich was back in Columbia finishing up his final exams.

Jeff Barns led off the game with a single off Clemson starter Oliver Whitaker. With one out, Joe Datin walked and Keith Killian, Scott Mackie and Price singled. Scott Lambert reached on an error. Riley Polk, in his first at bat at Clemson after transferring to South Carolina, delivered a two RBI single.

When relief pitcher Jerome Santivasci finally retired the side, South Carolina led 7-0. Clemson scored three runs in the bottom of the first, added a single run in the third on John Jay's 400 foot plus home run, and two in the seventh, when Sawyer relieved Boley to extinguish the Tiger rally after Boley had given up a home run to Steve Baucom and a double to Ray Williams.

South Carolina added single runs in the third, fourth and sixth, and two in the eighth. South Carolina lost leading hitter Rob Rinehart for the remainder of the series. The left fielder pulled a groin muscle when he stepped into a hole chasing a fly ball.

The attendance was announced at 1,856.

"We got an excellent job out of Steve (Boley). One thing you want going into a big game like this is to throw strikes and we studied our staff and knew Steve would throw the ball over the plate," June Raines said.

His strategy of bringing in lefthander Clint Sawyer worked as Clemson's Wilhelm lifted lefthanded batters John Jay and Bill Spiers for right handed pinch hitters, taking two of the Tigers' top hitters out of the game.

"Clemson's got a lot of lefthanded hitters and that big Jay can hit 'em out of sight," Raines said in explaining his strategy of bringing in Sawyer. "I didn't want him (Jay) coming up there with two or three men on again, so we put our lefty out there. Sawyer's pitched well for us. He really has."

Wilhelm second guessed himself by saying, "We got hung up on the platoon stuff and I don't know about the advisability of that. A righthanded hitter didn't get a hit off Boley until the seventh when Ray Williams got one down the third base line.

"We just weren't doing anything. That restores your faith in the platoon system, so then I get smart and put in the righthanded hitters against Sawyer. About all they could do was strike out."

Here's the way beat writers saw South Carolina's fourth consecutive win over Clemson:

David Newton, *The State* —"South Carolina doesn't want this baseball season to end and Clemson can't wait to get it over."

Mike Hunt, *The Greenville News*—"South Carolina continued its dominance over Clemson Tuesday with a 12-6 win against the Tigers in the first night game ever played here between the two rivals."

Beverly Phillips, *The Columbia Record*—"After losing two

straight in the Metro baseball tournament this past weekend, South Carolina didn't waste any time in getting back on the winning track, and the Gamecocks did it at the expense of the Clemson Tigers."

Rob Rinehart was on the bench nursing his pulled groin but Charlie Aldrich rejoined the Gamecocks from the examination room for the second game of the series.

Clemson made short work of South Carolina starting pitcher Brian Currie, reaching him for 2 walks, 2 hits and 2 runs in 1/3 of an inning and junior righthander Casey Reed was called to the rescue. He delivered 6 2/3 solid innings, although touched for 8 hits and 4 third inning runs, only 2 of them earned as the Gamecocks battled back with 2 runs each in the second and third to take a short-lived lead. Clemson's four run outburst in the third put the Tigers up 6-4, but the Gamecocks countered with 3 in the fourth and added 1 in the seventh to win 8-6.

Currie walked 2 of the first 3 batters he faced, then gave up a 2 run double to Chuck Baldwin. When Scott Dillon singled, Baldwin stopping at third, June Raines had seen enough. He called on Reed who promptly hit Tommy Thompson with a pitch to load the bases. Reed got out of the jam when Steve Baucom hit into a double play.

Walks to Keith Killian and Dave Hollins sandwiched around a single by Scott Mackie loaded the bases for South Carolina in the bottom of the first. Scott Lambert drove in two runs with a base hit.

Jeff Barns collected his 80th hit of the season, a school record, and Jeff Morris also singled in the third inning. Both scored on Joe Datin's double. South Carolina's 4-2 lead was short-lived as Clemson sent 10 batters to the plate in the bottom of the third, scoring 3 times.

Four hits and a wild pitch resulted in three fourth inning runs as the Gamecocks regained the lead, 7-6, and sent Clemson starter George Stone to the showers. Stone, who had a 9-4 record when he started the third game in Columbia, finished with a 9-9 mark.

Joe Datin hit his 22nd home run for South Carolina's final run in the seventh inning.

Reed, 2-5, got the win with Glenn Jenkins pitching the final two innings, retiring six consecutive Tigers, to earn his first save of the year.

"As the stakes, real or imagined, continue to grow for South Carolina, so too does the number of ways the Gamecocks come up with to beat Clemson," Mike Hunt's lead paragraph in *The Greenville News* stated.

"South Carolina's Gamecocks continued their baseball mastery of arch-rival Clemson Wednesday night, grabbing the lead in the fourth inning and holding on for an 8-6 victory over the Tigers," David Newton wrote in *The State*.

Newton added the fifth straight win over Clemson "moved Carolina a step closer to an NCAA tournament berth."

"After tightening up and tailing off at the end of last weekend's Metro Conference baseball tournament, South Carolina is swinging free and easy now," Beverly Phillips wrote in *The Columbia Record*.

"Its Clemson that appears to be uptight," she added.

Both coaches had their best pitchers available for the sixth and final game of the series, Mike Cook (13-2) for South Carolina and John Pawlowski (9-2) for Clemson.

"Cook will throw hard and Pawlowski will throw hard also," Bill Wilhelm predicted. However, he added, "They (South Carolina) are gonna swing, and they're gonna have fun doing it. They're going to watch the ball when they swing which is something we have had trouble doing."

In 7 2/3 innings, Clemson reached Cook for 8 hits, but 7 of them were singles with Steve Baucom getting a double. Cook struck out 9, walked 4, and gave up 3 earned runs. Pawlowski struck out 8 Gamecocks and allowed only 6 hits in 7 1/3 innings, but he was touched for 5 earned runs with relief pitcher John Burnett allowing 3 more runs as South Carolina completed the 6 game sweep with an 8-3 win.

Keith Killian hit his 14th home run and Jeff Morris his 10th for the Gamecocks, giving them 17 homers in the 6 game series, 13 at Columbia and 4 at Clemson.

"I really didn't have my best stuff," Cook commented about his performance. "I knew in the eighth inning I was getting the ball up high and it was only a matter of time before Coach Raines got me."

Clemson had pulled to within 1 run, 4-3, in the seventh when Bert Heffernan scored on a fielder's choice. South Carolina, as it had done throughout the series, quickly retaliated with a 3 run top of the eighth. Pawlowski, who had retired 12 straight Gamecocks, walked Datin. John Burnett relieved Pawlowski and walked Charlie Aldrich after a fielder's choice. Killian hit a 3 run home run over the 400 foot sign in center field.

"He had thrown me two curve balls for strikes," Killian said in describing the homer. "I figured he would come back with another and he hung one. If that one wasn't going out, none would. I got all of it."

The home run by Morris produced the final Gamecock run in the top of the ninth.

Clemson loaded the bases with two out in the bottom of the eighth but Glenn Jenkins, who picked up his second save in as many days, got McCollom to ground into a fielder's choice. Clemson stranded 14 runners in the game, 7 in the final 3 innings.

In post-game interviews, writers second guessed Wilhelm for removing Pawlowski who had settled down to pitch well after a rocky start. Wilhelm pointed out Pawlowski had thrown 138 pitches and had "given all we could get out of him."

Raines commented, "I'll be honest with you. I was glad to see him (Pawlowski) go."

"Mike Cook won his 14th game of the season....in beating Clemson 8-3 to complete a six game USC sweep of their intrastate rivals. But the key, Cook said, was teammate Keith Killian's three run homer in the eighth inning," Beverly Phillips wrote in *The Columbia Record*.

"I think that three run dinger took them completely out of the game," the Gamecock ace told the afternoon newspaper writer. Cook, making his third start in seven days, admitted he was tired. He had started twice in the Metro Conference tournament the previous weekend.

Killian, who came back from severe eye and other injuries suffered in an automobile accident his freshman season to have a su–perb senior year, said "it's uncanny the number of two strike home

Dave Hollins (L) as a Gamecock, 1985-87; (R) as a Philadelphia Phillie, 1990-95.—*USC Sports Information; Philadelphia Phillies*

runs I've hit this year. My level of concentration with two strikes is so much better. I should go up to the plate thinking I have two strikes."

When asked about Killian's game clincher, June Raines grinned and said, "Ah boy, that was a big home run by Killian. We really needed that."

In the six game series, South Carolina collected 74 hits in 220 at bats, a .336 team average, including 12 doubles and 17 home runs. The Gamecocks scored 59 runs with 54 runs batted in. The 3,127 fans who saw the three games at Clemson along with the 17,200 for three games at Sarge Frye Field totaled 20,327 for the six games.

Clemson ended its season with a 36-30-1 record, the most losses ever for a Tiger baseball team. South Carolina, with a 43-20 record, returned to Columbia to await a call from the NCAA. Four days later, the call came with double good news. South Carolina had a bid to the playoffs and would host the NCAA East Region tournament at Sarge Frye Field.

The Gamecocks swept through the regional with ease, defeating LaSalle 11-1, St. John's 13-6, Western Carolina 14-3, and LaSalle a second time, 7-2, to qualify for their fifth trip to the College World Series in eleven seasons and fourth under June Raines.

In Omaha, South Carolina played the second longest game in College World Series history, losing 1-0 to Arkansas in 14 innings, and then was outscored 16-11 by Oklahoma State to go out in 2 games. The final season record was 47-22, the 47 wins being the third most in school history.

Joe Datin hit a school record 23 home runs in 1985.
—USC Sports Information

The Gamecocks hit a school record 144 home run, second in the nation that season, and batted .318 as a team, led by Rob Rinehart's .390. Jeff Barns batted .351, Joe Datin .348, Scott Mackie .329, Charlie "Moose" Aldrich and Jeff Morris .325 each. Keith Killian hit .304, giving the Gamecocks seven regulars with above .300 batting averages.

Jeff Churchich batted .294, Lewis Jenkins .286, freshman Dave Hollins—a future major leaguer—.282, Scott Lambert .282, and Riley Polk .279.

Seven Gamecocks hit double figures on home runs, led by Datin's 23. Killian had 15, Rinehart—who had only two the year before— and Aldrich each hit 14, Jenkins 12, and Barns and Morris 10 each. Datin's 88 runs batted in were a school record as was the even 100 hits by Barns.

Cook led the pitching staff with a 16-2 record and a 1.91 earned run average. He struck out a school record tying 168 batters in 141 innings, was a first team All-America choice and a first round draft pick by the California Angels. He made it to the American League briefly on three occasions, pitching in 41 games between 1986 and 1993 with the Angels, Twins and Orioles.

Cook tied the school record with 19 starts and the only start in which he didn't figure in the decision was the 14 inning, 1-0, loss to Arkansas in the College World Series. He was forced to leave after seven innings due to a misinterpretation of the designated hitter rule with the game scoreless.

South Carolina

vs

Clemson

April 12, 1990—South Carolina 21, Clemson 2
At Columbia

The 1990 University of South Carolina baseball team was far from the best in school history. Although the Gamecocks had a winning record, finishing 33-25, the number of losses were the most ever by a Gamecock team.

However, on the night of April 12, 1990 at Sarge Frye Field, when the Gamecocks met arch-rival Clemson, they could do no wrong.

The Tigers had swept three games at Clemson, shutting the Gamecocks out 6-0 and 9-0 wrapped around an 11 inning 6-5 decision and were talking sweep of the six game season series. The series at Columbia was not scheduled in succession. Clemson visited Sarge Frye on April 12 and was scheduled to come back for two games May 5-6.

South Carolina had sputtered to a 19-16 record coming into the April 12 game.

Clemson Coach Bill Wilhelm had won 990 games in his 33 year career. Neither he nor Gamecock Coach June Raines was prepared for what happened.

"If it can happen on a baseball field, there's a good chance that Bill Wilhelm has seen it in his 33 years as Clemson baseball coach," Jeff Hartsell wrote in the Charleston *Post & Courier.*

"But even Wilhelm, 10 games shy of his 1,000th coaching victory, has never seen anything like what happened to his Tigers Thursday night," Hartsell added.

"Clemson's players might as well have laid their bats and gloves down on the train tracks that run behind Sarge Frye Field, for the rival South Carolina Gamecocks absolutely flattened the Tigers 21-2 before 4,298 spectators, most of them whooping USC fans."

The writer said the 19 run South Carolina margin made history in several respects, none of them good for Clemson.

"It was Wilhelm's worst loss ever in 1,480 games as Clemson's coach; it was South Carolina's biggest victory over Clemson since the two teams began playing each other in 1899; and it was the most one-sided blowout in the 205 games the two teams have played."

The last time South Carolina approximated such a whipping on the Tigers was in 1930, "the year Wilhelm was born," Hartsell reported. Coach Billy Laval's Gamecocks defeated Clemson 18-2 that season.

Mark McCallum covered the game for *The State*, Columbia's morning newspaper. His lead read:

"No. It wasn't another form of spring football.

"And nobody got trapped for a safety, but the University of South Carolina annihilated Clemson University 21-2 Thursday night before 4,298 fans at Sarge Frye Field.

'The score left even USC Coach June Raines expressing disbelief. "'This is unheard of to score 21 runs against a rival like that'," McCallum quoted Raines.

In amassing its highest score of the season, South Carolina scored in every inning except the fourth. In the third and fifth innings, USC combined for 14 runs and 10 of its 15 hits while Clemson committed 3 of 7 errors by the Tigers in the game.

"Nothing went right for them and we took advantage of everything they did wrong," Raines declared. "And we got a home run right when we needed it."

The score was tied 2-2 after 2 1/2 innings but South Carolina sent 11 batters to the plate in the bottom of the third and 8 of them scored, the final 4 coming on a grand slam home run by left fielder Skeets Thomas. The score rose to 16-2 after 5 innings as 11 more Gamecocks went to the plate and 6 scored.

Leadoff batter and Gamecock center fielder Mike McGee said, "The biggest thing was we got a few key hits. That got us sparked. Plus, they shut us out twice up there and we wanted to come out and prove we could beat them. We didn't let up all night."

Clemson played the game without three of its starters. Shortstop Tim Rigsby was out with a hamstring injury while first baseman Joe DeBerry and catcher Eric Macrina were serving suspensions for disciplinary reasons.

Clemson starting pitcher Tim Parker allowed 4 runs, 3 of them earned, in 2 1/3 innings to be charged with his second loss against 4 wins. He struck out 4 but walked 5 in his brief stint. It was Parker's shortest outing in 10 starts. Freshman Paxton Briley was raked for 6 earned runs in 1 2/3 innings and South Carolina reached 4 subsequent pitchers for 11 more scores.

Tim Peele pitched an inning, allowing 6 hits and 6 runs, only 3 of them earned. Aaron Jersild faced 4 batters without retiring any-one. He walked 2, allowed a hit and an error accounted for 3 un-earned runs. Chad Phillips worked 2 innings, allowing a hit and a run, and Brian Faw pitched a hitless inning but was charged with an unearned run.

The final count showed 6 Tiger pitchers issued 9 walks and 15 hits and 13 of the 21 Gamecock runs were earned.

Sophomore righthander Brian Williams pitched the first 6 in-nings for South Carolina, allowing 3 hits and both Clemson runs. He struck out 9 and walked 5. Ty Welch relieved Williams in the seventh and pitched a hitless inning, issuing one base on balls. Rob Mosser pitched the eighth and ninth, yielding 2 of Clemson's 5 hits and issuing 2 walks, but he held the Tigers scoreless.

Mosser struck out 4. Coupled with Williams' 9 strikeouts, 13 Clemson batters went down on strikes. Williams got the win, im-proving his record to 5-3.

Each player in the starting lineup collected at least 1 hit with designated hitter George Rush getting 3 of South Carolina's 15. Skeets Thomas, Mike McGee, catcher Dave Willman and short-stop Joe Gmitter had two hits each. Thomas' grand slam home run and doubles by Gmitter and second baseman Sandy Rickett were South Carolina's only extra base hits.

Every Gamecock starter except D. T. Cromer had at least one run batted in, with Thomas collecting 4, Rush 3, and Willman and Burke Cromer 2 each. Coach Raines substituted freely in the latter innings and used 18 players in the game.

Each team scored a first inning run and South Carolina took a 2-1 lead in the bottom of the second on some alert base running by Gmitter, who scored from second base on an infield out. Parker walked Gmitter and McGee with one out. Willman slapped a ground ball up the middle which Clemson shortstop Todd Stefan snared with a diving stop and threw to first base to retire Willman. Gmitter rounded third and kept running to score on the play.

Clemson tied it in the top of the third when designated hitter Chad Phillips, who later would come in to pitch, doubled down the left field line to drive in Brian Kowitz from second base.

Right fielder D. T. Cromer led off the South Carolina third inning with a single. With one out, first baseman Jeff Parnell walked and Wilhelm replaced Parker with the freshman Briley. The first batter he faced, third baseman Burke Cromer, slapped a single to score his brother with the run that put South Carolina ahead to stay, 3-2.

Briley walked Rickett to load the bases and Gmitter followed with a hard shot to Clemson third baseman Jimmy Crowley. His throw to the plate to force Parnell was in the dirt and the 210 pound

Parnell crashed into catcher Michael Spiers who was attempting to block the plate. The ball rolled to the screen and both Parnell and Burke Cromer scored to make the score 5-2.

Briley hit leadoff man Mike McGee in the back to again load the bases. Catcher Dave Willman beat out a high chopper to third base for an infield hit, scoring Rickett. Skeets Thomas then crushed a Briley pitch over the batter's background and 390 foot sign in straight away center field for a bases loaded home run that inflated the score to 10-2.

It was the sixth homer of the season for Thomas who also played wide receiver on the Gamecock football team.

Tim Peele, the third Clemson pitcher, gave up 6 hits and Clemson committed an error to account for 6 South Carolina runs in the fifth inning. The Gamecocks added 3 more in the sixth and 1 each in the seventh and eighth.

After the 21-2 game in Columbia, South Carolina won 8 of 13 games. Clemson won 10 of 13 and Coach Wilhelm registered his 1,000th with a 17-10 rout of Georgia Tech in Atlanta the game before Clemson returned to Columbia to resume the series with the Gamecocks.

The May 5 game was washed out and a doubleheader was scheduled for May 6 to make up the rainout.

Clemson led 4-2 in the fifth inning of the first game, primarily on Kevin Northrup's three run fourth inning homer, when Skeets Thomas tied it with a two run home run. Second baseman Sandy Rickett won it for South Carolina, 5-4, with a home run in the bottom of the ninth. Lefthander Will Lewis, who pitched four shutout innings in relief of starter Brian Williams, got the win to raise his record to 5-3.

In the seven inning second game, Charlie Young gave up three bases empty home runs—to Clemson's Jim Anderson, Joe DeBerry and Northrup—but South Carolina collected 11 hits off 4 Clemson pitchers to win 7-3, sweep the Columbia series, and gain a 3-3 split with the Tigers on the season.

Freshman first baseman Jeff Parnell hit a bases-empty home run for South Carolina. Young raised his record to 6-1.

"Consider Clemson paid back in full," writer Chris Thomasson declared in the *Spartanburg Herald.*

"Last month, after the South Carolina baseball team lost three games at Clemson, the Gamecocks resolved to get even. In fact, the Gamecocks were so eager to win three straight over the Tigers that they celebrated little after a resounding 21-2 win over Clemson.

"Yesterday, USC gained a split of the seasonal series by sweeping a doubleheader 5-4 in nine innings and 7-3."

South Carolina

vs

Georgia Tech

April 17, 1990—South Carolina 1, Georgia Tech 0
At Columbia

There was something about pitching against Georgia Tech that brought out the best in Brian Williams.

Drafted in the third round out of Lewisville High School, the 6-foot, 2-inch, 197 pound man child from Fort Lawn, S. C., turned down the offer of the Pittsburgh Pirates and would earn the nickname "The Natural" as the most versatile player ever to wear the uniform of the University of South Carolina.

As a freshman in 1988, Williams played every position except second base and catcher, and batted .332 with 8 home runs and 18 stolen bases. He saw action in 21 games at shortstop, 17 at first base, 9 as a designated hitter, 5 at third base, 2 in the outfield, and 8 as a pitcher. Scouts and other observers projected his professional future as a pitcher.

At the end of regular season play, however, he had only a 1-1 freshman year mound record and had pitched only 24 1/3 innings.

Coach June Raines started him against Southern Mississippi in the Metro Conference tournament at Tallahassee, Fla., and he struck out 12 and allowed 7 hits in a complete game, 6-2 victory.

That performance earned the freshman a start against Georgia Tech in the NCAA Atlantic Region tournament at Coral Gables, Fla. South Carolina was facing elimination, having lost to the Yellow Jackets 7-6 after defeating Towson State 3-2. The Gamecocks remained alive in the regional by defeating Towson State, 5-1, setting up a showdown rematch with Georgia Tech to reach the finals.

In another complete game performance, Williams allowed an infield single in the first inning, a clean single in the second, and no hits after that. He struck out 15, walked 2, and earned a 5-0 shutout victory. South Carolina advanced to the regional championship game but lost to Miami 10-3 to miss out on a sixth trip to the College World Series in Omaha.

Williams was named to the freshman All-America team.

As a South Carolina junior two years later, Georgia Tech was no stranger to Brian Williams when the Yellow Jackets visited Columbia April 17, 1990. He almost missed the assignment, however. Williams' mother was hospitalized at Lancaster and he returned to Columbia just two hours before game time after spending time at her bedside.

"I was tired. I wouldn't want to do it again," Williams said later. Tired or not, he carried a no-hitter into the ninth inning, but led only 1-0 on the strength of a double by catcher Dave Willman in the bottom of the eighth inning that scored third baseman Brian Lawler, who had walked.

Brian Williams, shown here with the Houston Astros, twice shut out Georgia Tech while pitching for the Gamecocks.—*Houston Astros*

Georgia Tech second baseman and leadoff batter Carlton Fleming led off the top of the ninth inning and slapped a ball off home plate that bounded high in the air toward shortstop Burke Cromer. Realizing he couldn't throw out the speedy Fleming and wanting to preserve the no-hitter, Cromer deliberately bobbled the ball in an attempt to draw an error.

Fleming was almost to first base when the ball came down and —as official scorer—I ruled it a hit, spoiling the no-hitter, and got a hearty round of boos from the Gamecock crowd of 2,117.

Williams promptly picked Fleming off first base, which prompted more booing for the official scorer from the partisan crowd. Williams retired Tom Green for the second out but then walked Darren Bragg to put the potential tying run back on first base.

Anthony Maisano, The Georgia Tech designated hitter who would finish the year with a school and Atlantic Coast Conference record 25 home runs, strode to the plate as the crowd held its breath. Maisano stroked a clean single to center field to take the official scorer off the hook. It also put the tying and go ahead runs on base.

Anthony Byrd ran for the slow footed Maisano and third baseman Andy Bruce was the batter. He hit a weak infield grounder to end the game.

"University of South Carolina pitcher Brian Williams went from the bedside to the ball park," Mark McCallum wrote in *The State.*

"After visiting his mother in Lancaster County Hospital, Williams returned to Columbia and came within three outs of his first collegiate no-hitter in a 1-0 victory over Georgia Tech."

The loss marked the first time Georgia Tech had been shut out in 106 games, since Williams blanked them 5-0 in the 1988 NCAA regional at Coral Gables.

"I think you saw why twenty scouts were out there and why he's one of the best pitchers in the country," Coach June Raines told reporters in post game interviews.

Mark McCallum commented, "Against Georgia Tech, none seemed better. In two career appearances against the Yellow Jackets, Williams, 6-3, holds a pair of two hit shutouts and 28 strikeouts.

He had 13 strikeouts and walked 5 in pitching the near no-hitter. He also had a string of 15 hitless innings against Georgia Tech, the final 7 innings of the 1988 win his freshman year and the first 8 innings as a junior.

"I tried to keep them off-stride and work it in and out," Williams said. "My curve ball was working and my change was getting over. That makes a pitcher effective."

Williams took a perfect game into the sixth inning, retiring the first 16 batters he faced before walking Georgia Tech catcher Jon Anderson.

Lost in the glamour of Williams' performance was a near equal performance by Georgia Tech pitcher Mike Hostetler, who lost his first decision after 8 wins. He allowed only 4 hits, struck out 10 and walked 3.

Aside from the ninth inning, Georgia Tech's biggest threat came in the seventh. Williams walked Fleming and Green moved the runner to second with a sacrifice. Williams struck out Bragg but worked the count to 3-0 on Maisano before walking him intentionally. He then struck out Bruce to end the threat.

Collegiate Baseball selected Williams as the Coppertone National Player of the Week for his performance against Georgia Tech.

The two Georgia Tech teams that Williams shut out were among the best in Yellow Jacket history, winning 91 games. The Yellow Jacket record was 45-24 in 1988 and 46-25 in 1990. Both teams were nationally ranked in the *Collegiate Baseball* and *Baseball America* final polls.

South Carolina played the 1990 Georgia Tech team twice in Atlanta after Williams' near no-hitter in Columbia, winning 7-4 and losing 11-1 to win two of three from the Yellow Jackets that season. Williams didn't pitch either of those two games but was the designated hitter in the first and played first base in the second.

Williams' activity in playing multiple positions throughout his collegiate career no doubt had an adverse affect on his pitching but he finished his junior season with an 8-4 record and had a career record of 14-8. In 222 2/3 innings his career earned run average was 3.11. His 277 strikeouts averaged out to 11.2 per 9 innings, a school record. His 11.91 strikeouts per 9 innings in 1988 set both freshman and team school records.

In three seasons as a Gamecock, Williams appeared in 34 games as a pitcher, 33 as a first baseman, 33 as an outfielder, playing all three outfield positions, 31 as a designated hitter, 21 as a shortstop, 5 at third base, and 1 game each as a pinch hitter and runner.

In 153 games, his career batting average was .309 on 154 hits which included 32 doubles, 6 triples and 17 home runs. He scored 102 runs, stole 47 bases, and drove in 72 runs.

Williams was a supplemental first round draft pick by the Houston Astros in 1990 and went on to a major league pitching career with the Astros and San Diego Padres.

South Carolina

vs

The Citadel

April 2, 1992—South Carolina 32, The Citadel 5
At Columbia

How often does the ninth hitter in the batting order drive in 9 runs, collect 5 hits, tie the school record for doubles in a game and hit a home run?

That was the night senior shortstop Randy Thompson had April 2, 1992 when South Carolina battered The Citadel 32-5 at Sarge Frye Field. Thompson came to South Carolina after two years at Spartanburg Methodist Junior College more renowned for his defense than for skills with the bat.

He hit only .203 as a junior in 1991 and wound up the 1992 season with a .238 average, but one day after April Fool's day was his night to shine.

Actually, Thompson's offensive star briefly flashed across the sky once before. On March 26, 1991 his eighth inning home run provided the only score in a 1-0 victory over Georgia. That feat paled, however, when compared to what the middle infielder from Easley accomplished slightly more than a year later.

Despite his low batting average and ninth spot in the batting order, Thompson did seem to have a knack for driving in runs. His 44 RBI in 1992 tied him for fourth on the Gamecock team with outfielder Jerry Shepherd who batted .346 and hit 17 home runs to Thompson's .238 and 4 homers. Shepherd usually batted cleanup.

Thompson's night began inauspiciously. He was hit by a pitch and scored in a 6 run Gamecock second inning. He doubled, drove in a run, and scored the other as South Carolina tallied twice in the third, and doubled with the bases loaded to drive in 3 runs in a 9 run fourth inning as the score mounted to 17-1.

In the fifth inning, Thompson hit his third consecutive double, driving in 2 runs. He hit a 3 run home run in the 8 run sixth inning to raise his RBI total for the night to 9. He singled and scored in the seventh inning and missed out on a perfect night at the plate when he grounded out to shortstop in the eighth.

Thompson tied 3 school records—Wes Westbrook's 1979 mark of 9 runs batted in a game; Joe McCarthy's 1980 record of 6 runs scored, and the record of 3 doubles shared by 7 other Gamecocks. His 5 hits were 1 shy of 1 of the oldest records in South Carolina's book. Bill Harley had 6 hits against Erskine in 1931.

"All weekend I was hitting the ball hard," Thompson said in explaining his career game. "The coaches told me to keep swinging the bat and they'd fall. I guess I got lucky tonight."

Randy Thompson
—USC Sports Information

The Gamecocks broke their 1980 record of 30 runs in a game, twice tied the 1980 record for most hits in an inning with 8, and tied the 1981 record for most doubles in a game with 10.

However, the Gamecocks fell short of two records set in a 25-10 win over The Citadel at Charleston in 1986.. The 1986 game produced 66 total bases to 54 in 1992, 33 hits to 31. In the 1986 game, South Carolina had 2 doubles, 5 triples and 7 home runs, 3 of them by designated hitter Charlie "Moose" Aldrich, who tied the record for homers and was one shy of the RBI record with 8.

Coach June Raines explained the 1992 offensive barrage by saying, "You've got to be greedy in baseball. You've got to want to hit every time up and pretend the ball game's nothing to nothing at all times. We did that. They came out aggressive and after every inning we kept telling them it was nothing-nothing. They kept swinging the bats for us."

Raines noted, "Everything we hit was hard and it all started with an error that gave us an extra at bat" in the 6 run second inning that started the onslaught.

"I'm just hoping this is catching," Raines added.

D. T. Cromer started the inning with a triple and scored on brother Burke's single. South Carolina loaded the bases with 2 out and Dave Willman grounded to third baseman Tony Skoles who bobbled the ball for an error, a run scoring, and Brian Lawler emptied the bases with a home run.

Fred Jordan, first year coach of The Citadel, said "Everything we threw they hit. Good pitches, bad pitches, all pitches."

In what was perhaps the understatement of the evening, Tony Skole, The Citadel third baseman, said, "It got out of hand."

Mark McCallum of *The State* said the game's "noteworthy items seemed as long as the Bulldogs' night—almost endless."

South Carolina first baseman Jeff Parnell, who played under Jordan at Stratford High School, had 4 hits in 5 at bats and scored 4 runs but didn't drive any in.

Right fielder Brian Lawler had his first collegiate grand slam home run and had 5 RBI. His 3 hits also included a double.

Left fielder Jerry Shepherd drove in 3 runs and scored 2. His 3 hits included his ninth home run of the season which tied him with Parnell for the lead in the Southeastern Conference.

Designated hitter D. T. Cromer had 3 hits, including a double and a triple, scored 3 times and drove in 2 runs.

His brother, third baseman Burke Cromer, had 2 hits, both doubles, and 3 RBI.

Second baseman Mike McGuire had a double and a single, walked 3 times, scored 4 runs and drove in 1. He moved to third base in the seventh inning when Burke Cromer took over the pitching mound.

The Gamecocks scored in every inning in which they batted except the first. They batted around in 3 different innings and sent at least 7 batters to the plate in 2 other innings. They finished with 31 total hits and 14 extra base hits.

Coach Raines announced before the game he would use at least 3 pitchers and Jim Stoops worked the first 3 innings to get the win. Stoops allowed 1 hit, struck out 3 and walked 2. He was followed by 5 pitchers with Wally Maynard working 2 innings and Scott Pace, Burke Cromer, Steve Kolbert and Rob Mosser pitching 1 inning each.

What a difference a week makes.

Seven days after South Carolina and The Citadel combined to score 37 runs in Columbia, the Gamecocks traveled to Charleston for the second game in the season series.

South Carolina won 1-0. The Gamecocks collected 7 hits, 24 fewer than they had scored a week earlier. The Citadel managed 5 hits off redshirt freshman Jim Stoops who worked 7 innings to improve his record to 4-0. Rob Mosser pitched the final 2 innings for his fourth save. he walked two but allowed no hits.

The only run of the game scored in the seventh inning. D.T. Cromer beat out an infield hit, stole second base, moved to third on a wild pitch and scored on a one out single by second baseman Stacy Stokes.

Randy Thompson, who had such a hot bat one week earlier, struck out twice and hit a fly ball to left field. He was lifted for pinch hitter Burke Cromer in the ninth inning.

South Carolina

vs

Florida

May 16, 1992—South Carolina 11, Florida 4
At New Orleans, La. (SEC Tournament)

South Carolina got off to a stumbling start in its first baseball season as a member of the Southeastern Conference but by the time the SEC tournament began in the New Orleans Superdome, the Gamecocks were hitting on all cylinders.

Before the twenty four game conference schedule began, South Carolina compiled a 19-4 record against non-SEC opponents and was in good shape until defending NCAA champion Louisiana State University came to Columbia and Sarge Frye Field for the Gamecocks' SEC baptism.

South Carolina got decent pitching in its first SEC series but the Gamecock bats couldn't solve the LSU pitching staff and scored only 2 runs in 3 games. The result was 3 losses by scores of 4-1, 3-1 and 5-0.

South Carolina whipped in-state rival Clemson 8-6 in a mid-week non-conference game before traveling more than 800 miles to Fayetteville, Ark., for its first road SEC series. The Gamecocks dropped the first two games, 8-3 and 7-2, to find themselves 0-5 in the conference before registering their first SEC win.

Jerry Shepherd hit two home runs and Dave Willman and Burke Cromer smashed one apiece as South Carolina clobbered the Razorbacks 20-11.

If the Gamecocks felt rejuvenated over breaking into the SEC win column it didn't show immediately. South Carolina traveled to Auburn for its third conference series and was swept by the War Eagles, Plainsmen, Tigers or whatever nickname Auburn was using that weekend, 4-1, 3-2 and 6-0.

Returning home, the situation got more desperate and the SEC record dipped to 1-9 when the Gamecocks dropped the opening game of a series with Georgia, 5-4. Then a ray of hope appeared on the horizon. South Carolina won 8-3 and 16-12 to take the series 2 games to 1.

South Carolina's first three All-Southeastern Conference players in 1992 were designated hitter D. T. Cromer (L), outfielder Jerry Shepherd (kneeling) and catcher Dave Willman.—*USC Sports Information*

On a trip to Nashville, the Gamecocks routed Vanderbilt 21-1, won the second game 7-5 with a dramatic final inning four run rally that featured Jeff Parnell's three run opposite field home run, and then swept the series with an 18-7 victory played in a steady rain. South Carolina sent 13 batters to the plate in the top of the first inning and led 9-0 before the Commodores came to bat.

The news media saw little hope for the Gamecocks qualifying for post-season play, even after South Carolina won the first two games of the Vanderbilt series. Jim Gilstrap wrote in the Anderson *Independent-Mail*:

"The University of South Carolina baseball team, ranked as high as 15th in the pre-season polls, is in danger of not qualifying for the Southeastern Conference baseball tournament.

"South Carolina is in last place (sixth) in the SEC's Eastern Division with a 5-9 record. To make the tournament the Gamecocks must finish at least fourth. Entering its three game series at Vanderbilt, South Carolina trailed Georgia and Vanderbilt. USC's sweep of Vandy (5-8) helped close the gap, but Georgia's sweep of Tennessee kept the Bulldogs (7-6) ahead in the race."

The three game sweep at Vanderbilt improved the conference record to 6-9 but the Gamecocks were still a second division club in the eastern division race. The surge from the depths caught the attention of Nick Gates of the Knoxville *News-Sentinel* and he wrote in an advance story on the Sarge Frye Field series with Tennessee:

"South Carolina knows the pressure of playing a must-win series in the Southeastern Conference. The Gamecocks have faced the dilemma the past two weeks and passed with flying colors."

Gates quoted Coach June Raines as saying, "We have to win 2 out of 3 everywhere we go the rest of the season. We were 1-9 at one time and our backs were to the wall."

In the Tennessee series, South Carolina was outscored 18-12 in a first game slugfest but rallied to win the next 2 games, 6-5 and 14-3 to reach the June Raines criteria of winning 2 out of 3 and pull within 2 games of .500 at 8-10.

At Gainesville, Fla., South Carolina faced the unenviable task of facing eighth ranked Florida's ace pitchers—Marc Valdes and John Burke—in the Saturday doubleheader that kicked off the series.

The Gamecocks beat both. Jared Baker bested Valdes 4-2, with ninth inning relief help from Rob Mosser, and the Gamecocks jumped on Burke for 4 first inning runs and held on to win 4-3 for a sweep that evened the SEC record at 10-10.

South Carolina lost the third game of the Florida series to again find itself below .500 with a 10-11 conference record, but, in the final series of the SEC regular season schedule, swept 3 home games from Kentucky, 11-4, 4-3 and 16-5, to climb above the break even mark, 13-11, and into second place in the final eastern division standings.

"Sometimes when you're on a roll, everything seems to work out right," Andy Friedlander wrote in the Spartanburg *Herald-Journal*. And the South Carolina baseball team is definitely on a roll."

It was a miraculous comeback from a 1-9 start, 12 wins in the final 14 conference games. The Gamecocks not only qualified for the conference tournament scheduled for the Superdome in New Orleans, but were seeded second in the eastern division. The top four teams in each division qualified for the tournament and South Carolina was paired against western division third seed Arkansas.

"We really feel we are the best team in the SEC right now," first baseman Jeff Parnell said in a media interview. "We're going down there to win the thing."

However, the Gamecocks—with an SEC leading team batting average of .320 and a 37-18 overall record—quickly found themselves in the loser's bracket. They lost to Arkansas 8-6 in the tournament's opening round.

The Greenville News foresaw the outcoming with a headline that read, "Arkansas May Have Edge on USC in SEC Opener," over a story written by Abe Hardesty.

"Norm DeBryin says his Arkansas team has never played in the Superdome but the Razorbacks have done two of the next best things," Hardesty reported. "Arkansas has played in an indoor facility this season—the Seattle Kingdome (in a tournament)—and has played all its home games on artificial turf."

Jeff Hartsell of the Charleston *Post & Courier* reported, "The Superdome, fake grass and the Arkansas Razorbacks" stood in the path of South Carolina's hopes for an SEC championship and a bid to the NCAA playoffs.

The score was tied at 6-6 with 2 out in the top of the ninth inning when pinch-hitter Carl Stall delivered a 2 RBI double to provide Arkansas' margin of victory. It was South Carolina's third loss in four games against the Razorbacks.

"The Gamecocks now are back in the same 'must win' situation in which they spent the second half of the season, when they battled back from a 1-9 start," Mark McCallum commented in *The State*.

"Junior righthander Matt Threehouse tied a Southeastern Conference tournament record with 14 strikeouts Thursday as South Carolina crushed Vanderbilt 14-1 to remain alive in the SEC baseball tournament," a sports information office dispatch from New Orleans reported.

Threehouse struck out every Vanderbilt batter at least once, left fielder Bart Nielsen 3 times, and threw only 112 pitches to improve his season record to 10-4. South Carolina battered 7 Vanderbilt pitchers for 18 hits, including 2 home runs by Jeff Parnell.

"I had command of all my pitches today," Threehouse said. "The umpire was calling my curve ball a strike and that was a key. I haven't thrown that pitch with that kind of control in two years. I'll remember this game for a long time."

The Gamecocks had to meet nemesis Arkansas in the third round as the Razorbacks dropped into the loser's bracket at the hands of Louisiana State. This time the Gamecocks prevailed, tying the tournament home run record in the process.

"South Carolina tied a Southeastern Conference tournament record with 4 home runs and banged out 15 hits Friday to eliminate Arkansas 9-5 and advance to the tournament's final 4," the sports information release from USC reported.

Brian Lawler hit his seventh home run in the third inning. D. T. Cromer hit his sixth, a 2 run shot, in the sixth, and Jerry Shepherd and Jeff Parnell hit back-to-back solo homers in the seventh. It was the 16th for each.

Florida knocked off LSU 3-1 to become the tournament's only unbeaten team and the Gamecocks faced the unenviable task of getting by the Gators in order to continue playing. After five innings prospects were dim.

Florida took a 3-0 third inning lead off South Carolina starter Jim Stoops on two walks and back to back doubles by Dave Majeski and Kevin Polcovich. The Gators made it 4-0 in the fifth when Majeski lashed his second double and rode home on Polcovich's single.

Florida starter Doug Brennan held South Carolina hitless until Brian Lawler singled with two out in the fifth inning. Stacy Stokes had walked and D. T. Cromer had reached on an error before Lawler's hit loaded the bases. Jerry Shepherd's ground ball to shortstop ended that threat.

Then came one of the most bizarre innings in collegiate baseball history with the Gamecocks as the beneficiary.

Jeff Parnell opened the top of the sixth with a bloop double down the left field line and continued to third base when Majeski couldn't handle the ball. Burke Cromer grounded to shortstop for the first out, Parnell scoring to make it 4-1.

Mark Gugino pinch-hit for Mac White who had struck out in his first two at bats and walked on a 3 and 2 count. Stacy Stokes also worked the count to 3 and 2 and drew a base on balls. Randy Thompson walked on a 3 and 1 count to load the bases. D. T. Cromer was hit by a pitch to force Gugino home with the second Gamecock run and the bases remained loaded with 1 out.

Joe Hasskew, who had replaced Florida starting pitcher Doug Brennan at the top of the inning, was relieved by Matt Parker who promptly walked Dave Willman and Brian Lawler, both on 3 and 2 counts, to force in 2 runs and tie the score at 4-4.

Exit Parker, enter Ron Scott who, like Parker, failed to retire a Gamecock. He faced 6. Jerry Shepherd drove in a run with an infield single, leaving the bases loaded. Parnell, up for the second time in the inning, walked on a 3 and 2 count to force in the sixth run. Burke Cromer got his second RBI of the inning with another infield hit. Gugino walked for the second time in the inning, again on a 3 and 2 count, and the score mounted to 8-4.

Stacy Stokes stroked a single to right field, the first ball hit out of the infield since Parnell's leadoff double. Stokes' hit drove in Parnell, making it 9-4 with the bases still loaded. Randy Thompson singled to left field, driving in Burke Cromer and Gugino for the 10th and 11th runs of the inning.

Bo Camposano, an outfielder who hadn't pitched since high school, came in as Florida's fourth pitcher of the inning and fifth in the game. He struck out D. T. Cromer and retired Dave Willman on a ground ball to shortstop to end the nightmare, but the damage had been done.

The summary on the top half of the sixth inning showed 11 South Carolina runs on only 5 hits, 1 Florida error and 2 runners left on base. Only 3 Gamecock hits left the infield but 7 walks, a hit batter and 4 wild pitches in the inning spelled disaster for Florida. Six of the seven bases on balls came after the count was three balls and two strikes.

South Carolina crammed all of its scoring into the sixth inning and lefthander Scott Pace pitched 4 2/3 innings of shutout relief for the victory, making his record 4-1.

"South Carolina erased a 4 run deficit with an 11 run sixth inning Saturday night to defeat Florida 11-4 and advance to the final day of the Southeastern Conference baseball tournament," the USC sports information release on the game reported.

"The Gamecocks had only 5 hits in the inning but 3 different Florida pitchers walked 7 and hit 1 batter in the 52 minute half inning. The win boosted South Carolina's record to 40-19 and moved the Gamecocks a step closer to an NCAA bid. Florida, which already has a bid sewed up, is 43-17."

As the tournament's last undefeated team, Florida could sit back, lick its wounds, and await the outcome of South Carolina's showdown battle with LSU to see who the Gators would meet for the SEC tournament title.

Gator coach Joe Arnold wasn't too concerned over the bizarre loss, treating it as a blessing in disguise.

"You never want to lose but this is really the way it works out best for us," he told writer Bill King of *The Gainesville Sun*. If Florida had eliminated South Carolina and then lost to LSU the Gators would have been faced with playing a second game against LSU the next day.

"We don't have enough people available to play two more ball games," Arnold added. "If we win tomorrow, fine. If we don't, we're still playing in the (NCAA) regional."

South Carolina Coach June Raines' reaction to the 11-4 trouncing of Florida was, "If that win doesn't get us in the NCAA regionals, I'm going to Kansas City and blow the building up."

Umpires ejected Skip Bertman in the fifth inning, but the absence of their coach didn't hamper the LSU Tigers as they eliminated South Carolina 6-3, despite home runs by Dave Willman and D. T. Cromer, to move into the championship game against Florida.

The rest that Joe Arnold had talked about as an asset after his team's 11-4 loss to South Carolina didn't help as Florida's pitching was just as ineffective in a 12-1 loss that crowned LSU as the SEC tournament champion.

After the loss to LSU eliminated South Carolina from the SEC tournament, June Raines said he told his team, "Clean your stuff

Jeff Parnell (L) and Jerry Shepherd were the top two home run hitters in the Southeastern Conference in 1992.—*USC Sports Information*

and keep it packed. We're going somewhere."

He was right. South Carolina landed two players—outfielder Jerry Shepherd and third baseman Burke Cromer—on the SEC all-tournament team and went home to await a bid to the NCAA playoffs. Earlier, Shepherd, designated hitter D. T. Cromer and catcher Dave Willman had been named to the regular season All-Southeastern Conference team.

South Carolina—which had played many times in Mark Light Stadium in Coral Gables, Fla.—was assigned to the Atlantic regional hosted by Miami and met Notre Dame, which brought a 45-13 record into the NCAA playoffs, in the opening round.

Matt Threehouse was magnificent against the Irish. He struck out 11, walked 5 but allowed only 5 hits in a 5-1 victory that improved his season record to 11-4. The only Notre Dame batter that gave Threehouse trouble was designated hitter Edwin Hartwell. He hit a bases empty second inning home run to stake the Irish to an early lead and added a fourth inning walk and a one out triple in the sixth inning.

Jeff Parnell's fourth inning home run tied the score and the Gamecocks took a 2-1 lead in the fifth on successive singles by Randy Thompson, D. T. Cromer and Dave Willman. Brian Lawler led off the bottom of the sixth inning with a home run. Jerry Shepherd singled, Jeff Parnell doubled, and both scored on Mac White's single to make the final score 5-1.

Jared Baker walked 6, was reached for 12 hits and allowed 6 runs, 5 of them earned, in 7 2/3 innings but managed to pick up the win as the Gamecocks ripped six North Carolina State pitchers for 14 hits and a 9-6 decision in second round action. Rob Mosser pitched 1 1/3 hitless innings to earn his 11th save of the season.

Parnell hit his 18th home run with the bases empty in the sixth inning. The Gamecocks also got doubles from Dave Willman, Jerry Shepherd, Burke Cromer and Randy Thompson. Willman had 3 RBI and Shepherd drove in 2.

South Carolina ran out of pitching and was blasted by host Miami 17-2 and Notre Dame 11-2 to finish its season with a 42-22 record.

Freshman lefthander Tom Price—with the same name but no relation to the South Carolina sports information director and author—pitched a 7 hitter for Notre Dame. He struck out 7 and walked none.

Jerry Shepherd hit his 17th home run for the Gamecocks, one behind Jeff Parnell, as South Carolina finished with the top two power hitters in the SEC. Shepherd was the only Gamecock named to the regional all-tournament team.

South Carolina

vs

Florida

May 9, 1993—South Carolina 7, Florida 1
At Columbia

Jason Haynie's nickname was "Magic" and he threw some sleight of hand at the Florida Gators on Sunday, May 9, 1993.

It was Mother's Day and the freshman lefthanded pitcher had promised his mom a Mother's Day present. Haynie was born in Savannah, Ga., and lived at Hilton Head, S. C., before his family moved to St. Petersburg Beach, Fla., where he attended Lakewood High School. On Mother's Day 1993, Haynie was South Carolina's starting pitcher against his home state university.

He earned the nickname "Magic" when he was an amateur magician. His sleight of hand and fire eating act often entertained members of the Junior Gamecock Club and other organizations. Back home he had performed with the Florida Children's Circus.

Haynie took a 6-2 record into his starting assignment against Florida. South Carolina's team record was 34-15-1 and the Gamecocks were battling Tennessee for the eastern division lead in the Southeastern Conference with a 12-7-1 conference mark.

Florida shut out the Gamecocks 5-0 in the opening game of the three game series but South Carolina won the second game 11-7. Sunday's game was the series rubber match.

Things began a little shaky as Haynie walked leadoff batter Brian Duva on a 3 and 2 count to begin the game. He picked Duva off first base and retired the next four batters before walking Chris Kokinda, again on a 3 and 2 count, with 2 outs in the second inning. He retired the next 9 Gators before issuing a 2 out walk to David Valdes on 4 pitches in the fifth inning. Valdes was left stranded when Haynie struck out Shane McGinnis to end the inning.

Haynie walked James Ramos, again with the count 3 and 2, to open the sixth inning before retiring 9 Gators in a row to finish 8 innings without having allowed a hit. He completed the eighth with a flourish, striking out McGinnis and Ramos.

Meanwhile, Florida starter Doug Brennan held South Carolina scoreless until the roof fell in on him in the sixth inning.

Brennan walked Stacy Stokes to open the bottom of the sixth. Joe Biernat singled to right field and Mac White beat out a bunt. Stokes scored on a bad throw by Florida third baseman McGinnis on White's bunt hit. Designated hitter Ted Rose tripled to drive in 2 runs with his third hit of the game.

Jeff Parnell, South Carolina's top long ball hitter hadn't homered in five weeks, since an April 7 two run shot against Clemson. He surprised everyone with a squeeze bunt that scored Rose. Mike McGuire singled before Mike Dezenzo struck out to end the inning. South Carolina led 4-0.

Brennan was replaced by Ron Scott when South Carolina came to bat in the bottom of the seventh but he lasted only one third of an inning. Mark Gugino flied out to right field but Scott walked Stokes and Biernat hit a two run home run to increase the Gamecock lead to 6-0. Darren McClellan replaced Scott and retired the Gamecocks after giving up a bunt single to White.

Parnell broke his home run drought when he led off the bottom of the eighth inning with a homer off Eddie Soto, Florida's fourth pitcher of the day, and Haynie went to the ninth inning with a 7-0 lead, a no-hit game in the works, and the top of Florida's batting order coming up.

Brian Duva hit a routine ground ball to shortstop but Biernat's throw to first base was in the dirt for an error. Tripp Mackey dribbled a slow ground ball to third baseman McGuire who nipped Mackey for the first out but Duva advanced to second base. Chan Perry hit a soft fly ball to left fielder Gugino for the second out.

But for the error the game would have been over and Haynie would have pitched South Carolina's first no-hit, no-run game since 1975.

Florida right fielder and cleanup batter Bo Camposano, probably the Gators' best hitter, swung at Haynie's first pitch and stroked a soft line drive into short right field for a clean single. Duva scored on the play and the bid for the no-hitter, as well as the shutout, was history.

With the no-hitter gone, pitching coach Randy Davis took Haynie out of the game and brought on relief ace Rob Mosser. Alex Diaz hit Mosser's first pitch off the right centerfield fence for a double with Camposano stopping at third base. Chris Kokinda hit a ground ball to second baseman Stacy Stokes to end the game.

Haynie settled for a 7-1 win that improved his record on the season to 7-2 and left South Carolina in first place in the SEC's eastern division, half a game ahead of Tennessee.

Sportswriter David Newton of Columbia's *The State* had this to say about the near historic performance:

"On any other day, South Carolina Coach June Raines would have spent the postgame interview talking about Jeff Parnell's first home run in more than a month, Joe Biernat's .571 average during a 14 game hitting streak, Ted Rose's 3 hits and the apparent end of USC's slump at the plate.

"But this day belonged to freshman lefthander Jason Haynie."

June Raines was exuberant in his praise of the freshman lefthander.

"Jason Haynie was the story of the game," Raines enthused. "I thought he was a dominating type pitcher. I was pulling like crazy for him to get the no-hitter."

Newton said so were most of the Sarge Frye Field crowd of 2,615 which was on its collective feet and "clapping in anticipation of USC's first no-hitter since 1975 when Bo Camposano lined an 86-mph fast ball into the opposite field in right."

Haynie's post-game comment was, "I knew it was going to happen. You see it all the time. The last pitch. Almost a no-hitter."

Pitching Coach Randy Davis didn't think Haynie had his best stuff of the season.

"He basically pitched with his fast ball today," Davis commented. "We threw a few sliders, I think 5 or 6 curve balls. He's had a lot better stuff than that."

Despite Davis' assessment, David Newton said Haynie "hasn't had a much better fast ball. He moved it inside and out almost at will, getting 12 of the 26 outs he recorded on grounders, 8 on strikeouts and one in a rundown" (the pickoff play).

"That was pretty much all I had," Haynie said of his fast ball. "I could put it where I wanted for the first time in a long time."

As for the error that prolonged the Florida ninth inning, Haynie refused to speculate on whether that cost him a no-hit game.

"Maybe. Maybe not. You never really know," he said.

Jason Haynie—*USC Sports Information*

203

Joe Biernat said he "felt terrible" about committing the error. "I decided to hurry up and throw it and I lost control," he said.

Biernat said Haynie pitched better than he had seen him all season.

"He was in total control the whole time. he put us in a position to win. All we had to do was score some runs."

"I promised my mom a mother's day gift," Haynie said. "She said, 'Get me a win and I'll be happy'."

Haynie was named Southeastern Conference pitcher of the week and was one of Mizuno's National Players of the Week. He finished his freshman season with an 8-2 record and a 2.68 earned run average. He struck out 86 batters in 77 1/3 innings, was named to Mizuno's Freshman All-America team, and was a second team All-SEC choice.

South Carolina edged Tennessee by half a game for first place in the Southeastern Conference's eastern division at the end of regular season play with a 15-8-1 conference record to Tennessee's 15-9. South Carolina played one tie game against Louisiana State University. The regular season overall record was 38-16-1.

In the SEC Eastern Division tournament which the Gamecocks hosted, however, South Carolina went out in two games, losing 3-1 to Georgia and 11-7 to Vanderbilt.

Despite the early exit from the conference tournament, the Gamecocks received their 14th bid to the NCAA playoffs, 11th under Coach June Raines, and competed in the Atlantic Region tournament hosted by Georgia Tech in Atlanta.

South Carolina defeated East Carolina 6-5 with a dramatic 2 out, 2 run rally in the bottom of the ninth inning, with Wally Maynard getting the win in relief of Jason Haynie, but lost a close one, 3-2, to Wichita State, and then was shut out 12-0 by Georgia Tech to end the season with a 39-20-1 record.

Wichita State defeated Georgia Tech to advance to the CollegeWorld Series in Omaha.

Joe Biernat won the Southeastern Conference batting championship with a .403 average, one point shy of the modern school record of .404 set in 1981 by Rob Lowery. Biernat had 94 hits in 233 at bats. Jeff Parnell hit 10 home runs as a senior and ended his career with 45, third on South Carolina's all-time list and 3 less than Hank Small's record of 48.

Biernat, senior lefthanded pitcher Rich Pratt, who had an 11-3 record, 2.83 earned run average and 101 strikeouts, and center fielder Mac White, who batted .355 with 7 home runs and 21 stolen bases, were first team All-Southeastern choices and—as previously mentioned—Haynie made the second team.

South Carolina

vs

Clemson

April 13, 1994—South Carolina 5, Clemson 4 (17 Innings)

At Columbia

In 182 games, South Carolina outfielder Mike Dezenzo hit only 11 home runs in his career, but when he did hit for the circuit he often did so with a flair for the dramatic.

For example, consider the first two homers that Dezenzo registered as a Gamecock. On Feb. 19, 1993 the game with Charleston Southern was scoreless when Dezenzo led off the third inning with a home run. South Carolina batted around and, with 2 out and a runner on base, Dezenzo hit a 2 run homer to wrap up an 8 run inning and the Gamecocks went on to a 14-1 win.

Through the 1995 season, Mike Dezenzo remained the only South Carolina player ever to hit two home runs in the same inning.

On April 18, 1995, Dezenzo led off the first inning with a home run to start South Carolina on the way to a 9-4 win over Georgia Southern at Statesboro.

On May 5 the same season, South Carolina trailed Florida 4-3 in the fifth inning when Dezenzo hit a 2 run homer in a game which South Carolina eventually won 8-7 with a 3 run rally in the bottom of the ninth inning. Dezenzo didn't homer in that inning but his single started the rally.

No home run by any player was more dramatic, however, that the two run shot with one out in the bottom of the ninth inning that Dezenzo hit against Clemson on April 13, 1994 at Sarge Frye Field.

Both teams had excellent records and were nationally ranked going into their third meeting of the season, but Clemson was ranked substantially higher than the Gamecocks. The Tigers had a 36-7 record and were judged the fifth best team in the nation. South Carolina's record was 27-11 and the Gamecocks were ranked twentieth.

The two teams had split two earlier meetings, each winning on the other's field. On March 16, South Carolina ended a string of 14 consecutive losses at Clemson's Tiger Field with a 7-4 win. The

Gamecocks used 2 big innings, scoring 4 times in the sixth and twice in the ninth to offset a 3 run Clemson seventh inning.

Lefthander Scott Pace pitched 6 1/3 innings to get the win before a crowd announced at 1,500 and Craig Ross worked the final 2 2/3 for his sixth save. Walk on catcher Brian Hucks eased the pressure by driving in two runs with a two out ninth inning pinch hit double.

That win not only broke South Carolina's long losing streak at Clemson, it also broke a twelve game win streak by the Tigers.

Three weeks later, before a Sarge Frye Field crowd of 4,202, Clemson evened the series by downing the Gamecocks 7-2. The third game was scheduled a week later, April 13.

South Carolina claimed a 1-0 lead in the bottom of the first inning. Mark Gugino led off with a single to left field, moved to second base on Stacy Stokes' ground out to the right side of the infield, and scored on Mac White's single to right. That was all the Gamecocks would get off Clemson starter Andy Taulbee through eight innings.

In fact, the only hits off Taulbee between the second and ninth innings were a 1 out third inning double by Gugino, a bad hop single by Mike Dezenzo in the fifth, an infield 2 out single by Ted Rose in the sixth, and a 2 out single to center field by Rose in the eighth. Taulbee didn't walk anyone although he hit 2 batters, Rose in the fourth and Randy Stegall in the sixth inning. One Gamecock reached on an error.

Meanwhile, Clemson was collecting 10 hits and 3 runs off Scott Pace and relief pitcher Wally Maynard. Pace worked 6 innings, allowing 7 hits and 2 runs, only 1 of them earned. Maynard pitched through the top of the ninth inning, allowing 3 hits and a run and South Carolina trailed 3-1 going to the bottom of the ninth before a crowd announced at 3,806.

Singles by Mike Eydenberg and Jason Embler, a sacrifice by Seth Brizek—who reached on an error to load the bases—and Eric Demoura's single tied the score at 1-1 in the fifth inning. Dexter McLeon hit into a double play, Embler scoring, to give Clemson a 2-1 lead.

The Tiger margin grew to 3-1 in the top of the eighth inning. Shane Monahan struck out but reached first base on a wild pitch. He was sacrifice to second by Mike Hampton and scored on David Miller's single.

Chris Diaz grounded out to shortstop to begin South Carolina's last opportunity to stay in the game. Brian Hucks, as he had done in an earlier pinch hitting role at Clemson, doubled down the left field line and was replaced by pinch runner Sean Edwards. Dezenzo, representing the tying run, came to the plate.

He crushed Taulbee's first pitch, hitting a towering drive about thirty feet fair down the left field line for a game-tying home run. Taulbee was replaced by Scott Winchester who retired Mark Gugino on an infield pop up and struck out Stacy Stokes to send the game into extra innings.

Craig Ross relieved Wally Maynard to begin the 10th and pitched four innings. He gave up a base hit and hit a batter in the tenth but Clemson didn't score. Ross walked David Miller in the 11th but doubled him off first base on a pop to the mound.

South Carolina loaded the bases with 2 out in the bottom of the 10th on Mac White's single and 2 walks, but couldn't score. The Gamecocks left 2 base runners in the 11th. Mark Gugino singled and Stacy Stokes walked with 1 out. Michael Holtz replaced Winchester as Clemson's pitcher. Holtz struck out White and Rob DeBoer.

Clemson took the lead, 4-3, with an unearned run in the top of the 13th. Mike Eydenberg led off the inning with a double off Ross. Jason Embler grounded to third baseman Randy Stegall, Eydenberg remaining at second. He move to third base on Seth Brizek's ground ball to second baseman Stacy Stokes. Stegall booted Demoura's ground ball for an error allowing Eydenberg to score the tie breaking run.

With their backs to the wall, the Gamecocks tied it up again in the bottom of the 13th. With one out, Gugino singled to left center field. Stokes blooped a single over shortstop Brizek's head. White forced Stokes for the second out but Clemson second baseman Demoura threw the ball away attempting to complete the double play and Gugino scored, White moving to second with the potential winning run. Rob DeBoer was walked intentionally and Ted Rose struck out to send the game, once again tied, to the 14th inning.

Jim Stoops came on to pitch for South Carolina. He retired six consecutive Clemson batters. The Gamecocks went down in order in the 14th, but got two base runners in the 15th on Dezenzo's single and a two out walk to White. Jamie Eggleston came on to pitch for Clemson and covered first on DeBoer's ground ball which second baseman Demoura handled to retire the side.

Lefthander J.J. Pearsall became South Carolina's fifth pitcher of the game in the top of the 16th. He walked Jason Dawsey on four pitches with two out but retired the side when Shane Monahan grounded to first baseman Ray Baksh. Eggleston retired the Gamecocks in order in the bottom of the 16th.

Pearsall flirted with disaster in the top of the 17th when David Miller singled with 1 out and Mike Eydenberg walked with 2 out.

Jason Embler grounded out to Stegall at third to strand 2 Clemson runners. On to the bottom of the 17th inning as the length of the game approached 5 hours.

Freshman Craig Dour, who had replaced pinch runner Sean Edwards, who had replaced pinch hitter Brian Hucks, who had replaced shortstop Ryan Szwejbka in the ninth inning, singled to left center field. Dezenzo bunted him to second base and Dour moved to third as Mark Gugino grounded to second base.

With the winning run at third base and two out, Ken Vining became Clemson's fifth pitcher of the night. Stacy Stokes worked him for a 3 and 2 count, fouled off a pitch and then hit a high, slow chopper to shortstop. Seth Brizek charged the ball. His hurried throw eluded first baseman Jason Embler but it wouldn't have retired Stokes who was a step past the bag when the throw arrived.

It was scored as an infield hit. Dour crossed the plate 4 hours and 59 minutes after the first pitch was thrown and South Carolina was a 5-4 winner. The game tied with two earlier Gamecock wins as the longest in South Carolina history. The Gamecocks also went 17 innings to beat North Carolina 6-5 in 1967 and Georgia 3-2 in 1968.

Leadoff batter Mark Gugino set a school record with 9 official at bats in the game. He had 4 of the 16 Gamecock hits. Thirty five players saw action, 19 for South Carolina and 16 for Clemson with each team using 5 pitchers.

"After South Carolina's Mike Dezenzo drilled a two run homer with one out in the ninth inning to tie the game, it took Stacy Stokes' infield single off reliever Ken Vining in the 17th inning to determine a winner as the No. 20 Gamecocks outlasted No. 5 Clemson 5-4 Wednesday night at Sarge Frye Field," Mark McCallum reported in *The State.*

"With two outs and a runner at third, Stokes chopped the ball toward short. Clemson shortstop Seth Brizek charged and grabbed it on the big hop but sailed his throw past Jason Embler at first."

Clemson Coach Jack Leggett said, "It's always tough when you are the visiting team. When you don't score, then you're always on the edge in the bottom of the inning."

McCallum noted the winning rally followed "nine combined threats since the ninth in which each team stranded runners in scoring position by going 0-for-21 with the lead run waiting."

Clemson left runners in scoring position in the 10th, 12th, 13th and 17th. South Carolina left them there in the 10th, 11th, 12th, 13th and 15th innings.

McCallum recounted that Clemson's Andy Taulbee appeared on the brink of pitching his first complete game.

"After allowing a first inning run, he had bottled the Gamecocks on seven hits and no walks. Just three USC players reached second over the final eight innings until pinch hitter Brian Hucks doubled to left with one out in the ninth.

"Dezenzo hit the next pitch out, just the third USC homer in 14 games."

Dezenzo said he told Rob DeBoer "I was going to hit a homer" in the ninth inning and DeBoer "just laughed about it."

A week after the seventeen inning marathon the Gamecocks and Clemson met for the fourth time in 1994. South Carolina built a 4-0 lead through eight innings before a Tiger field crowd estimated at 4,000.

Mike Dezenzo—*USC Sports Information*

The Gamecocks jumped ahead 2-0 in the first inning when Mark Gugino led off with a single and Rob DeBoer hit a two out, two run homer. Mike Dezenzo singled in the fifth inning, raced to third on a bad throw by Clemson second baseman Eric Demoura, and scored on a ground ball by Stacy Stokes. Mac White hit a solo home run in the eighth inning to make it 4-0.

Jason Haynie held Clemson to 3 hits over the first 6 innings. J. J. Pearsall pitched a hitless inning and stopper Craig Ross took over the Gamecock mound when Mike Eydenberg reached on an error by shortstop Ryan Szwejbka to open the Clemson eighth.

Ross retired the next three batters and struck out Jason Dawsey to open the bottom of the ninth. Shane Monahan and Mike Hampton singled and both moved up on Mike Miller's ground ball to second base for the second out.

Andy Monin hit a three run home run to pull Clemson to within one, but Ross got Eydenberg on a ground ball to Szwejbka to end the game.

South Carolina finished the season with a 35-23 record and went out of the Southeastern Conference Eastern Division tournament at Lexington, Ky., with consecutive losses, 6-5 to Kentucky and 8-1 to Tennessee. Clemson finished with a 57-18 record, won the Atlantic Coast Conference championship and hosted the NCAA East Region tournament.

However, the Tigers were eliminated by SEC member Auburn which advanced to the College World Series.

South Carolina won three of four games from the Tigers, including two game a sweep at Clemson, and a record tying seventeen inning marathon in Columbia.

The seventeen inning game was the 699th career win for Coach June Raines. Two games later, he collected number 700 with a 24-12 slugfest over Georgia.

South Carolina

vs

Clemson

March 28, 1995—South Carolina 4, Clemson 2
At Columbia

History repeated itself March 28, 1995 at Sarge Frye Field.

Clemson, which had won 25 consecutive games since a season opening loss to Oklahoma State, came to Columbia needing 1 victory to equal its longest winning streak in history. The Tigers had opened the 1977 season with 26 consecutive wins before Gamecock All-America righthander Randy Martz beat them 2-1 at Clemson on March 28.

Exactly eighteen years later the Tigers were on the verge of equaling that school record. Clemson had just moved into the number one spot in the national baseball rankings compiled by both *Collegiate Baseball* and *Baseball America.*

Following its season opening loss to Oklahoma State, Clemson had defeated Old Dominion 5 times, had won 3 games each from George Mason, Duke, Wake Forest and Maryland, had defeated Tennessee and James Madison twice each, and had won 1 game each from Western Carolina, Appalachian State, Texas Arlington and Arkansas State.

South Carolina had turned things around after its slowest start in 34 years, and showed an 18-9 record which paled in comparison to Clemson's 25-1.

The Gamecocks lost 6 of their first 9 games but then reeled off 8 wins in a row. After a loss, South Carolina put together a 6 game win streak before losing 2 of 3 to Alabama in the first Southeastern Conference series of the season prior to the non-conference clash with Clemson.

Coach June Raines sent junior lefthander Jason Haynie to the mound to try and stop the Clemson win streak before an overflow Sarge Frye Field crowd of 4,953. After posting records of 8-2 as a freshman and 8-6 as a sophomore, Haynie had struggled in his junior season and didn't have a decision to show for his seven previous

1995 pitching assignments. His earned run average was 5.29.

Clemson Coach Jack Leggett called on tall righthander Kris Benson, a 6-4, 182 pound sophomore with a 5-0 record and an ERA of 1.17. South Carolina quickly jumped on him for two first inning runs.

After Haynie retired Clemson in order in the top of the first, Mike Dezenzo led off the bottom of the inning with a base hit. He moved to third on Randy Stegall's one out double. Dezenzo scored and Stegall moved to third base on a sacrifice fly to right field by Mark Mapes. Stegall scored on a wild pitch. Benson retired 7 of the next 8 Gamecock batters, yielding only a 2 out second inning single to Jason Reynolds.

Gary Burnham led off Clemson's second inning with a single but Haynie struck out Matt LeCroy and Will Duffie hit into a double play. Haynie walked Paul Galloway with one out in the third, but struck out Jerome Robinson and Shane Monahan ended the inning with a fielder's choice.

Clemson tied the score in the top of the fourth inning. Doug Livingston walked and David Miller hit a line drive that looked like a single, but the ball bounced over right fielder Dezenzo's head for a triple, scoring Livingston. Burnham doubled, scoring Miller, but was left stranded when LeCroy again struck out, Duffie grounded to second base, sending Burnham to third, and Seth Brizek flied to center field.

South Carolina quickly got the two runs back in the bottom of the inning. Mapes reached on an error by Livingston, the Clemson second baseman, and moved to second when Benson's attempted pickoff was thrown away. Brian Hucks was hit by a pitch, putting Gamecocks at first and second with no outs.

South Carolina first baseman Craig Ross laid down a bunt, attempting to sacrifice, but beat it out for a hit to load the bases. Craig Dour took a called third strike but Mapes scored and the other runners moved up on Jason Reynold's ground out to shortstop. Ryan Szwejbka beat out an infield hit, driving in Hucks. Dezenzo ended the inning with a hit to shortstop but South Carolina led 4-2.

Haynie retired Clemson in order in the fifth inning, but with one out in the sixth, David Miller singled and Gary Burnham walked. Jim Stoops replaced Haynie as South Carolina's pitcher. LeCroy forced Miller at third base but he moved to second and Burnham to third when South Carolina third baseman Dour made a bad throw attempting to complete the double play.

Stoops struck out Will Duffie to end the Clemson threat. He then retired five Tigers in a row before giving up a two out double to Burham in the eighth inning. LeCroy grounded out to Dour at third

Coach June Raines makes a point with an SEC umpire.
—USC Sports Information

base to end that threat and Stoops set Clemson down in order in the top of the ninth.

South Carolina posed a two out threat in the bottom of the fifth but couldn't add to its lead. Randy Stegall walked with one out but was thrown out attempting to steal. Mark Mapes and Brian Hucks followed with singles, but Craig Ross flied out to center field .

In the bottom of the eighth inning, Hucks singled with one out. Ross struck out and Dour doubled into the left center field gap. Hucks, attempting to score on the play, was out at the plate, left fielder Burnham to first baseman Miller to catcher LeCroy.

"Jason Haynie and Jim Stoops combined to hold nationally top ranked Clemson to five hits Tuesday night and South Carolina broke a 2-2 tie with two unearned runs in the fourth inning for a 4-2 win that halted the Tigers' 25 game win streak," the release from the South Carolina sports information office reported.

"Haynie, 1-0, picked up his first decision of the season in his eighth appearance and Stoops earned his first save, as South Carolina improved its record to 19-9. Clemson dropped to 25-2.

"All of Clemson's hits were by David Miller and Gary Burnham. Miller had a triple and a single and Burnham was 3 for 3 with 2 doubles and a single. Each drove in a run."

Sports Editor Bob Spear of *The State* watched the upset from the press box and produced a column that quoted me, the official scorer and retired sports information director:

"The caller to the Sarge Frye Field press box late Tuesday night asked for the score and Tom Price replied, '4-2, Gamecocks.'

"The retired South Carolina sports information director paused a moment to listen, then cheerfully scolded, 'Don't sound so incredulous'."

But, Spear continued, "This—South Carolina 4, Clemson 2 —does sound impossible, unbelievable and, yes, incredulous.

"The Tigers rolled into town with a 25 game winning streak and the No. 1 spot in the college baseball polls. They averaged nine runs a game, and their pitchers had been more miserly than Scrooge.

"How could Carolina compete?

"Yes, the Gamecocks had been playing better. But this is the team that a few games into the season received the last rites from the talk show scholars, who seized the opportunity to scream for coach June Raines' scalp.

"How, indeed, could they compete against the No. 1 team?

"Easy. Quality pitching covers a multitude of sins, and that the Gamecocks got Tuesday night."

Haynie and Stoops held Clemson to a season low five hits and the game marked only the second time in 1995 that Clemson had scored just two runs. The Tigers entered the game with a .346 team batting average and had averaged 9.0 runs and 11.7 hits per game.

In a sidebar story which *The State* printed on page one, Spear wrote, "In one of those games that make sports so wonderful, South Carolina's Gamecocks jolted the nation's top-ranked college baseball team Tuesday night.

His sidebar went on to say, "The Gamecocks have this habit of snapping long Clemson winning streaks in baseball, putting an end to the Tigers' 26 game streak in 1977 and a 21 game string in 1988."

Beat writer Mark McCallum of *The State* wrote, "The dash started as soon as South Carolina first baseman Craig Ross caught Paul Galloway's foul pop for the final out.

"The Gamecocks raced toward second base en masse like a team celebrating a national championship."

Bob Lang of Charleston's *Post & Courier* reported, "Clemson won 25 straight games and rose to No. 1 in the baseball polls playing solid defense and getting steller pitching along with timely hitting. Tuesday night, South Carolina turned the tables on the Tigers."

"South Carolina did it again," beat writer Rick Scoppe wrote in *The Greenville News.*

"So they're not exactly No. 1 in the country, but for one night, South Carolina felt on top of the collegiate baseball world," wrote Cedric Harmon in the *Spartanburg Herald-Journal.*

June Raines reflected calmly on the win, saying "I was worried they would be too emotional early. But they stayed focused and used it as a plus. They proved it to themselves that they could win. I believed in them."

Clemson coach Jack Leggett said he knew the streak would eventually end but it hurt just a little more to have it end at the hands of the Tigers' in-state rival.

"It's just tough to swallow," Leggett said. "It was going to end some time. You just don't want it to end here. But it did. But we're going to be all right tomorrow.

"You're not going to win every ball game," Leggett added. "We can't let it affect us the rest of the season. One game does not a season make. Their team did a good job, but we didn't play our best game and you have to play your best game in this environment. I hope we learn something from this."

Tiger third baseman David Miller said having the streak end might be a blessing in disguise.

"We were playing more not to lose to keep the streak going instead of trying to kick a lot of butt," Miller said. "We can start over again and do what we did when we started the streak."

Jim Stoops, who overcame an arm injury that sidelined him for a year, was too excited to talk immediately after his 3 2/3 innings of shutout relief pitching.

"Hold on a second. Give me a minute to catch my breath," he told reporters who surrounded him as he crossed the foul line.

When he calmed down enough to talk, the fifth year senior from Somerset, N.J., who came to South Carolina as a walk on infielder, said, "I can't even describe it right now. I wish it was all like this."

The Gamecocks, on the 18th anniversary of the ending of Clemson's 26 game win streak, denied the Tigers a chance to equal that record. Actually, South Carolina has defeated the Tigers to end the three longest streaks in Clemson history.

The Gamecocks beat Clemson 11-7 April 23, 1988 to break a 21 game win streak.

Clemson recovered from the loss to win the three remaining 1995 games from South Carolina. That evened Leggett's personal record against June Raines at 4-4. South Carolina had won 3 of 4 games played in 1994, Leggett's first season as Clemson's head coach.

The Tigers were regular season Atlantic Coast Conference champions but were unseated by Florida State in the ACC tournament. Clemson received an at large bid and hosted the NCAA East Region tournament.

The Tigers won the regional to advance to the College World Series but lost their first two games there to finish with a 54-14 record.

South Carolina, meanwhile, broke even in regular season Southeastern Conference play with a 12-12 record, but lost two straight in the SEC East tournament finish with an overall record of 32-25.

South Carolina lost its top relief pitcher and utility player Craig Ross for five weeks in the heart of the SEC schedule. Ross, frustrated after striking out while playing first base April 2 against Mississippi, punched his bat in a fit of anger and fractured a bone in his pitching hand.

He was out of action until the Florida series, May 5-7, when he returned to the mound to save two games and win one in a three game sweep of the Gators. Before the injury, Ross had been used at third base, first base, in the outfield and as a designated hitter and pinch hitter in addition to relief pitching duties. After the injury, he was used only out of the bull pen.

While it was far from the best Gamecock year, it marked South Carolina's 25th consecutive winning season and kept alive Coach June Raines' string of never having won fewer than 31 games in 19 years as the Gamecock baseball coach.

Index